The Structure of Monetarism

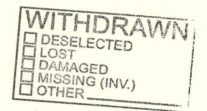

The Structure of Monetarism

Thomas Mayer
University of California, Davis

with contributions by

Martin Bronfenbrenner, Duke University

Karl Brunner, University of Rochester and Universität Bern

Phillip Cagan, Columbia University and
National Bureau of Economic Research

Benjamin Friedman, Harvard University

Helmut Frisch, Technical University, Vienna

Harry G. Johnson, late of the University of Chicago and
Graduate Institute of Advanced International Studies

David Laidler, University of Western Ontario

Allan Meltzer, Carnegie-Mellon University

W · W · Norton & Company · *New York* · *London*

FIRST EDITION

Library of Congress Cataloging in Publication Data
Mayer, Thomas, et al
   The structure of monetarism.
   Includes index.
   1.   Money—Addresses, essays, lectures. 2.   Monetary
policy—Addresses, essays, lectures. 3. Keynesian
economics—Addresses, essays, lectures. I. Bronfen-
brenner, Martin, 1914– II. Title.
HG221.M42 1978   332.4   78–12766
ISBN 0–393–09045–0

Note: a German translation of this book is published as a supplement
to *Kredit und Kapital, 1978*.

1 2 3 4 5 6 7 8 9 0

Contents

To the memory of
Harry G. Johnson

Preface

The most prominent development in macroeconomics in recent years has been the rise of monetarism. But monetarism is not a clear-cut doctrine set forth in one particular place; it has no *General Theory*. Instead it comprises a set of propositions held to greater or lesser extent by a group of economists who are far from forming a monolithic school. As David Laidler points out in this volume, monetarism "is not some rigid orthodoxy but rather an ongoing, expanding, and above all pragmatic body of doctrine."

This volume represents not so much an attempt to establish the validity or invalidity of monetarism as to clarify the issue between monetarists and Keynesians, and hence to pave the way for further investigations that may confirm, modify, or run counter to monetarist hypotheses. The propositions described here as monetarist are not ones which *every* monetarist accepts, and every Keynesian rejects, rather they represent the general thrust of monetarist thinking. Thus there is a tendency for Keynesians to reject any single one of them because of its association with monetarism, while monetarists show the opposite tendency.

Understandable as such tendencies may be, and convenient, too, in reducing search costs (such as reading articles written by the other side), they are not justified. An all-or-none stand would be justified only if the relation between the various monetarist propositions were one of logical entailment; that is, if the truth value of one proposition would necessarily imply the truth value of the others. But this is not the case, the various monetarist propositions are connected only in the probabilistic sense, that if it were shown that proposition *A* is correct then this would raise the probability that proposition *B* is also correct.

Accordingly, the first essay in this volume selects twelve propositions that characterize monetarism, discusses their interrelations, and shows how they form a meaningful whole. But it also shows that one need not accept, or reject, all twelve propositions as a unit, but can, without any logical difficulty, accept some, and reject others.

This paper appeared originally as a two-part article in 1975 in *Kredit und Kapital,* a leading German journal specializing in monetary economics and publishing papers in both German and English. Dr. Wolf-Dieter Becker, the co-editor of *Kredit und Kapital* then suggested that some other economists be invited to comment on this issue. The eight following papers, also

i

published in *Kredit und Kapital,* are these comments. The authors range from firm monetarists to critics of monetarism.

In his essay Martin Bronfenbrenner prefers to juxtapose monetarism to fiscalism rather than to general Keynesian theory. He adds a thirteenth monetarist proposition, that the central bank has responsibility for, and independent power over the money stock, and he draws out the implications of distinguishing between volatility and stability. Karl Brunner's paper is one of the most detailed. He discusses the monetarist transmission process and the critical issue of the relative substitutability between money, bonds, and real assets. He discusses the role of fiscal policy and the problem of "crowding out" in his monetarist model, which differs sharply from the Chicago model. He also takes up the question of how much allocative sectoral detail one should include in a model as well as the implications of different assumptions about the Phillips Curve and the stability of the private sector. Phillip Cagan reviews the way the profession has been led to attach much more importance to the stock of money, and discusses its importance relative to fiscal policy. He presents the case for fixed rules governing fiscal policy as well as monetary policy. Benjamin Friedman shows that the dispute is not so much a matter of different theoretical conceptions, but is essentially empirical. His essay focuses on the transmission process, particularly on the Brunner-Meltzer transmission process which he compares to Tobin's.

Helmut Frisch discusses the acceleration theorem, that is, the monetarist belief that there is no long-run trade-off between inflation and unemployment, and also the formation of expectations. He takes up "crowding out" and the concept of the stability of the private sector. Harry Johnson's essay brings out the critical role of the stability of the demand for money function, and relates the current discussions of monetarism to the monetary theory discussions of the interwar period, thus adding a much needed historical background. David Laidler adds the international perspective by bringing in the complications that arise in an open economy. He also reviews the British debate on monetarism, a debate that stresses the question of whether one can reduce unemployment by accepting more inflation. In his detailed paper Allan Meltzer discusses the distinguishing characteristics of Keynesian theory, the quantity theory and monetarism, and relates the discussion to classical monetary theory. He points out that monetarists stress relative prices much more than quantity theorists or Keynesians do. He also presents a monetarist interpretation of the concept of involuntary unemployment, an approach that focuses on permanent income, and thereby greatly reduces the scope of involuntary unemployment.

I would like to acknowledge my gratitude to all of these essayists for their contributions. Our joint enterprise will have succeeded if it makes the debate between monetarists and Keynesians less dogmatic.

Thomas Mayer

The Structure of Monetarism

The Structure of Monetarism (I)

By Thomas Mayer*

In recent years the term "monetarism" has come into vogue[1]. Defined in a very narrow sense it is the view that changes in the money stock are the predominate factor explaining changes in money income, and hence is merely a new term for "quantity theory". But used in a broader sense the term "monetarism" encompasses a number of other propositions apart from the quantity theory of money. Unfortunately, this whole set of views is commonly judged as a single unit. This contributes to an unfortunate division of economists into monetarists and Keynesian schools with a resulting polarization. It is my impression that the Keynesians have a predisposition to reject all monetarist propositions on the basis of their "guilt by association" with other monetarist propositions, while monetarists have the opposite tendency. I will therefore try to do two things in this paper. One is to show the interrelations between the various monetarist propositions, and to illustrate that they do indeed form a coherent whole. The other is to show that despite this, the connection between various monetarist propositions is loose enough so that one can judge each one on its own merits rather than having to accept or reject monetarist doctrine as a whole. However, I will not try to judge the validity of monetarism.

* I am indebted for helpful comments to Karl *Brunner*, Thomas *Cargill*, H. *Cheng*, Benjamin *Friedman*, Milton *Friedman*, Michael *Hamburger*, Michael *Keran*, Allan *Meltzer*, Franco *Modigliani*, Manfred J. M. *Neumann*, Roger *Spencer*, Edward *Shaw*, Daniel *Vencill*, and to members of workshops and seminars at the Board of Governors, Federal Reserve System, the San Francisco Federal Reserve Bank, and M. I. T., none of whom are responsible for any remaining errors.

[1] The term "monetarism" was originated by Karl *Brunner* ("The Role of Money and Monetary Policy", Federal Reserve Bank of St. Louis, Review, Vol. 50, July 1968, pp. 8 - 24), and was popularized by David *Fand;* see for instance his "Monetarism and Fiscalism", Banca Nazionale del Lavoro, Quarterly Review, Number 94, September 1970, pp. 3 - 34 and „Ein monetaristisches Modell des Geldwirkungsprozesses", Kredit und Kapital, Vol. 3 (1970), pp. 361 - 385.

1

To do this it is necessary as a first step to define the set of propositions which characterize monetarists and distinguish them from Keynesians. Unfortunately there is no single place where one can find a listing of all monetarist propositions, and I have therefore had to construct my own list[2]. In doing so I have tried to err on the side of inclusiveness rather than exclusiveness, and I am dealing therefore with monetarism in the broad sense of a "Weltanschauung". Any such listing is, of course, quite arbitrary and the reader may want to add or to delete items from the following list[3].

1. The quantity theory of money, in the sense of the predominance of the impact of monetary factors on nominal income.

2. The monetarist model of the transmission process.

3. Belief in the inherent stability of the private sector.

4. Irrelevance of allocative detail for the explanation of short-run changes in money income, and belief in a fluid capital market.

5. Focus on the price level as a whole rather than on individual prices.

6. Reliance on small rather than large econometric models.

7. Use of the reserve base or similar measure as the indicator of monetary policy.

8. Use of the money stock as the proper target of monetary policy.

9. Acceptance of a monetary growth rule.

10. Rejection of an unemployment-inflation trade-off in favor of a real *Phillips*-curve.

11. A relatively greater concern about inflation than about unemployment compared to other economists.

12. Dislike of government intervention.

---

[2] Similarly, there is no authoritative listing of Keynesian propositions. I have interpreted Keynesian theory as a theory represented by the views of such economists as James *Duesenberry*, Franco *Modigliani*, Paul *Samuelson*, and James *Tobin* rather than by the more extreme views which can be found in the writings of economists such as Alvin *Hansen*. Hence, what I am calling "Keynesian theory" is to some extent a synthetic theory which has probably been influenced by monetarism.

[3] Throughout my discussion deals only with monetarist school as it exists in the United States.

The first four of these items are ones listed by Karl *Brunner* in his description of monetarism[4], while items 2 and 7 - 9 can be found in David *Fand's* survey of monetarism[5]. On the other side of the debate James *Tobin* has characterized it by items 1, 7, 8, 9, and 10 in the above list[6]. Item 5, the focus on the price level as a whole, while usually not explicit, is implicit in typical monetarist discussion of inflation, particulary in their rejection of cost-push inflation. Item 6, the preference for small models, while certainly not a basic part of monetarist doctrine, is something which most monetarists seem to have in common. Item 10, the real *Phillips*-curve, is listed by Leonall *Andersen*[7]. Item 11, concern about inflation, is admittedly a rather questionable item, based only on my general impression of monetarist writings and verbal tradition[8]. The final item, dislike of government regulation, is a view that seems to be generally shared by monetarists, at least in the United States.

---

[4] *Brunner*, "The 'Monetarist Revolution' in Monetary Theory", Weltwirtschaftliches Archiv, Vol. 105, Number 1, 1970, pp. 1 - 30.

[5] *Fand* also mentions another item, the monetarist's belief in long and variable lags. But at present many Keynesians also believe that monetary policy has long lags. David *Fand*, "Monetarism and Fiscalism", loc. cit.

[6] James *Tobin*, The New Economics One Decade Older (Princeton, N. J., pp. 58 - 59). Actually, as far as item 7 is concerned *Tobin* refers to the money stock rather than total reserves, but this is a minor difference. Also, item 8 is implicit, rather than explicit in *Tobins's* list. Paul *Samuelson* ("Reflections on the Merits and Demerits of Monetarism" in James *Diamond*, editor, Issues in Fiscal and Monetary Policy, Chicago, Illinois, 1971, pp. 7 - 21) lists the quantity theory and the monetary growth rate rule as the two basic propositions of monetarism. To these he adds the belief in wage and price flexibility, and in the response of the interest rate to inflation (two propositions which can be treated as part of the quantity theory) and a belief in the real nature of the *Phillips*-curve with the associated belief in a natural rate of unemployment. He then stated (p. 20) that "there is no reason why monetarists should believe this except that all of these notions happen to be believed by one man, Professor *Friedman*". (For a similar statement see James *Tobin*, op. cit., p. 62.) This not only ignores the work of *Brunner* and *Meltzer*, but also ignores the various linkages discussed below.

[7] "The State of the Monetarist Debate", Federal Reserve Bank of St. Louis, Review, vol. 56, September 1973, pp. 5 - 6. Although *Andersen* states that it is also accepted by "many other economists" it is frequently rejected by Keynesians.

[8] For a typical example see James *Tobin's* criticisms of the policy recommendations made by the, mainly monetarist, "Shadow Open Market Committee" (James *Tobin*, "Monetary Policy in 1974 and Beyond", Brookings Papers on Economic Activity, 1974: 1, pp. 219 -2 32.

These twelve items are, of course, not all equally significant. The first four are the basic ones and can be used to define monetarism. Monetarists need not accept any of the other eight[9]. But monetarists do tend to accept these other eight propositions too. And my purpose here is to describe a set of beliefs which are shared by economists who call themselves monetarists (and to a much lesser extent by other economists) rather than to set out a set of beliefs which are the sufficient and necessary conditions for an economist to be called a monetarist[10].

The way I will now proceed is to start with the quantity theory, and then take up each of the other components in the order listed, and see to what extent they are dependent or independent of the previously dis-

---

[9] Thus Allan *Meltzer* wrote (private communication) "I do not accept any but points 1 to 4 as part of monetarism. The other points are, for me, propositions that I accept to varying degrees. Many are unrelated to monetarism. For example, your point 5 is a Hicksian proposition about composite goods. It should be accepted by all economists." It is certainly true that item 5 can be considered as a theorem about composite goods, but there is still a decision to be made as a matter of research strategy, rather than as a matter of formal theory, whether one analyzes the general price level as a single unit or by looking at individual prices.

[10] However, I have omitted the international aspect of monetarism, the proposition that with fixed exchange rates a country's money stock and price level depend not on its own monetary policy, but on the whole world's monetary policy. At least in the United States, this proposition has not played much of a role in monetarist discussions. But adding it to my list would not change my conclusions because, as Harry *Johnson* has pointed out, "a properly understood Keynesian approach to the system as a whole would produce the same conclusion". (H. G. *Johnson* and A. R. *Nobay* (editors), Issues in Monetary Economics, London, Oxford University Press, 1974, p. 50.) Besides, it is essentially part of the first proposition, the quantity theory. I have also omitted an item mentioned by *Brunner* ("The Role of Money and Monetary Policy", op. cit., p. 9), the belief that the monetary authorities can control the stock of money. This is now accepted by many Keynesians as well, though admittedly, Keynesian tend to qualify it more than monetarists do.

The various hypotheses I describe as monetarist do, of course, predate the development of the term "monetarism". The quantity theory, together with its transmission process, has an ancient history, as do, though perhaps to a lesser extent, the next three items. Items 6, 7 and 10 are newer because the problems they present are newer. A hundred years ago nobody was worried about the proper size of an econometric model, or about the correct monetary indicator. Debate about items 8 and 9 can, to some extent, be traced back to the banking school-currency school debate. The final two items again, do have a long history. What is new about monetarism is therefore primarily its combination of hypotheses into a single doctrine.

cussed components. In Part I of the paper I will deal with the first six propositions. In the second part of this paper, to be published in the subsequent issue of this journal, I will deal with propositions 7 - 12 and will summarize the results obtained in both parts.

I. The Quantity Theory

The quantity theory is the most basic component of monetarism. By the quantity theory I mean the proposition that changes in the money stock are the dominant determinant of changes in money income[11]. This is a very general version which does not commit one to a specific theory of the transmission process, a process treated separately in the next section. A very important aspect of the quantity theory-Keynesian dispute involves the speed of adaption of the economy[12]. Keynesians would not — or at least should not — deny that in the long run changes in nominal income are dominated by changes in the money stock.

The above definition of the quantity theory clearly fits both the Friedmanian and the *Brunner-Meltzer* versions. It is not at all clear, however, that it also fits the *Patinkin* version. This is due to two characteristics of *Patinkin's* model. First, while changes in the stock of money ultimately bring about equivalent changes in the price level we are not told how long this process takes. Hence someone may completely accept the *Patinkin* model, and yet, in forecasting next year's money income might not pay very much attention to recent changes in the money stock because these changes will have their effects only in some far-off equilibrium[13]. Second, while *Patinkin's* model tells us that changes in the money supply have proportional effects on money income, this does not necessarily deny that changes in other variables also affect money

---

[11] The modern Keynesian theory differs from the quantity theory in denying that changes in the money stock dominate changes in income, but it does not claim that changes in the money stock are unimportant. According to J. R. *Hicks* (The Crisis in Keynesian Economics, Oxford, 1974, pp. 31 - 32) *Keynes* himself "must surely in some sense, perhaps a very weak sense, have been a monetarist. He has nevertheless been read to imply that there is nothing to be done with money."

[12] Thus the growing literature on search costs is relevant to the monetarist-Keynesian debate and monetarists attach more importance to search costs than do Keynesians.

[13] To be sure, if there are long lags in the effects of money on income then one might predict next years's income by changes in the money stock in previous years, but if the lags are highly variable, even this would not work.

income. And if changes in these other variables have important effects on income, then the essential monetarist proposition that variations in money income are explained mainly by changes in the money stock need no longer hold. Thus a Patinkian might well use a Keynesian model for ordinary forecasting purposes instead of a quantity theory model.

This is not to deny that *Patinkin's* model is a quantity theory model, but it is a quantity theory model in a different sense from the way I am defining the quantity theory here. His model has, to a large extent, a quantity theorist's "engine of analysis"[14], but the conclusions he reaches are not necessarily those of the quantity theory in the short run as distinct from the long run[15]. Since monetarism is a policy-oriented doctrine, concerned very much with the short run, *Patinkin's* version of the quantity theory can be excluded from it.

II. The Transmission Process

The monetarist's version of the transmission process by which changes in the money stock affect income follows naturally from his research strategy which is to focus on the supply and demand for real money

---

[14] *Patinkin's* model uses the quantity theory's analytic procedures insofar as it focuses on the gap between desired and actual real balances. However, it is Keynesian in its use of capital theory since, as *Patinkin* has argued, the Cambridge school did not use capital theory in its monetary analysis to any significant extent. (See Don *Patinkin*, "Keynesian Monetary Theory and the Cambridge School", in H. G. *Johnson* and A. R. *Nobay*, op. cit., pp. 3 - 30.)

[15] This difference between looking at the quantity theory as an engine of analysis and looking at it as the conclusion that money matters a great deal is at the heart of a dispute between *Friedman* and *Patinkin*. *Patinkin*, focusing on the fact that *Friedman* — like *Keynes*, but unlike pre-Keynesian quantity theorists — uses capital theory in his monetary analysis, has argued that *Friedman's* theory is more a Keynesian than a quantity theory. (Don *Patinkin*, "The Chicago Tradition, the Quantity Theory and *Friedman*", Journal of Money, Credit and Banking, Vol. I, Feb. 1969, pp. 46 - 70, and "*Friedman* on the Quantity Theory and Keynesian Economics", Journal of Political Economy, vol. 80, September/October 1972, pp. 883 - 905.) *Friedman's* reply was to object to *Patinkin's* "propensity to take the 'quantity theory' to mean one thing, and one thing only, namely the long-run proposition that money is neutral, even though he fully recognizes, indeed insists, that quantity theorists (myself included) were concerned mostly with short-run fluctuations". ("Comments on the Critics", Journal of Political Economy, vol. 80, September/October 1972, p. 932.) Perhaps the point should be stated differently by saying that *Friedman* classifies theories on the basis of the conclusions they reach, while *Patinkin* classifies them on the basis of the analytic method used.

balances[16]. If the public finds itself with excess balances it will reduce them by increasing expenditures, presumably on both goods and bonds. By contrast, the Keynesian focuses on relative yields, and therefore phrases the story differently. If the public has excess money balances this must mean that the yield on its money balances is less than the yield it can obtain on other assets, and hence it buys other assets. Such a portfolio realignment to bring yields (adjusted for risk, etc.) into equality is likely to involve primarily assets which are similar to money, that is securities rather than goods. Hence, monetarists and Keynesians typically have a different range of assets in mind when they think of the transmission process. This difference is illustrated by the Keynesian calling the price of money the interest rate since he thinks of money as a fund which can be either held as money or lent, while the monetarist thinks of the price of money as the inverse of the price level, since money is used to buy goods[17].

Unfortunately, this genuine dispute, as well as disputes relating to the measurement problem discussed below, are often obscured by a spurious dispute about whether money affects income "directly" or only "indirectly". This difference is terminological; one can reformulate the

---

[16] I will not describe the monetarist transmission processes here in any detail. *Friedman's* variant stresses substitution effects, and the influence of changes in the money stock on the nominal interest rate while the *Brunner-Meltzer* variant stresses relative price and stock effects. Both variants attach much importance to the distinction between nominal and real rates of interest, and more generally, pay greater attention to price changes than Keynesians typically do.

I am discussing only the transmission process for changes in the quantity of money, and not for fiscal policy etc. The monetarist argument that fiscal policy changes result in counteracting changes, such as "crowding out", which offset them after some time, is really part of the previously discussed monetarist proposition, that changes in money income are explained largely by changes in the money stock.

[17] Thus in commenting on a draft of this paper Milton *Friedman* wrote (private communication) "I believe an important distinction between Keynesian and monetarist views is one that I have not myself stressed sufficiently but that comes out in the course of some of your comments. This is the distinction between money and credit and most particularly in what one regards as the price of money. The Keynesian approach invariably regards the interest rate as the price of money whereas the quantity theory approach regards the interest rate as the price of credit and the inverse of the price level as the price of money. This is exremely important in connection with the way in which the demand curve for money is used."

monetarist story in terms of the interest rate and the Keynesian story in a way that omits the interest rate. An increase in the real stock of money lowers the imputed real interest rate on money balances. Hence, a monetarist, instead of saying that the public has more money than it wants to hold, and thus increases expenditures, can say that the public's imputed interest rate on money holdings has fallen while the yield on other assets is constant. Thus, directly to equalize marginal yields, and indirectly because of the increase in the money stock, the public increases expenditures. Conversely, the Keynesian can use his liquidity preference diagram to show that an increase in the public's money stock means that the public is now holding more than its optimal stock of money, and hence, to equalize rates of return on the margin, buys securities. Essentially the point here is the following: Given a demand curve, whether for a commodity such as apples, or for the holding of money, we can described any change either in terms of price (the interest rate) or in terms of quantities (the stock of money). As long as we have a given demand curve it does not matter; we must get the same answer regardless of which axis of the diagram we look at. Hence, on a level of formal theory where one can ignore measurement problems, it is unimportant whether one formulates the analysis in terms of the money stock or in terms of the interest rate[18]. This dispute is spurious. It is therefore not surprising that Y. C. *Park* in his careful survey of the transmission process concluded that "at the level of general description there appear to be no significant differences in the transmission process of monetary influences among a variety of monetary economists"[19].

A genuine aspect of the dispute, however, relates to the stability of the demand for money which is part of the previously discussed hypothesis that nominal income changes are dominated by changes in the money stock. If the demand for money is unstable (in a numerical sense), perhaps because of shifts in the marginal efficiency of investment, then knowledge that the supply of money has increased no longer allows us to predict with any degree of confidence that expenditures will actually increase. This is so regardless of whether one phrases the process in Keynesian or monetarist terms. The real difference between

---

[18] Cf. Milton *Friedman,* "A Theoretical Framework for Monetary Analysis", National Bureau of Economic Research, Occasional Paper, number 112 (New York, 1971), p. 28.
[19] Y. C. *Park,* "Some Current Issues on the Transmission Process of Monetary Policy", International Monetary Fund, Staff Papers, March 1972, p. 38.

the two schools is that the Keynesian tends to take the possibility of an unstable demand for money much more seriously than does the monetarist, in part because he has a different theory of the interest rate[20]. Hence, in predicting expenditures the Keynesian prefers to look at what is happening to the rate of interest, thus taking account of changes in both the demand for, and the supply of, money. The monetarist, on the other hand, though he would agree in principle that changes in the money supply may give a misleading answer because of changes in money demand, does not treat this danger as seriously as does the Keynesian.

However, one must beware of exaggerating this difference. Although in "The General Theory" *Keynes* did give the impression that the demand for money is highly unstable, modern Keynesians no longer seem to believe this, and instead treat the demand for money as fairly stable. On the other hand, *Friedman* has stated that the quantity theorist looks upon the demand for money as being a stable function of other variables, rather than as necessarily being stable in a numerical sense[21].

Since changes in the interest rate register demand as well as supply shifts they clearly have more information content than changes in the money supply. One might, therefore, ask why anyone would look at the money supply rather than at the rate of interest. This question brings us to the second substantive issue, the measurement problem. The above discussion has assumed implicitly that both "the" interest rate and "the" money stock can be measured without error, or that they are measured with equivalent errors. But this is questionable. Monetarists prefer to use the money stock rather than the rate of interest because they believe that the money stock can be measured much better. The term "the rate

---

[20] Many monetarists believe that if the quantity of money is increased the nominal interest rate declines only very temporarily. It soon rises back to its previous level, and, due to the *Fisher* effect, even exceeds it. The monetarist therefore looks upon the expected real interest rate as fairly stable. Hence, one of the factors which can cause fluctuations in the quantity of money demanded, changes in the expected real interest rate, seems much less important to the monetarist than to the Keynesian. Another important reason why monetarists take the demand for money as stable is that, as discussed below, the monetarist treats expenditure incentives as much more stable than the Keynesian does, and hence considers the expected real rate of interest, and therefore the demand for money, to be stabler than Keynesians do.

[21] "The Quantity Theory of Money: A Restatement", reprinted in Milton *Friedman*, The Optimum Quantity of Money, op. cit., ch. 2.

of interest" as used in formal theory is a theoretical term, and for any empirical work with it it is necessary to find an accurately measureable counterpart. The monetarist typically believes that this creates insuperable difficulties. One difficulty is that "the" rate of interest is an amalgam of a vast number of specific long term and short term rates, and that there is no clear way in which these rates can all be combined into a single measure. Term structure theory is not a completely reliable guide. The second difficulty is that by no means all the rates which should be combined into "the" interest rate can be observed in the market. Imputed rates used internally by households and firms should be included, and due allowance should also be made for borrowing costs other than the measured interest rate, for example the cost of deteriorating balance sheet ratios. Third, what is relevant for economic decisions is the expected real rate of interest, which cannot be observed in the market, and cannot be approximated reliably by econometric techniques. Since changes in the inflation rate are frequently large relative to changes in the real interest rate, changes in the nominal rate may be a very poor guide to changes in the expected real rate. Hence, monetarists argue, in practice the money stock is a much better measuring rod than is the interest rate.

It is, of course, open for Keynesians to reply that the money stock is also measured badly. Again the problem is that the theoretical term, "money", as used in the quantity theory does not have a clear-cut empirical counterpart. Should it be approximated by M_1 or M_2? This is an issue on which monetarists disagree among themselves[22]. Presumably, the proper counterpart is some weighted mean, but there exists no reliable way of estimating it[23]. Furthermore, as in the case of the interest rate one should make some adjustment for the anticipated inflation rate. Surely, it does affect how the public feels about the adequacy of its cash balances. Hence, it is open to the Keynesian to argue that despite the

---

[22] In the United States in recent years the growth rates of M_1 and M_2 have diverged widely, presumably in large part due to restrictions on interest payments on deposits. For example, between December 1972 and December 1973 M_1 grew at a 6.1 percent rate while M_2 (excluding large certificates of deposit) grew at an 8.9 percent rate, that is at a 69 percent greater rate.

[23] Some attempts have been made to settle this issue by seeing whether M_1 or M_2 have a closer correlation with income. But these attempts founder on the fact that the "reverse causation" bias may be greater for one measure than for the other.

difficulties of measuring "the" rate of interest, it can be measured more accurately than "the" money stock.

Problems of measuring the money stock are likely to seem more serious to a Keynesian than to a quantity theorist because someone who believes that the money stock cannot be measured accurately is likely to be skeptical of the empirical evidence claiming to show that changes in the money stock explain changes in money income. But it does not necessarily follow from this that a Keynesian need be more worried about the difficulty of measuring the money supply than about measuring the interest rate. He may well take the position that, while neither variable can be measured accurately, the interest rate is measured with a greater error than is the money stock. There is certainly nothing in Keynesian theory to deny this. The exposition of the argument in terms of the interest rate rather than the money stock, both in the "General Theory" and the subsequent Keynesian literature, can often be explained by the argument being on a high level of abstraction where measurement problems can be ignored. Thus, while it is hard to see why a quantity theorist would prefer to use the interest rate in his description of the transmission process, it is not hard to see why a Keynesian may agree with a quantity theorist in looking at the money stock rather than the rate of interest.

A third substantive difference between the Keynesian and monetarist transmission processes relates to the range of assets considered. The monetarist looks at an increase in the money supply as having raised the public's money holdings relative to its holdings of securities and all types of real assets. Hence, to bring marginal yields into equilibrium the public now spends these excess balances to acquire securities, capital goods and consumer goods. The Keynesian, however, typically treats the increase in the money stock as affecting only investment, and not consumption[24]. There are two reasons for this. First, by looking at the interest rate the Keynesian adopts a borrowing-cost interpretation; an increase in the money stock lowers interest rates, and this lower cost of borrowing stimulates demand for goods which are bought with credit; that is, it stimulates business investment, residential construction, and

---

[24] To be sure, in the mainly Keynesian Federal Reserve-M.I.T.-Penn model the interest rate has a strong effect on consumption. But this is not true for the more typically Keynesian models.

perhaps investment in consumer durables[25]. Demand for nondurables is not directly affected because they are usually not bought on credit. A second reason is that the Keynesian often makes the simplifying assumption that the propensity to consume is not directly affected by the interest rate, so that an increase in the money stock affects only investment[26].

How does this difference in the range of assets relate to the magnitude of the impact of changes in the money stock, and hence to the question whether changes in money income are dominated by changes in the money stock? On a level of rather causal empiricism there is a direct relationship. If monetary changes affect consumption as well as investment then money probably has a much greater effect on income than is the case if it can affect only "investment" including perhaps consumer durables[27]. But this reasoning while suggestive is hardly conclusive. Someone might accept the Keynesian transmission process, believing that changes in the money stock operate only via investment, and yet he might think that, due to a high interest elasticity of investment, this effect is very powerful. On the other hand, someone might believe that changes in the stock of money affect both consumption and investment, but that this total effect is quite weak.

Another substantive difference is newer. Recently Karl *Brunner* and Allan *Meltzer* have developed a new version of the monetarist transmis-

---

[25] According to Karl *Brunner* ("The Monetarist Revolution in Monetary Theory", op. cit., p. 3) the borrowing-cost interpretation is post-Keynesian rather than part of *Keynes'* own thought.

[26] *Keynes'* evidence for the interest inelasticity of consumption is extremely casual (The General Theory, London, 1936, pp. 93 - 94), but this rather arbitrary judgement allowed him to make a great simplification. This is to dichotomize his model into decisions made about the disposition of income (to save it or consume it) and decisions made about asset composition (to hold money or bonds). He did not have to consider the feedback effect of asset decisions on consumption through changes in the propensity to consume as the interest rate changes.

[27] Although this is no more than a surmise I suspect that the debate about the channels of monetary influence received some of its impetus from the fact that at one time empirical studies of business investment behavior showed the interest rate as playing, at best, a very small role. Hence, monetarists had a strong reason to argue that changes in the money stock do not operate just through business investment, while Keynesians had an incentive to treat business investment as the only link between changes in the money stock and income.

sion process[28]. They argue that the Friedmanian version, which is really what was discussed above, is essentially Keynesian in its underlying theory, and they have set out a theoretical critique of this Keynesian transmission process. It focuses on a relative price process and stock effects which tend to bring the system towards a classical rather than a Keynesian equilibrium[29].

Thus there are four links between the hypothesis of the primacy of changes in the quantity of money and the monetarist — as opposed to the Keynesian — version of the transmission process. One is the stability of the demand for money, the second is the relative measurability of money and interest rates, the third is the range of assets considered, and the fourth concerns the relative price effects and stock effects discussed by *Brunner* and *Meltzer*.

Are these links compelling in the sense that someone who accepts the monetarist story on one must also accept it on the other? The answer is, no. Clearly, one can accept the Keynesian version of the transmission process and yet believe that monetary factors dominate money income. All one has to do is to believe that the interest elasticity is high for investment and low for the liquidity preference function. Conversely, one can accept the monetarist transmission process, and yet reject the quantity theory as an explanation of most observed changes in income. Thus, while the demand for money may be relatively stable (compared to the seriousness of the errors introduced by the measurement problem), the stock of money may be even more stable. And while someone who believes in the primacy of the monetary impulse is likely to believe that money can be measured fairly well, he could also believe that the interest rate can be measured just as well or better. Moreover, changes in the quantity of money could exert all their (strong) effects on income through investment. Finally, someone may consider the *Brunner-Meltzer*

---

[28] Karl *Brunner* and Allan *Meltzer*, "Money, Debt and Economic Activity", Journal of Political Economy, vol. 80, September/October 1972, pp. 951 - 977; Karl *Brunner*, "A Survey of Selected Issues in Monetary Theory", Schweizerische Zeitschrift für Volkswirtschaft und Statistik, Vol. 107, 1971, pp. 1 - 146.

[29] Y. C. *Park* (op. cit., p. 31) has argued that "*Brunner* and *Meltzer* — contrary to their claim — accept the Keynesian view of the nature of the transmission process; what they seem to reject is the heuristic simplification of reality with regard to the range of assets considered in the Keynesian income/expenditure theory." This statement is very much open to question if one treats as "Keynesian" not every single factor mentioned in the "General Theory" and post-Keynesian writings, but only those which are stressed.

analysis of the relative price and stock effects to be valid, but might believe that in the short run and intermediate run these effects are relatively minor. In other words, one cannot logically infer how money affects income from the strength of the monetary impulse and vice versa.

III. Stability of the Private Sector

Monetarists generally believe that the private sector is inherently stable if left to its own devices and not disturbed by an erratic monetary growth rate. Many, probably most, Keynesians deny this. The nature of this dispute is complex. Keynesian typically do not deny that the private sector is stable in the sense that it is damped rather than explosive. As Lawrence *Klein* has pointed out, some leading Keynesian econometric models show the economy to be stable in its response to stochastic shocks[30]. However, Keynesian look upon the private sector as being unstable in another sense. This is that it is inherently subject to erratic shocks, primarily due to changes in the marginal efficiency of investment. To a Keynesian many factors can, and do, cause substantial changes in aggregate demand, changes which may then lead to damped oscillations.

By contrast, the monetarist treats aggregate demand as the resultant of a stable demand for money and an unstable supply of money. He looks upon the private sector as stable because its demand for money is stable, and attributes most, though certainly not all, the actually observed instability to fluctuations in the money supply induced by the monetary authorities[31]. Thus, this dispute about the stability of the private sector is tied directly into the basic dispute about the quantity theory, the extent to which changes in aggregate demand are explained

---

[30] "The State of the Monetarist Debate: Comment", Federal Reserve Bank of St. Louis, Monthly Review, Vol. 55, September 1973, p. 11.

[31] An approach which looks at expenditure incentives is likely to come up with different results than one which focuses on the demand for money. The latter — on an intuitive level at least — seems stable, while — again on an intuitive level — expenditure incentives seem highly variable. Obviously, these two intuitions are in conflict due to *Walras'* Law. Perhaps the resolution of this conflict is that while the incentives for particular expenditures looked at one at a time seem unstable, much of this instability averages out in the sense that one sector may be depressed while another is in a boom.

primarily by changes in the money supply rather than by changes in the marginal efficiency of investment, etc.[32].

But even so, the tie between the quantity theory and the stability of the private sector is not complete; someone can reject the quantity theory, and yet believe in the inherent stability of the private sector. For example, a Keynesian who believes that fiscal policy is so badly timed that it is destabilizing, and that monetary policy has also not been a net stabilizer, would have to believe that the private sector is stabler than is indicated by the actually observed fluctuations in GNP. Yet there is nothing about such a view which is contrary to Keynesian theory, or which requires the quantity theory as its foundation. Thus one can be a Keynesian in one's basic theory, and, at the same time, accept the monetarist proposition that the private sector is inherently stable or at least stabler than the private and government sectors combined. Admittedly, it is much harder to see how a quantity theorist could believe in the instability of the private sector.

IV. Irrelevance of Allocative Detail and Belief in the Fluidity of Capital Markets

One of the points of distinction between the monetarists and the Keynesians is that in trying to determine short-run changes in income the Keynesian, unlike the monetarist. typically focuses on what happens in particular sectors of the economy. With unstable private sectors (in the sense defined above) fluctuations can start in various sectors, or be conditioned by the particular characteristics of a sector. For example, a rise in the interest rate may have different effects on residential construction, and hence on total output, at a time when mortgage lending institutions are already short of liquidity than at a time when they have a large liquidity buffer. More fundamentally, the Keynesian predicts, or explains, income by looking at expenditure motives in each sector. Hence, he has to analyze each sector.

The monetarist, by contrast, looks upon expenditures as determined by the excess supply of, or demand for, real balances. He therefore has

---

[32] Leonall *Andersen* ("The State of the Monetarist Debate", Federal Reserve Bank of St. Louis, Monthly Review, Vol. 55, September 1973, pp. 2 - 8) has pointed to another factor as the difference between Keynesian and monetarist views on the stability of the private sector, the length of time it takes to return to the neighborhood of equilibrium when the economy is subjected to a shock.

to look at the behavior of only a single market, the market for real
balances[33].

The Keynesian's concern with allocative detail, that is the behavior
of different sectors, is reinforced by a frequent tendency among Keynesians to treat the capital market as imperfect so that capital rationing
can occur. Hence, in estimating aggregate demand the Keynesian is not
satisfied with knowing the total amount of liquidity in the economy.
He also wants to know the liquidity of specific sectors, such as financial
institutions serving the mortgage market[34]. This emphasis on imperfect
capital markets and credit rationing is also connected with the common
Keynesian emphasis on borrowing conditions as the only channel
through which monetary policy operates[35]. Hence, he wants to know a
great deal about various interest rates and financial markets in assessing
the influence of monetary factors on money income. And his belief that
capital markets are imperfect explains why Keynesians seem much more
interested in flow of funds analysis than are most monetarists, despite
the fact that the flow of funds deals with the monetarist's item of
central concern, money.

Another reason for the Keynesian emphasis on sectorial detail is
probably the tendency of many Keynesians to favor government intervention. Efficient government intervention obviously requires detailed
knowledge of many sectors since the intervention is likely to focus on
specific "troubles" in particular sectors. Finally, as will be discussed in
the next section, many Keynesians look upon inflation as sometimes
being due, at least in part, to developments in particular sectors rather
than as due to the monetarist's single pervasive factor.

By contrast, in explaining short-run changes in income, the monetarist
usually expresses little interest in allocative detail[36]. He makes a sharp

---

[33] This does not mean that the monetarist can ignore all institutional detail.
He has to consider numerous institutional factors (which differ among countries) in his analysis of the money supply process. But this is different from
concern with allocative detail.
[34] Thus in the, mainly Keynesian, Federal Reserve-M.I.T.-Penn model, one
of the major channels by which monetary changes affect income is credit
rationing.
[35] Obviously, a large sophisticated model, like the above mentioned one,
can have several channels, and is not confined to borrowing costs. But for most
Keynesian expositions borrowing costs are the channel.
[36] This does not mean that the monetarist is uninterested in allocative detail
per se. He is often strongly interested in it because he looks upon government

distinction between relative prices which are affected by the fortunes of various sectors, and the general price level which is affected by the quantity of money. He does not build up his estimate of national income by adding up incomes in various sectors as Keynesians do, but rather, he works "from the top down". Using changes in the money stock he estimates total expenditures, and then, if he happens to be interested in it, he might investigate the allocation of this fixed expenditure total among various sectors. His assumption of a fluid capital market fortifies the monetarist in his belief that a given increase in the money stock will have more or less the same effect on aggregate incomes, though not of course, on the relative incomes of various sectors, regardless of where it is injected[37]. And his belief in the stability of the private sector and in the absence of a need for government intervention gives the monetarist little incentive to focus his attention on developments in various sectors[38]. This is reinforced by the fact that the monetarist, unlike the Keynesian, does not typically try to specify the channels through which monetary factors operate, and hence does not try to gauge the impact of monetary factors by looking at their impact on different sectors.

Hence, the monetarist's disregard of allocative detail in explaining short-run income changes is a natural outgrowth of his basic position. It results from his belief in the quantity theory, i. e. in the primacy of money supply changes in explaining income. It is also connected with his view of the transmission process, in which expenditure motives and the peculiarities of individual sectors are unimportant and the borrowing cost approach to gauging the influence of monetary factors is

interference with financial markets as creating very serious problems. Thus he opposes the suppression of financial deepening. In the United States monetarists are much more critical of Regulation Q (the limitation of interest payments on bank deposits) than are Keynesians. It is only with respect to the use of allocative detail as a predictor of short-run changes in income that monetarists have shown less interest in it than Keynesians.

[37] But to the extent that the velocity of money differs in various sectors the monetarist has an incentive to analyze the distribution of money between various sectors. For a notable example see Richard *Selden,* "The Postwar Rise in the Velocity of Money", Journal of Finance, vol. 16, December 1961, pp. 483 - 545.

[38] This statement is subject to one qualification. The monetarist is likely to pay a great deal of attention to the efficiency of one sector, the financial sector, and to point out the distortions created in this sector by government regulations.

rejected. But this does not mean that a monetarist must necessarily deemphasize allocative detail in his prediction of income fluctuations. Someone might accept all the other basic and characteristic monetarist positions, and yet believe that the capital market is highly imperfect, that capital rationing is important, and that the flow of funds between various sectors therefore plays some role in determining income[39]. Similarly, a monetarist might favor government intervention either because he is skeptical of the stability of the private sector, or because he favors government intervention for some other reason; in principle one could certainly be a monetarist and also a socialist.

At the same time, a Keynesian need not believe in the imperfection of the capital market and the importance of capital rationing. Neither of these ideas plays a role in the "General Theory". More significantly, one can accept the general framework of Keynesian analysis without believing in the instability of the private sector, and in the advisability of government intervention, and hence not be concerned with allocative problems on these grounds. It is only the Keynesian focus on expenditure motives that provided a basic reason for the Keynesian's interest in allocative detail.

V. The Price Level versus Individual Prices

One major distinction between monetarists and most Keynesians is the way of looking at the price level[40]. This is a subtle distinction that is seldom, if ever, made explicit. Basically there are two ways of approaching the price level. One is to treat it as an aggregate phenomenon, determined by the interaction of only two factors, aggregate demand and aggregate output. This view draws a sharp distinction between the price level as a whole and relative prices. Specific events in particular industries, such as an increase in the degree of monopoly, union pressure, or bad harvests obviously affect relative prices. But they affect the price level only to the extent that they also affect either aggregate demand or output. Thus if prices rise in industry A without raising

---

[39] Admittedly, capital rationing tends to make the demand for money less stable.

[40] One way of determining whether someone is a Keynesian or a monetarist is to ask him for a quick and intuitive answer to the following question: "Suppose the price of petroleum rises. What will this do to the average of other prices?"

aggregate demand, this rise in the price of A has to be matched either by a reduction of output, or by a decline in the average of all other prices.

The alternative way of treating the price level is to approach it as the weighted sum of individual prices. These prices are then explained by the interaction of supply and demand in individual industries with the pricing policies of various industries. Changes in aggregate demand are certainly not ignored in this framework since they affect the demand curve faced by each industry, but there is considerable emphasis on the particular behavior of individual industries.

Both of these ways of looking at the price level are formally correct. While, they must therefore yield the same answers to someone who possesses all the required information, they do lead to different research strategies, and are therefore likely in practice to provide different answers.

Monetarists clearly use the aggregative approach to the price level. They look at changes in the quantity of money to determine changes in aggregate demand, and then allocate changes in aggregate demand between changes in prices and changes in output[41]. In this approach, at least in its simple version, the pricing decisions made by any particular industry have no effect on the overall price level, but affect only relative prices[42]. Hence, the monetarist typically rejects cost-push explanations of inflation.

It might be worth noting in passing that this rejection of all cost-push phenomena may well be unwarrented even within the monetarist framework. If industry A (with an inelastic demand) raises its prices, and thus reduces the aggregate demand that is available for other industries, these industries may respond, at least in part, not by cutting prices, but by cutting output. Insofar as this occurs, the general price level is raised by the behavior of industry A, and not just the relative price of commodity A. The extent to which this happens is an empirical question, and is likely to depend upon the degree of inflation in the economy. If prices in general are rising then, as industry A raises its

---

[41] See, for example, Keith *Carson,* "A Monetarist Model for Economic Stabilization", Federal Reserve Bank of St. Louis, Review, Vol. 52, April 1970, pp. 7 - 25.

[42] This is subject to the caveat that the central bank might raise the money stock to maintain output when some prominent industries raise their wages and prices, or when unemployment develops.

prices other industries can adjust their prices for this merely by not raising them by as much as they otherwise would. On the other hand, at a time when prices are generally stable they would have to lower their prices absolutely in order to offset the rise in the price of commodity A, and there is considerable evidence that prices are sticky downward.

The monetarist's macroeconomic, rather than microeconomic, approach to the price level fits in well with two of the previously discussed characteristics of monetarism. First, insofar as the rise in the price of one particular industry results in a price decline in other industries the economic system is inherently stable, at least as far as cost-push inflation is concerned. Second, if the price behavior of individual industries has no effect on the general price level, then this is one more reason for ignoring allocative detail. However, it should be noted, that while the monetarist's approach to the price level therefore goes along well with his belief in the stability of the private sector and the irrelevance of allocative detail, in neither case is the relationship one of logical entailment. One can accept the monetarist's hypotheses about the irrelevance of allocative detail, and the stability of the private sector, and yet, at the same time, accept the Keynesian approach to the price level[43].

The typical Keynesian's view of the price level is quite different from the monetarist view. To be sure, in the Keynesian model the price level is also determined by aggregate demand and supply, but to the Keynesian this formulation is not useful because he cannot take aggregate demand as given[44]. The monetarist, by contrast, can do this; if industry A raises its price, this does not change aggregate demand which depends upon the money stock[45]. But to the Keynesian the money stock is only

[43] The private sector may be stable even in the sense of being immune to cost-push inflation even if individual price increases do not result in corresponding price decreases in other sectors. This is so if, and only if, the forces making for cost-push are weak. Similarly, erratic shifts in expenditure motives could destabilize the private sector even if the monetarist's approach to the price level is correct. And allocative detail would then be important.

[44] Cf. Sidney *Weintraub,* Keynes and the Monetarists (New Brunswick, N. J., 1973) Ch. 7.

[45] Admittedly, this reasoning is only a first approximation, for it ignores the fact that an increase in the price level, by raising the interest rate, raises velocity. However, a monetarist may feel justified in ignoring this effect as minor because he may believe that the interest elasticity of the demand for money is low.

one of several factors determining aggregate demand. Thus while the rise in the price of commodity A lowers the real money stock, it may also raise the marginal efficiency of investment, particularly in industry A. In other words, while to the monetarist aggregate demand, as determined by the quantity of money, functions as a budget constraint, in the Keynesian system it is a variable. Hence, to the Keynesian it is at least possible that a rise in the price of commodity A raises aggregate demand enough so that other prices (and outputs) will not have to fall, and might even rise.

Since the aggregate demand effects of a rise in the price of commodity A are uncertain, the Keynesian is tempted to ignore them. And this temptation is frequently not resisted. A typical example is a study by Otto *Eckstein* and Gary *Fromm* in which they investigated the effect on the wholesale price index of the rise in the price of steel. They considered both the direct effect as well as the indirect effect of the steel price increase being passed forward by steel users, and concluded that "if steel prices had behaved like other industrial prices, the total wholesale price index would have risen by 40 percent less over the last decade ..."[46]. To a monetarist such a statement gives us only an arithmetic relationship which has no economic meaning because it ignores aggregate demand, and hence other prices[47]. And, indeed, it is hard to see how a Keynesian can really justify ignoring the indirect repercussions.

But the roots of this oversimplification can already be found in the "General Theory" since *Keynes* looked upon prices as determined by the wage rate and the marginal physical product of labor. Indeed *Keynes* specifically tried to bring the theory of the price level into contact with microeconomic factors such as marginal cost, and to eliminate the dichotomy between the determination of individual prices by marginal cost etc., and of the price level by macroeconomic factors such as the quantity of money and its velocity. Thus he wrote in Chapter 21 of the "General Theory": "One of the objects of the foregoing chapters has been to escape from this double life and bring the

---

[46] Otto *Eckstein* and Gary *Fromm*, "Steel and the Postwar Inflation", Study Paper Number 2, U.S. Congress, Joint Economic Committee, 86th Congress, 1st Session, Washington, D. C., 1959, p. 34.

[47] See Denis *Karnosky*, "A Primer on the Consumer Price Index", Federal Reserve Bank of St. Louis, Review, Vol. 56, July 1974, p. 7.

theory of price as a whole back to close contact with the theory of value[48]."

This Keynesian tendency to look at the price level as determined by costs in various industries has been furthered in recent years by an extensive empirical literature which estimates prices more on the basis of shifts in costs than on the basis of shifts in demand[49]. (However, this evidence is not always easy to interpret because changes in costs may be the result of changes in demand[50].) In addition, it has probably gained in acceptability from the use, as a first approximation or as an elementary teaching tool, of the Keynesian supply curve dichotomized at full employment. If changes in aggregate demand affect only output and not prices until full employment is reached, then if one is trying to explain the price level under conditions of less than full employment, the fact that a price rise in industry A changes the demand experienced in other industries can be ignored.

But while many — perhaps most — Keynesians treat the price level in the way just described, this way of looking at the price level is far from being a necessary implication of the Keynesian model. A Keynesian could focus on the overall price level rather than on its individual component prices to the same extent as a monetarist does without abandoning any basic part of Keynesian theory. As pointed out above, the only way a Keynesian can ignore the effects of the rise in the price of commodity A on the demand left over for other commodities is to assume that this rise in the price of commodity A generates an exactly offsetting increase in demand. But there is nothing in Keynesian theory that requires this to occur. The increase in the price of commodity A reduces real balances thus lowering demand. To be sure, this may be offset by

[48] "The General Theory", op. cit., p. 293.

[49] See William *Nordhaus*, "Recent Developments in Price Dynamics", in Board of Governors, Federal Reserve System, The Econometrics of Price Determination, Conference (Washington, D. C. 1972). See also W. *Godley* and W. *Nordhaus*, "Pricing in the Trade Cycle", Economic Journal, Vol. 82,, September 1972, pp. 853 - 882. Perhaps this tendency of Keynesians to treat prices as cost determined represents a partial fusion of the Keynesian and institutionalist schools.

[50] A leading monetarist, Phillip *Cagan*, has recently suggested that the dependence of price changes on changes in costs can be explained as a short run phenomenon resulting from the difficulties which firms have in coordinating their price changes. (Phillip *Cagan*, "Inflation: the Hydra-Headed Monster", Washington, D. C., 1974, pp. 21 - 24.)

an increase in the marginal efficiency of capital, but this need not happen. The effect of the increase in the price of commodity A on the marginal efficiency of investment may even be negative, or if it is positive, it need not be great enough to offset all the effect of the decline in real balances. Keynesian theory is silent on this. Strange as it may seem, there appears to be virtually no Keynesian literature on the effect of a rise in a particular price on income[51]. It is, of course, true that a change in demand for other commodities could affect the output of other commodities rather than their prices, but whether this happens or not depends upon where we are along the aggregate supply curve[52].

Thus, this dispute about the determinants of the price level is not so much a dispute between monetarism and Keynesianism as it is a dispute between monetarism and a particular specification of Keynesianism. And while this specification is a popular one, and is perhaps accepted by most Keynesians, it represents only one line of development of the basic Keynesian model.

Moreover, a monetarist too need not accept the typically monetarist position discussed above. He may argue that while a rise in the price of commodity A will eventually lower the prices of other commodities, in the short run it will lower their outputs rather than their prices. Hence, a Keynesian can accept the typically monetarist view on this issue, and a monetarist can adopt the typically Keynesian view, without either one abandoning his fundamental Keynesian or monetarist position[53].

---

[51] The only serious Keynesian discussion of this issue I know of is Abraham *Bergson's* "Price Flexibility and the Level of Income", Review of Economics and Statistics, Vol. XXV, February 1943, pp. 2 - 5.

[52] It is not clear whether a Keynesian is more likely than a monetarist to believe that the change will be in output rather than in prices. On the one hand, a Keynesian is more likely to stress price inflexibility and situations of underemployment. On the other hand, many monetarists stress expectational effects, and anticipatory pricing in inflation. Insofar as prices are set in anticipation of inflation, a decline in demands is likely to affect output rather than prices even during an inflation when downward price flexibility is not a problem.

[53] And while monetarists frequently consider prices to be fairly flexible, one can be a monetarist without this belief.

VI. Large versus Small Models

While Keynesians usually prefer large-scale structural models, monetarists prefer small reduced-form models[54]. This dispute on model size
involves many issues which are extraneous to the monetarist debate. To
a large extent it is an issue in theoretical econometrics concerned with
the validity of the single equation approach, rather than an issue in
monetary economics. Moreover, as *Friedman* has pointed out, it involves
also the question of whether we know enough to be able to represent
complex reality by the greatly simplified systems used even by large
models[55]. Hence, *Friedman* considers the debate about large versus small
models to be "almost entirely independent of the monetarist versus
Keynesian point of view"[56].

But even so, there are several ways in which the use of a reduced-
form model goes along well with monetarist hypotheses. One way relates to the transmission process. If changes in the money stock affect
income through a limited number of channels then it is tempting to cover
each of these channels, and thus to use a structural model. But if monetary changes affect the economy in a very large number of ways, as
the monetarist claims, then even a large structural model is not likely

---

[54] However, a number of fairly small Keynesian models do exist. It may be
worth noting that if one is trying to evaluate the Keynesian-monetarist debate
by comparing the predictive powers of monetarist and Keynesian models one
should compare the monetarist model (i. e. the *Andersen-Jordan* model), not
with large Keynesian models such as the *Wharton* model, as is sometimes
done, but with small Keynesian models. Thus, the finding that the *Andersen-
Jordan* model does well compared to the *Wharton* and O. B. E. models (Cf.
Yoel *Haitovsky* and George *Treyz*, "Forecasts with Quarterly Macroeconomic
Models, Equation Adjustment and Benchmark Predictions: The U.S. Experience", Review of Economics and Statistics, Vol. LIV, August 1972, pp. 317 -
325) is not as important for the Keynesian-monetarist dispute as is the finding
that the *Andersen-Jordan* model's performance is not outstanding when compared to that of small Keynesian models. (See S. K. *McKnees*, "A Comparison
of the GNP Forecasting Accuracy of the Fair and St. Louis Econometric
Models", in Federal Reserve Bank of Boston, New England Economic Review,
September/October 1973, pp. 29 - 34, and J. W. *Elliot*, "A Direct Comparison
of Short-Run GNP Forecasting Models", Journal of Business, Vol. 46, January
1973, pp. 33 - 60). The trouble with the *Wharton* or O. B. E. model may be its
structural, rather than its Keynesian, characteristics.
[55] See Milton *Friedman*, "Comment" in Universities-National Bureau Committee for Economic Research, Conference on Business Cycles (New York,
1951), pp. 112 - 114.
[56] Private communication.

to pick up all of them. Hence a reduced-form approach is likely to be more reliable.

Second, one of the great advantages of large structural models is that they provide detailed information on various economic sectors. This makes large structural models attractive to Keynesians, who are interested in allocative detail, but does little to recommend them to monetarists who are not interested in allocative detail. Furthermore, by focusing on expenditure motives, and looking upon people as being consumers, investors in inventories etc., the Keynesian is naturally concerned with many sectors. The monetarist, on the other hand, is concerned with people only as money holders, and hence is interested in only one sector, the supply of and demand for money. Third, someone who is concerned about the instability of the private sector in the sense that erratic shifts in expenditure incentives cause serious fluctuations, is likely to believe that to predict income one needs a large model which allows for the impact of these erratic factors on various sectors.

The relationship between the quantity theory per se and the choice of structural models versus reduced-form models is much less clear. "Ex ante", there is little, if any, reason why someone who believes in the strength of the monetary impulse, should necessarily believe in the desirability of reduced-form models. But there is an "ex post" relationship due to the fact that the most famous of all reduced form models, the *Andersen-Jordan* model, yields monetarist conclusions while structural models generally yield Keynesian conclusions. But the relationship between model size and the results obtained from the model are far from firm. Edward *Gramlich* has shown that *Andersen-Jordan* type models can generate not only monetarist results. but also Keynesian, or in-between, results depending on the monetary variables used[57].

Thus there are many links between various monetarist propositions and a preference for reduced form models. But as indicated above this linkage is not strong. A monetarist might well reject the use of reduced form models, while a Keynesian might prefer such models since the dispute is largely a matter of choice of estimation technique.

This concludes the discussion of the six monetarist propositions which relate to theory and techniques of analysis. In Part II of this paper I will discuss the remaining six policy-oriented propositions.

---

[57] "The Usefulness of Monetary and Fiscal Policy as Discretionary Stabilization Tools", Journal of Money, Credit and Banking, Vol. III, May 1971, Part 2, pp. 506 - 532.

The Structure of Monetarism (II)

By Thomas Mayer

In Part I of this paper which appeared in the previous issue of this journal* I selected twelve propositions characterizing the monetarist outlook, and discussed six of them. I will now discuss the remainder, and then summarize both parts of this paper. Three of these propositions relate to monetary policy. They are the choice of an indicator, the choice of a target, and the use of a monetary growth rule[58].

VII. Monetary Indicators

A monetary policy indicator is a variable that measures the thrust, that is the direction and magnitude, of monetary policy. It should therefore be a variable which is closely controlled by the central bank rather than being endogenous to the economy. Accurate data on it should be available without delay, and it should have a very high correlation with the target, or goal, variables. These requirements rule out both the money stock and the long term interest rate as monetary indicators. To be sure, to a monetarist the stock of money is the ultimate indicator of monetary policy in a different sense, because changes in the money stock foretell changes in income. But, at least in the United States, accurate data on the money stock are not available quickly, and besides, the money stock is partly endogenous, being some distance removed from central bank actions. Hence, it cannot be used as an indicator as the term is defined in this context. Similarly, for the Keynesian the long-term interest rate is not an adequate indicator because it is not under the close control of the central bank. Thus, neither monetarists nor Keynesians can use as their indicators those variables which would fit best into

---

* pp. 190.

[58] The indicators-targets dichotomy has recently been challenged by Benjamin *Friedman* ("Targets, Instruments and Indicators of Monetary Policy", Journal of Monetary Economics, forthcoming). However, since I am dealing here with the dispute between monetarists and Keynesians both of whom generally use this dichotomy, I am accepting it without questioning its validity.

their models. Both of them have to select other indicators which are closer to the tools used by the central bank.

Monetarists favor some measure of total reserves such as the reserve base adjusted for changes in reserve requirements or else unborrowed reserves. These are clearly under the control of the central bank, they are measured accurately without delay, and they have a powerful effect on the money stock, the monetarists' target variable. Keynesians, on the other hand, probably use the short-term interest rate as their favored indicator[59]. The short-term rate can then be related to one of their target variables, the long term interest rate, via term structure theory. And in addition, the short-term rate is a target in its own right to Keynesians since it affects flows into depository institutions, and hence residential construction. But this does not make it an indicator.

But it is important to note that the choice of a monetary policy indicator is to a considerable extent isolated from the rest of the Keynesian-monetarist dispute. The monetarist chooses a monetary base measure for two reasons. One is that his analysis of the money supply process tells him that this is the variable which best reflects monetary policy actions. The second is that he believes the monetary base (adjusted for reserve requirement changes) to be the best indicator of future changes in the money stock. As far as the first of these reasons is concerned this involves little dispute with Keynesians if only because few Keynesians have bothered to formulate a money supply hypothesis.

Turning to the second reason, the predictive power of a base measure, it is certainly true that one can predict the money stock fairly well in this way. But suppose that it were shown that changes in the short-term interest rate are an even better indicator of changes in the money stock. In this case, the monetarist should use the short-term interest rate as his indicator to predict the money stock. And the possibility that the short term interest rate is a better predictor of the money stock than are various reserve measures is by no means farfetched[60]. Furthermore, if it

---

[59] I have phrased this statement in such a tentative way because I am far from certain that most Keynesians really prefer the short term rate as their indicator. Unlike the monetarists, Keynesians have not written much on this topic.

[60] See Richard *Davis* and Frederick *Schadrack,* "Forecasting the Monetary Aggregates with Reduced Form Equations", in Federal Reserve Bank of New York, Monetary Aggregates and Monetary Policy (New York, 1974), pp. 60 - 71. See also Fred J. *Levine,* "Examination of the Money-Stock Control

were somehow shown that monetary policy changes are reflected better by the Federal Funds rate than by a reserve base measure, the monetarist could abandon his money supply hypothesis without thereby weakening his belief in any of the other monetarist propositions.

Conversely, a Keynesian could select total reserves as his policy indicator, and use this variable, rather than the short-term rate, to predict long term interest rates. The unsettled state of term structure theory hardly provides us with much confidence in trying to predict the long rate on the basis of the short term rate. Empirically, David *Fand* has shown that while there is a fairly high correlation between long term and short term rates, "in a cyclical context, the long rate is relatively independent of the short-run movements in the short rates"[61].

In addition to its use in gauging policy, a monetary indicator can also be used to measure the thrust of the monetary impulse regardless of whether this arises in the private or public sector. For this a monetarist may want to use the money stock, while a Keynesian may want to use a short term interest rate. Thus, if the money stock is growing at, say, a 10 percent rate, while the Federal Funds rate is 12 percent, a monetarist would call this a situation of monetary ease, while a Keynesian would call it tight money.

This distinction has some superficial relation to the dispute about the transmission mechanism because the Keynesian is looking at an interest rate while the monetarist is using the money stock. But, as discussed above, this dispute is, in part, a matter of terminology rather than a genuine dispute. (And, as will be shown below, in part it is the result of many Keynesians not being faithful to their Wicksellian tradition.)

Another connection is that to the Keynesian the short term interest rate is a valid partial indicator because it affects the flow of funds into financial intermediaries, and hence residential mortgage lending and construction. (This is a channel stressed strongly in the FMP-model.)

Approach of *Burger, Kalish,* and *Babb*", Journal of Money, Credit and Banking, vol. V, November 1973, pp. 924 - 938; and James *Pierce,* and Thomas *Thomson,* "Some Issues in Controlling the Stock of Money", in Federal Reserve Bank of Boston, Controlling Monetary Aggregates II: The Implementation (Boston n. d.), pp. 115 - 136.

[61] David *Fand,* "A Time Series Analysis of the 'Bills-Only' Theory of Interest Rates", Review of Economics and Statistics, vol. XLVIII, November 1966, p. 369.

Thus, here we have a component of monetarism which has only a limited relationship to the other components. The dispute about the proper indicator is to a considerable extent an isolated technical issue. Its intrusion into the monetarist-Keynesian debate can perhaps be explained as an historical accident. In the past the Federal Reserve has used short-term interest rates and money market conditions as its indicator in a different sense from the way the indicator concept is defined here. Instead of treating short term rates and money market conditions as an intermediate step on the way to long-term interest rates or to the money stock, it looked at short term rates and money market conditions as an immediate guide to how its policy is affecting income. In this way — which does not allow the money stock to be a recognized part of the process — the use of short term rates and money market conditions is, of course, contrary to monetarism. But as a result of the insights which monetarists have brought to this debate indicators are no longer thought of in this way.

VIII. Monetary Policy Targets

Obviously monetarists want to use the money stock as the target of monetary policy. Keynesians, on the other hand, prefer to use long term interest rates or, in some cases, bank credit or total credit. The extent to which each of these targets fits into the underlying theories of both schools can be seen best by considering the arguments for each of these targets.

To start with a comparison of the interest rate target and the money stock target there is again the measurement problem previously discussed in connection with the transmission process.

But with respect to the problem of chosing a target, the Keynesian is less worried about the difficulties of measuring the interest rate. This is so because one important Keynesian channel for the impact of monetary policy operates through the flows of funds into depository institutions. And since such flows depend upon a comparison of interest rates of depository institutions with open market rates, the problem of infering the expected real rate from the nominal interest rate does not arise. (And the problem of combining various observed and imputed rates into "the interest rate" is also less serious.) Furthermore, another channel is the effect of interest rates on the market value of the households' stock of securities, and hence on consumption. Here too, the problem of measuring the interest rate is not serious. However, for the traditional "cost of capital" effect of interest rates on investment, the measurement problem still exists.

Apart from the measurement problem the choice of a target involves another issue which arises from our inability to predict precisely changes in the liquidity preference schedule and in expenditure incentives[62]. If we would know very accurately the liquidity preference curve as well as expenditure incentives, then the central bank could easily select the interest rate which would optimize its objectives. Since with a known liquidity preference curve we can infer a particular quantity of money for each rate of interest and vice versa, leaving aside the above discussed measurement problem, it would be a matter of complete indifference whether the central bank picks a particular interest rate target or a money stock target.

But in actuality the central bank does not know the liquidity preference schedule and the strength of the expenditure incentives accurately. Suppose that the liquidity preference curve shifts outward unexpectedly. All the central bank observes is a rise in the interest rate. If it uses an interest rate target it responds to this rise in the interest rate by increasing the quantity of money sufficiently to lower it back to its previous level[63]. What it does is to satisfy the increased demand for money, or in terms of the cash balance equation, it offsets the rise in the Cambridge "k" by raising "M", thus keeping "PT" constant. If it had used a money stock target instead of its interest rate target, it would have kept the money stock constant and allowed the interest rate to rise. This increase in the interest rate would then have reduced income below its previous (presumably optimal) level.

On the other hand, suppose that the liquidity preference curve is predictable, but that expenditure incentives increase unexpectedly[64].

---

[62] For a detailed exposition of this argument see William *Poole,* "Optimal Choice of Monetary Policy Instruments in a Simple Stochastic Macro Model", Quarterly Journal of Economics, vol. 84, May 1970, pp. 197 - 216; and "Rules of Thumb for Guiding Monetary Policy" in Board of Governors, Federal Reserve System, Open Market Policies and Operating Procedures, Staff Studies, Washington, D. C., pp. 135 - 189.

[63] The assumption that the money growth rate and the interest rate are negatively correlated is justified by the analysis being only very short run.

[64] It is worth noting that what is relevant is not the stability of either the IS or LM curve, but its predictability since the central bank can readily offset predictable fluctuations.

This too raises the rate of interest. If the central bank has an interest rate target and counteracts this rise in the interest rate it allows income to rise in an unintended way. In other words, if expenditure incentives increase the interest rate should also increase, thus acting as an automatic stabilizer. Hence, if it is expenditure motives rather than the liquidity preference function which changes in an unpredicted way, then an interest rate target does harm, and a money stock target is preferable. But if it is the liquidity preference function which is the unpredictable one, then an interest rate target is superior[65].

On both of these issues a monetarist prefers a money stock target. Regarding the measurement problem, someone who accepts the monetarist transmission process believes that the money stock can be measured more accurately than can the interest rate. On the relative predictability of the liquidity preference function and the expenditure functions a quantity theorist considers the liquidity preference function (i. e. the demand for money) to be the stabler of the two[66]. Hence, the monetarist's preference for a money stock target over an interest rate target can be seen as an implication of the quantity theory and its transmission mechanism.

Apart from the money stock and the long term interest rate there is a third major potential target for monetary policy. This is a credit measure, such as bank credit or total credit. Here too, the quantity theory and the monetarist's version of the transmission process decide the issue for the monetarist. As a quantity theorist he believes that the effect of changes in the money stock on income is more imporant than the effect of changes in bank credit, for otherwise he would hold a quantity theory of bank credit rather than a quantity theory of money.

---

[65] A third aspect of the choice between a money stock target and an interest rate target relates to the problem of lags in the effects of monetary policy. Since many types of expenditures respond only slowly to a change in the interest rate the effects of monetary policy tend to be delayed. But this delay can be offset if interest rates initially overshoot their new level. (See Donald *Tucker*, "Dynamic Income Adjustments to Money Supply Changes", American Economic Review, vol. LVI, June 1966, pp. 433 - 449.) Insofar as the central bank follows a money stock target such an overshoot occurs automatically. But with an interest rate target, the central bank may fail to allow for the required overshoot. And even if it aims for an overshoot, it does not know how large it should be.

[66] The monetarist looks upon expenditure motives as stable too, unless disturbed by variations in the money growth rate, since he treats the private sector as stable, but even so, he takes the demand for money as the stabler one.

Moreover, in his analysis of the transmission process the monetarist rejects a credit and borrowing cost interpretation[67].

The matter is more complex for a Keynesian. As indicated above, the problem of measuring the interest rate is of serious concern to him only with respect to the cost of capital channel. Since different Keynesians attach different weights to this channel, it is hard to say how significant the measurement problem is for the Keynesian's choice of a target. Furthermore, a Keynesian may — or may not — be concerned about the difficulties of measuring the money stock.

With regard to the second issue, the relative predictability of the liquidity preference and expenditure functions, *Keynes* originally considered both the liquidity preference function and the investment function to be erratic without indicating which was the more unstable. Modern Keynesians, on the other hand, have deemphasized the speculative motive for liquidity preference which for *Keynes* was the source of its instability, and appear to believe that the liquidity preference function is fairly stable and predictable. On the other hand, Keynesians also believe that investment and consumption, while unstable, are predictable. It is therefore not really clear whether Keynesians typically consider the liquidity preference function or the expenditure functions to be the more predictable. Perhaps there is a presumption that, on the whole, they consider the demand for money to be the more predictable variable which should make them prefer a money stock target.

Moreover, insofar as they are the intellectual heirs of the Wicksellian tradition, Keynesians should prefer a money stock target to an interest rate target. It was *Wicksell* who taught us the dangers of keeping the money rate of interest fixed (as happens with an interest rate target) when the natural rate of interest changes. All in all, Keynesian theory is more or less neutral on the issue of the money stock versus the interest rate as the target.

The third potential target is the volume of bank credit, or total credit. Some Keynesians have accepted such targets and they, of course, differ sharply from the monetarists. But one can be a good Keynesian while rejecting the reasoning of the *Radcliffe* Report.

---

[67] A fourth potential target, and money market conditions, is hardly taken seriously anymore, at least in the United States.

IX. The Monetary Growth Rule

The next component of monetarism is the constant money growth rule. Such a rule fits well into the monetarist framework on several counts. First, it is closely related to the quantity theory. If the demand for money is indeed constant when adjusted for trend, then a constant growth rate of the supply of money would result in income too growing at a constant rate[68]. Hence, someone who accepts the quantity theory of money is much more likely to favor constant money growth then is someone who believes either that the demand for money is unstable, or that fluctuations in income are largely due to nonmonetary factors, factors which the central bank can offset[69]. Second, a belief in constant money growth also fits in with the monetarist's belief that the private sector is inherently stable. If this is the case there is at best a limited amount of good that could be accomplished by variations in the money growth rate. Third, belief in a constant money growth rate requires acceptance of a money stock target, for the monetary growth rule is really only a special version of the use of a monetary target; it merely sets a specific, unvarying target.

In addition, the constant money growth rule also has some connection, albeit a looser connection, with two other components of monetarism, the disinterest in allocative detail, and the monetarist view of the price level. Someone who is interested in allocative detail is likely to be concerned, from time to time, with the impact of financial stringency on a particular sector, such as residential construction. He is therefore likely to feel, at least occasionally, that the monetary growth

---

[68] A monetary growth rule is supposed to provide a growth rate of money income which is stable, though this may be a stable rate of inflation or deflation.

[69] This conclusion is subject to the caveat that in their formal theory monetarists consider the demand for money to be stable only in a functional sense. Hence, if many of the variables in the money demand functions fluctuate, the demand for money, and therefore income, would also fluctuate under a constant money supply rule. But according to *Friedman*, and perhaps to most monetarists, this distinction between the functional stability and the constancy of the demand for money does not create a serious problem. Insofar as the demand for money is a function of permanent income or wealth it is likely to grow at a steady rate. To be sure, it is also a function of the nominal rate of interest. But fluctuations in the nominal interest rate are largely the result of previous fluctuations in the money growth rate and prices. Hence, given a constant money growth rule, velocity would tend to be fairly stable in a numerical, as well as a functional, sense.

rate should be changed to protect a particular sector. A monetarist who believes that allocative detail is outside the purview of macroeconomic stabilization policy is much less likely to feel this way. The monetarist view of the price level reinforces the case for a monetary rule by implying that one of the factors which might cause someone to favor variations in the monetary growth rate, cost-push inflation, does not occur.

Having seen how the monetary growth rule fits into the rest of monetarism let us see to what extent it conflicts with Keynesian theory. It does conflict in one way because the Keynesian looks upon velocity as being variable; a belief connected with his view that the private sector is unstable, and with his emphasis on the interest elasticity of the demand for money. Hence, to the Keynesian a constant rate of monetary growth would not result in an acceptable degree of income stability. However, a Keynesian may well accept some of the other arguments mentioned above which cause a monetarist to favor a constant growth rate. Thus, a Keynesian need not consider it desirable to change the money growth rate to accommodate particular sectors of the economy. And similarly, he need not accept the likelihood of cost-push inflation, or he may feel that while cost-push inflation is a serious possibility it should be resisted by not creating the additional money stock demand at higher prices. Moreover, as pointed out above, a Keynesian may well accept the use of a money stock target.

Despite the fact that the monetary growth rule fits in so well with a large number of monetarist propositions it is in a very important way a separate issue, independent of the validity of all other monetarist propositions. This is so because the main arguments for a constant monetary rule are essentially quite different from what has been discussed so far. They are that monetary policy affects the economy with long and unpredictable lags, or that the central bank is likely to be inefficient and follow goals other than income stabilization[70]. These hypotheses are not derivable from other monetarist propositions, nor do they conflict in any important way with Keynesian propositions. Yet while, strictly speaking, these two hypotheses are neither necessary nor sufficient conditions for the desirability of a monetary rule, they are close to it[71].

---

[70] Another reason sometimes given for a monetary growth rule is that it reduces arbitrary government interference, substituting as it does the rule of law for the rule of men.

[71] They are not really necessary conditions, because someone might advocate the monetary growth rule solely on the basis that it curbs arbitrary government

Thus, if it were shown conclusively that the lags of monetary policy are so long and variable that discretionary monetary policy is likely to be destabilizing, or that the central bank is too inefficient to operate a successful stabilization policy, then many — probably most — Keynesians would support a monetary rule. And concern that a discretionary stabilization policy may be destabilizing is far from being a monetarist monopoly. In fact, a classic article warning of this danger was written by a Keynesian, A. W. *Phillips*[72].

Conversely, if it were shown conclusively that discretionary policy can stabilize the economy, then probably most monetarists would reject the monetary growth rule. To be sure, a monetarist with his beliefs in a stable demand for money, and in the inherent stability of the private sector, is likely to expect that even a successful stabilization policy will do relatively little good, but it could still do some good. Hence, it is not surprising that belief in a stable monetary growth rule is not a component of *Friedman's* definition of monetarism[73]. Thus, the debate about a monetary growth rule transcends the issue of monetarism versus Keynesianism[74].

---

power. They are also not really sufficient conditions because someone might reject the rule, even though it would stabilize income, because he believes that monetary policy should be used to stabilize particular sectors of the economy, to help government finance, or to obtain balance of payments equilibrium, etc.

The belief that stabilization policies are actually destabilizing may appear to conflict with one Keynesian proposition, the instability of the private sector. If the government sector has been a net contributor to instability it would seem that the private sector must be relatively stable. But this reasoning is questionable. At least in the United States, discretionary fiscal policy has frequently not behaved countercyclically; government expenditures have frequently risen at times of high activity. Similarly, if one accepts a money stock measure of monetary policy it also has usually not been countercyclical in the post-war period.

[72] "Some Notes on the Estimation of Time-Forms of Reactions in Interdependent Dynamic Systems", Economica, Vol. 23, May 1956, pp. 99 - 113.

[73] The Counter-Revolution in Monetary Theory (London 1970), p. 26.

[74] In any case, the debate about stable money growth versus discretionary policy is in the process of becoming technologically obsolete. Recent work suggests that an intermediate position, a stable central bank reaction function to changes in income, may well be superior to both a fixed money growth rule and to ad hoc discretionary policy. (See J. Phillip *Cooper*, Development of the Monetary Sector, Prediction and Policy Analysis in the FRB-MIT-Penn Model, Lexington, Mass., 1974.)

X. Absence of an Inflation-Unemployment Trade-Off

Having looked at the basic theory of the monetarists, their choice of estimation procedures, and their views on monetary policy there remain three monetarist propositions having to do with economic policy in general. One of these is the monetarists' belief that, except in the short run, the *Phillips*-curve is in real terms, so that, at most, there exists a very limited trade-off between inflation and unemployment.

The real *Phillips*-curve is related to three of the previously discussed monetarist propositions, the quantity theory, the stability of the private sector, and the stable monetary growth rate. If the *Phillips*-curve (over the time span relevant for analysis) is in real terms, then an increase in the quantity of money does not affect real income, but affects only prices since it merely changes the wage unit. Moreover changes in Keynesian variables such as fiscal policy then have no lasting effect on real income[75].

But a Keynesian could accept the real *Phillips*-curve' and still claim that changes in the marginal efficiency of investment are more important than changes in the monetary growth rate in explaining short run fluctuations in real income. This is so because, with his belief in the instability of the private sector, a Keynesian believes that much of the time the economy is in a situation where the marginal efficiency of investment has changed, and the nominal wage has not yet adapted to this change, so that real income is affected.

The stable money growth rate rule too has a connection with the real *Phillips*-curve. One objection to it is that it would not allow the central bank to intervene when unemployment becomes too high. But if there exists only a very short-run trade-off between unemployment and inflation such intervention would do little good, and hence a monetary growth rate rule becomes more acceptable[76].

---

[75] Cf. Jerome *Stein*, "Unemployment, Inflation and Monetarism", American Economic Review, Vol. LXIV, December 1974, pp. 867 - 887. Two other ways in which the real *Phillips*-curve fits in well with the quantity theory are the quantity theory's emphasis on the distinction between real and nominal magnitudes, and the use of adaptive expectations in both the modern quantity theory and the real *Phillips*-curve analysis.

[76] The direction of the connection between the real *Phillips*-curve and the monetary growth rule is from the real *Phillips*-curve to the growth rate rule rather than vice versa.

Having seen that the real *Phillips*-curve fits into the monetarist framework, to what extent is it inconsistent with the Keynesian framework? One obvious inconsistency arises in an historical context. In the "General Theory" *Keynes* sharply rejected *Pigou's* assumption that workers bargain for a real wage (which is what the real *Phillips*-curve says), and argued instead that workers bargain for a certain money wage.

A second inconsistency relates to the current Keynesian, or neo-Keynesian, model. In this model the *Phillips*-curve fixed in nominal terms is used to determine the price level. If a real *Phillips*-curve is substituted for the nominal *Phillips*-curve a Keynesian has no way of determining the equilibrium price level[77]. In this way, the acceptance of the real *Phillips*-curve would weaken Keynesian theory.

But despite this, the debate about the real or nominal nature of the *Phillips*-curve is to a considerable extent independent of the Keynesian-monetarist debate. It is essentially an empirical issue which has to be resolved by detailed studies of the labor market, rather than by settling the monetarist-Keynesian debate in some other way, and then deducing the nature of the *Phillips*-curve from the result reached in the monetarist-Keynesian debate. If empirical studies were to show conclusively that the *Phillips*-curve is in real terms a Keynesian could surely accept this result without abandoning Keynesian theory in favor of monetarism. Conversely, if the empirical evidence were to show that the *Phillips*-curve is fixed in nominal terms, a monetarist could easily live with this conclusion.

XI. Concern about Inflation

Monetarists appear to be more concerned than are Keynesians about the disadvantages of unanticipated inflation, and to be relatively less concerned about the disadvantages of unemployment[78]. This choice

---

[77] Insofar as prices are changing a Keynesian could use an expectational adjustment model to derive a modified *Phillips*-curve which would then allow him to determine the price level. But if the inflation rate stays constant long enough for expectations to have fully adapted a Keynesian could predict neither the price level nor the unemployment rate unless he has independent information on what the natural rate of unemployment is. However, the same is true for a monetarist. He also needs a specialist in labor markets to tell him the natural rate of unemployment.

[78] And there are monetarist objections even to fully anticipated inflation. As *Friedman* has pointed out (The Optimum Quantity of Money, op. cit., Ch. 1)

between these two evils can be related to several of the foregoing characteristics of monetarists. One is that the quantity theorist pays much more attention to the likelihood of price changes than does the Keynesian. Indeed, one of the standard criticisms which monetarists make of Keynesians is to accuse them of assuming that the price level is constant[79]. And someone who considers price level changes to be a serious possibility will obviously be concerned much more about potential inflation than someone who more frequently takes the price level as constant.

Second, there is the belief in the inherent stability of the private sector at an acceptable rate of unemployment. While the modern Keynesian may readily concede that underemployment cannot be an equilibrium, he still stresses that serious underemployment may occur frequently, and continue for a very long time. The monetarist, by contrast, has a stronger belief in the corrective forces that bring the private sector close to full employment if it is left undisturbed by government policy. Hence, the monetarist worries less about unemployment than the Keynesian does.

Third, there is the monetary growth rule. A stable monetary growth rule would limit the potential inflation rate by denying the economy the additional liquidity needed during an inflation. Hence, someone who is very concerned about inflation, and the inflationary bias of the political process, might be led by this to favor the monetary growth rule[80]. On the other hand, if velocity falls or productivity increases to an extent unanticipated when the monetary rule is instituted, substantial unemployment might result. Hence a Keynesian who is very concerned about unemployment may, for this reason, reject a stable money growth rule.

A fourth, rather tenuous, connection is that, by accepting a real *Phillips*-curve the monetarist abandons any hope of being able, except in the short run, to lower unemployment at the cost of inflation. And while this may not make the monetarist more concerned about inflation,

---

the price level should be falling to induce the public to hold the optimum quantity of money.

[79] See, for example, Milton *Friedman*, "Comments on the Critics", op. cit., pp. 917 - 918.

[80] Admittedly, a constant monetary growth rate, if set at too high a level, might result in inflation. But this would be a fully anticipated inflation.

it causes him to oppose as essentially useless inflationary policies which aim at raising employment.

But again, the issue under discussion is far removed from the main area of monetarist-Keynesian contention. For example, if we had conclusive evidence on the validity of the quantity theory and the monetarist transmission process, it would probably do little to change our relative degree of concern about inflation and unemployment. This depends much more on other issues, such as the effects of inflation on income distribution, and on fundamentally ethical judgments.

XII. Dislike of Government Intervention

The final characteristic of monetarists, at least in the United States, is a dislike of government intervention. This is not limited to macro-economics; in general monetarists appear to be much more satisfied with the outcome of market processes than most Keynesians are. There is, of course, no way of proving that this attitude should be considered a component of monetarism, rather than a characteristic which those economists who are monetarists happen to have for extraneous reasons. However, a dislike of government regulations fits very well with most of the previously discussed components of monetarism. Thus, a belief in the quantity theory implies that there should be no countercyclical fiscal policy. Moreover, a countercyclical fiscal policy might result in the government sector expanding in a recession more than it shrinks in the expansion, so that it grows secularly[81]. In any case, if the private sector is inherently stable no countercyclical policy may be needed or be desirable. Someone who objects to government regulations is less likely to be interested in allocative detail than someone who has to have information about various sectors to plan government policy. And conversely, if the behavior of various sectors does not matter for macroeconomic policy, some government regulations should be abolished. Furthermore, if the behavior of the price level is essentially independent of the pricing policies and wage policies followed in "strategic in-dustries" then this is another reason why some government regulations are unnecessary.

Using the money stock rather than interest rates or bank credit as the target of monetary policy means that the government can leave the

---

[81] See James *Tobin*, op. cit., p. 63. However, *Tobin* also points out a negative relationship; insofar as fiscal policy has little, or no, effect on income, inflation cannot be used as an excuse for cutting the budget.

determination of interest rates and bank credit to free market, and can confine its attention to the stock of money, something just about always considered outside the domain of the private market. A monetary growth rule, obviously reduces the need for discretionary policy. And if the *Phillips*-curve is such that one cannot successfully trade off unemployment and inflation then here is another task the government should not attempt.

Finally, there are several links between a concern about inflation and concern about the growth of government. One is that inflation can easily lead to political pressures for the imposition of wage and price controls. A second is that, given a progressive tax system, inflation raises the share of the government sector with the resulting temptation to increase government expenditures. A third link is that since one way government expenditures have risen is through inflationary finance, prevention of inflation may indirectly limit government expenditures. Fourth, deficit expenditures when financed by newly created money, as is so often the case, tend to be inflationary.

A critic of monetarism might therefore be tempted to claim that monetarism is basically an "ideological" doctrine; that it consists of finding seemingly technical reasons to hide a basic commitment in favor of unfettered capitalism. But this temptation to play amateur psychoanalyst should be firmly resisted. A monetarist can reply to it very easily by reversing the argument, and claiming that the ideological element in the debate rests with the Keynesians; that it is their ideological commitment to government regulations and the growth of bureaucracy that makes them reject the monetarist's sound arguments on various technical issues of monetary economics.

On a more worthwhile level than such name-calling it should be noted that while opposition to government regulations fits in well with monetarism, it is still a very loose connection in one important sense[82]. One can be a radical and yet accept all the other monetarist propositions discussed above. Thus, a radical might even accept the constant monetary growth rule on the basis that this is the best one can do under capitalism[83]. In fact, a planner in an almost totally controlled economy,

---

[82] See *ibid.*, p. 63.

[83] A radical, unless he is Marxist, need not reject the monetarist's belief in the inherent stability of the private sector since his objection to capitalism could be founded on grounds other than instability.

such as China, should find the quantity theory more useful than the Keynesian theory[84]. Conversely, one can be a right-wing extremist without being a monetarist.

XIII. Some Other Differences

If one wants to look for a common thread connecting various monetarist propositions one need not confine oneself to an ideological consideration since there is a methodological element available.

We live in a world too complex for our intellectual apparatus. We must therefore do either of two things. One is to take account of a great many factors at the cost of being able to see their interrelations only in a vague, clouded way. The other is to simplify drastically, and to look at only a few factors. Along these lines one can classify economists into "cloud makers" and into "oversimplifiers", to use two derogatory terms. Using this dichotomy the Keynesian is a cloud maker while the monetarist is an oversimplifer[85]. Thus the quantity theory is simpler than the Keynesian theory in the sense of taking account of fewer variables[86]. The picture is less obvious as far as the monetarist transmission process is concerned. The monetarist view of this process is certainly more cloudy and less clear than the Keynesian one, since the monetarist believes that it works through a large number of channels, some of which he cannot specify. However, a vague transmission

---

[84] The Keynesian's marginal efficiency of investment and the multiplier play little, or no, role in determining income in a controlled economy. On the other hand, since the public has freedom to adjust its money holdings the quantity theory is relevant.

[85] This does not imply that the quantity theorist thinks we live in a simple world. One may want to use simple models precisely because the world is so complex that no complex, but still manageable, model can do it justice. This can be seen readily on an empirical level. If we try to forecast a variable which has determinants of only moderate complexity we tend to use a standard "explanatory" regression. But if we try to forecast a variable with extremely complex determinants were are more likely to use a naive model or some other autoregressive scheme.

[86] The *Brunner-Meltzer* version of the quantity theory gives the impression of being more complex than the Keynesian theory since it criticizes Keynesian theory for ignoring some important effects. But this appearance is due, in part, to the fact that when *Brunner* and *Meltzer* criticize the Keynesian model they focus on the greatly oversimplified IS, LM diagram which does not give the full Keynesian story. Although they introduce some additional variables, they omit some of the Keynesian variables.

process, when combined with *Friedman's* methodological views results
in a simple, rather than a complex, view of the world. *Friedman* finds
a close relationship between changes in money and in nominal income,
and presumably does not feel greatly worried by the fact that it is difficult to specify the transmission process[87]. He stresses predictive power
rather than descriptive realism[88].

The monetarist's hypothesis that the private sector is inherently
stable also helps to simplify the analysis, since, if true, this means that
we do not have to concern ourselves in macroeconomics with fluctuations in expenditure motives. Hence, one can dispense with the detailed
Keynesian analyses of consumption and investment, as well as many
complex business cycle theories. The monetarist's disinterest in allocative
detail obviously also simplifies macroeconomics. The same is true for his
use of small, rather than large, econometric models, and for his focus
on the overall price level rather than on the prices charged in individual
industries.

Using total reserves rather than a combination of short term interest
rates and money market conditions as an indicator of monetary policy
helps to simplify the analysis of monetary policy. Indeed, monetarists
have criticized the use of money market conditions because of the
complexity and vagueness it introduces[89]. The use of a stable money
growth rate also obviously simplifies the conduct of monetary policy.
Indeed, one of the leading monetarist arguments for it is that we do not
have the required information, such as knowledge of lags, to do better
with discretionary policy than a simple growth rate rule does. And a
Phillips-curve that does not allow for any unemployment-inflation
trade-off simplifies macroeconomics by removing one very difficult

---

[87] To be sure, *Friedman* believes that the mere correlation of money and income is not enough to establish the quantity theory, that a plausible transmission process is needed. (See Milton *Friedman* and Anna *Schwartz*, "Money and
Business Cycles", Review of Economics and Statistics, Vol. XLV, February
1963, Supplement, p. 59.) However, a vague, generalized sketch of the transmission process may suffice for this.

[88] Karl *Brunner* too, has rejected the type of descriptive realism that tests
theories by evaluating the validity of their assumptions. (See his "Assumptions'
and the Cognitive Quality of Theories", Synthese, Vol. 20, 1969, pp. 501 - 525.

[89] See Karl *Brunner* and Allan *Meltzer*, Some General Features of the Federal
Reserve's Approach to Policy, U.S. Congress, House, Committee on Banking
and Currency, Subcommittee on Domestic Finance, 88th Congress, 2nd Session
(Washington, D.C. 1964).

Figure 1: Interrelation of Monetarist Propositions

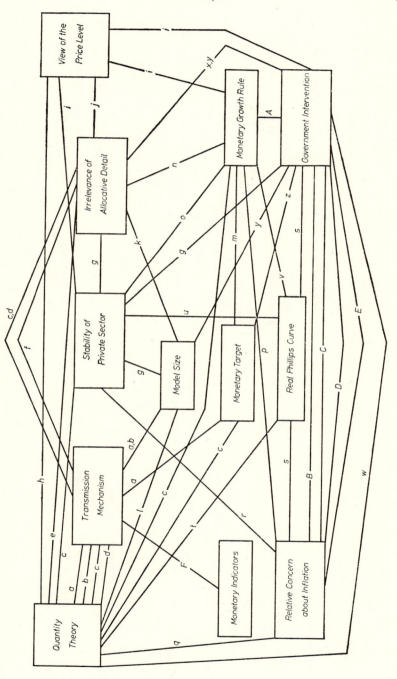

Notes:

a measurement problems
b range of assets considered
c stability of demand for money
d relative price and stock effects
e disinterest in expenditure motives
f unimportance of expenditure motives and of peculiarities of sectors
g little concern about instability
h aggregate demand determined by quantity of money
i immunity to cost-push inflation
j irrelevance of price behavior in individual industries
k disinterest in particular sectors
l results reached by models
m growth rule as special type of monetary target
n no need to help particular sectors
o little need to offset fluctuations
p prevent unanticipated inflation
q focus on price flexibility
r natural rate of unemployment

s absence of unemployment-inflation trade-off
t adaptive expectations and emphasis on distinction between real and nominal magnitudes
u real variables unaffected by inflation
v absence of trade-off ameliorates potential loss from monetary rule
w ineffectiveness of fiscal policy
x information on sectors not needed
y intervention in sectors not needed for macroeconomic policy
z no interference with interest rates or credit volume
A no discretionary monetary policy
B less danger of wage and price controls
C inflationary impact of government expenditures financed by new money creation
D inflation raises government receipts
E inflationary finance facilitates additional expenditures
F focus on the money stock rather than on interest rate and disregard of the financial intermediation-residential construction channel

question, selection of the optimal trade-off. Only two components of monetarism, the use of a money stock target, and the concern about inflation do not fit the picture of monetarism as simplification.

There exists also another element that links six monetarist propositions. This is the monetarist's skepticism about how much we really know about the short run workings of the economy. Monetarists generally seem to be less optimistic about this than are Keynesians. If we really do know little about the short-run behavior of the economy, then the monetarist transmission process is less subject to the criticism that it does not try to spell out the channels of monetary influence in any detail. Any attempt to do this could then be considered presumptuous. Second, if our knowledge of short-run economic behavior is limited, then we may not have an adequate framework for using information about allocative detail. Third, we then do not know enough to build useful large scale econometric models. Fourth, the less our knowledge, the weaker is the case for "fine tuning", and the stronger is the case for a monetary rule[90], and hence the use of a money stock target. Finally, the less we know about the economy the less likely are government regulations to improve it.

XIV. Conclusion

This paper has dealt with various propositions that make up monetarism, broadly defined, and showed that they form a coherent whole. With one exception (the use of a total reserve measure as the indicator of monetary policy) they fit together in the sense that definitive proof of the validity of one of the more basic propositions would increase the plausibility of some of the other propositions. Figure 1 shows relations which have been traced here between the various propositions.

But this does not mean that monetarism is a paradigm which must be accepted or rejected as a whole. As pointed out above, with the exception of the quantity theory itself, and perhaps its transmission process, every single proposition of monetarism is one which a Keynesian could accept while rejecting others, and still maintain his adherence to basic Keynesian theory. In particular, the policy propositions are

---

[90] This statement is subject to the objection that a great deal of knowledge is required to decide on the correct long run growth rate rule. But monetarists believe that the economy can adapt itself to any monetary growth rate as long as this rate is stable.

readily detachable from the theoretical propositions of monetarism, and can be accepted without qualms by a Keynesian. Conversely, someone who accepts some of the monetarist propositions, including the two most basic ones (the quantity theory and the monetarist version of the transmission process) need not therefore accept all the others.

Hence, a good case can be made for abolishing the term "monetarism" altogether, and for treating each proposition independently. This would reduce the unfortunate polarization of economists into monetarists and anti-monetarists, with the accompanying tendency to accept or reject various propositions on a basis other than the empirical evidence bearing on them[91]. Admittedly, this may well be the counsel of perfection since the term "monetarism" is now so well established and convenient. But eclecticism is fully justified[92].

[91] As Cyrus *Gordon* (Riddles in History, New York, 1974, p. 156) has put it, "all schools of thought are in reality 'schools of un-thought' to the extent that they prevent us from going to where the facts should lead us".

[92] Thus Karl *Brunner* has argued that: " ... the four major issues [in the monetarist debate] allow a variety of combinations. ... The evolution of such a spectrum with a 'middle ground' should enrich our future research activities. Such activities should yield substantive results over the years to the extent that economists successfully avoid the 'media propensity' of equating all issues with ideological positions." "Commentary on 'The State of the Monetarist Debate' ", Federal Reserve Bank of St. Louis, Review, Vol. 55, September 1973, p. 14.

Thomas Mayer on Monetarism

By Martin Bronfenbrenner

> When I use a word it means just what I want
> it to mean — neither more nor less.
>
> *Alice in Wonderland*

I.

Professor *Mayer* and I collaborated amicably and — I hope — usefully during our Michigan State days in the 1950's.[1] He has since gone West from Michigan, while I have gone East. It nevertheless seems strange to sit in judgement on his work — even at his own invitation. I have accepted the invitation mainly in the hope of clarifying some of my own ideas as a by-product of considering his.

II.

Mayer's essay on "The Structure of Monetarism"* is a long exercise on the nature and inter-relationships of twelve propositions which he treats as comprising contemporary monetarism. The first four of these propositions — the quantity theory of money, some distinctly monetarist transmission mechanism between monetary and income changes, belief in the inherent stability of the private economy, and the unimportance of allocative (distributive) disaggregation for the explanation of short-run macroeconomic effects — he sees as necessary conditions for monetarism but offers no formal proof which might satisfy a professional logician. The other eight — including such well-known facets as preference for monetary rules, unconcern with guaranteed full employment, distrust of the *Phillips* curve and "incomes policies," dislike for inflationary finance — are either arguments in support of his "big four' or policy conclusions or corollaries from them, which most but not all monetarists do in fact support. The entire edifice is summarized

---

* Kredit und Kapital, Vol. 8 (1975) pp. 190 and pp. 293.
[1] M. *Bronfenbrenner* and Thomas *Mayer*, "Liquidity Functions in the American Economy." Econometrica (April, 1960.)

diagrammatically in a figure which seeks to include not only all twelve propositions but also the principal relations *Mayer* believes to exist between them. Any such construction is inevitably subjective, but *Mayer* hopes it may nevertheless be objectively helpful to his professional colleagues.

III.

Mayer sets monetarism against the conventional "Keynesianism" of, say, the Northern wing of the American Democratic party and its economic spokesmen. I should myself have preferred the antithesis to have been "fiscalism" without quite so much emphasis on the doctrines of the late Lord *Keynes*, either in the "General Theory" of 1936[2] or as they may have been developing in the inflationary milieu at the time of his death ten years later.[3]

Let us denote by pure fiscalism the doctrine that "money does not matter." This implies that 1. the economic effects of a fiscal measure are independent of the way that measure is financed, and that 2. changes in the stock of money have no effect on the level of economic activity unless embodied in a fiscal measure for introducing the new money into the economy (or withdrawing money from it). Similarly, let us denote by pure monetarism the doctrine that "only money matters." This implies that (1) the economic effects of a change in the money stock are largely independent of the methods by which the positive or negative increment is injected into or withdrawn from the economy, and that (2) fiscal policy measures have negligible effects on the economy apart from their monetary consequences.

Let us also suppose, without asking embarrassing questions about measurement, that a continuum could somehow be set up, with pure fiscalists at one end (if any exist) and pure monetarists at the other (subject to the same restriction). Taxonomic exercises like *Mayer's* are valuable if, as I think he believes, economists tend to be bunched at the

---

[2] Even in the depths of depression, there is room for doubt that "the economics of *Keynes*" was so fiscalist as "Keynesian economics" subsequently became. There doubts constitute, in part, the *Clower-Leijonhufvud* reinterpretation of the "General Theory", which I interpret as shifting emphasis from the *shapes* to the *volatilities* of certain crucial functions. See Axel *Leijonhufvud*, "Keynesian Economics and the Economics of Keynes" (New York: Oxford University Press, 1968).

[3] J. M. *Keynes*, "The Balance of Payments of the United States," Economic Journal (June, 1946).

two ends of this continuum, with relatively few eclectics in the middle. They are less useful if, as I have come increasingly to intuit[4], the distribution would be more or less even throughout the continuum (except perhaps at the two extremes) with no gaps or bald spots open for other-than-arbitrary cuts between monetarists and fiscalists.

Difficulties are compounded by at least two other considerations:

1. A fiscal measure (an expansion) is accompanied by a monetary expansion to keep interest rates down and prevent multiplier attenuation. Is the resulting income increase to be attributed to the fiscal expansion — in Hicksian terms, the shift in the *IS* curve — or to its monetary corollary — the shift in the *LM* curve?[5]

2. Assume that the *Mundell* assignment of policy tools is correct[6] — fiscal policy to the internal balance and monetary policy to the external balance. Is this fiscalism or monetarism? Since *Mayer* is dealing with the closed economy at least 95 per cent of the time, I presume he would call *Mundell* a fiscalist; I am not sure of my own stand, especially for small countries with high international dependence.

IV.

Accepting the risk of pedantry, I wish more macroeconomists — including *Mayer* — would distinguish carefully between *stability* and *volatility* in describing the functions with which they are dealing. To

---

[4] Of my own colleagues at Duke University, perhaps seven (including myself) have recently taught or written in the macroeconomics — monetary policy — fiscal policy triangle. Of these, I should classify three as decidedly more fiscalist that I, two as decidedly more monetarist, and the other as located close to myself on my hypothetical continuum.

[5] In my own eclectic and unoriginal view, the answer depends on the interest-elasticities of the two functions. An inelastic *IS* and/or an infinitely-elastic *LM* leads to fiscalist answers. An infinitely-elastic *IS* and/or inelastic *LM* leads to monetarist answers. The real world of the 1970's is "just a little bit in between", although the real world of the 1930's — when *Keynes'* "General Theory" was written — may indeed have conformed to fiscalism. What one might call "normative" fiscalism, however, depends not at all on the shapes of the macroeconomic functions. Whatever these shapes may be, it requires monetary policy to "validate" expansive fiscal policy by keeping nominal interest rates from rising. I am unaware of any corresponding normative monetarism.

[6] Robert A. *Mundell*, "The Appropriate Use of Monetary and Fiscal Policy for Internal and External Stability", IMF Staff Papers (March, 1962).

classify the distinction, suppose that a Hicksian IS - LM model in (Y, r) space, with error terms (shift parameters) e_t and ε_t may be written :

$$IS \quad \text{curve} \quad r_t = a - bY_t + e_t \quad (a, b > 0)$$

$$LM \quad \text{curve} \quad r_t = \alpha + \beta Y_t + \varepsilon_t \quad (\alpha < a, \beta > 0)$$

Solving for Y_t, we have:

$$Y_t = \frac{(a - \alpha) + (e_t - \varepsilon_t)}{b + \beta}$$

This is a macrostatically *stable* solution by all the usual definitions I know about. (Neither IS nor LM slopes the wrong way, in other words.) But at the same time, the stable equilibrium value of Y_t is highly *volatile*, particularly if the error terms (e_t, ε_t) are negatively correlated. Similarly, solving for the interest rate r_t, we derive:

$$r_t = \frac{\beta(a + e_t) + b(\alpha + \varepsilon_t)}{b + \beta}$$

which is also stable but volatile, particularly if the error terms are positively correlated.

What difference does this point make? Primarily, that the case for intervention and direct control is much stronger in unstable markets than in merely volatile ones. And secondarily, that a number of conceptually stable functions (investment functions, *Phillips* curves, possibly even liquidity functions) may exist but be so volatile over a wide range of shift parameters (not only economic but social and political) as to be disappointing when used for modelling, planning, tracking, and allied uses. (This, I fear, is particularly true of the once-so-promising *Phillips* curve with its neat unemployment — inflation trade-off.)

V.

Mayer's footnotes reveal a running debate with leading monetarists on the justifiability of *Mayer's* eight subordinate propositions. They are admittedly not logically essential to monetarism although many (probably most) monetarists accept them. *Mayer's* critics object to *Mayer's* excluding from their ranks the minority who do not accept one or more of this group of eight.

Here, I think, I am on *Mayer's* side on Schumpeterian grounds. For in raising the Schumpeterian question, what grand "vision" of the economic process inspired the development of monetarist ideology, it is to this group that we must look, rather than to the relative abstraction and aridity of *Mayer's* primary quartet. And if I select among the eight, I should select (1) a monetary growth rule as at least a "second best" guide to monetary policy (*Mayer's* # 9), (2) the corollary use of a money stock rather than an interest rate monetary target (his # 8), (3) a willingness to tolerate unemployment as a cost of price disinflation (# 11) coupled (after *Phillips'* 1958 paper)[7] with rejection of the *Phillips* curve as a reliable trade-off indicator (# 10) and an essentially libertarian abhorrence of "suppressed inflation" and such direct controls as incomes policies, rationing, and allocations (# 12).[8]

VI.

I might myself suggest, again on Schumpeterian grounds, one additional (ninth) member for *Mayer's* team of secondary propositions, raising his total to 13.[9] This is the debatable proposition that the monetary authority — meaning the Federal Reserve in contemporary America — does in fact have the power, and accordingly the responsibility, to regulate the money supply. The aspect of monetarist vision involved here is that monetary mismanagement by the Federal Reserve has been and is the prime cause of the great booms and contractions of the American past and present, which have been unjustly blamed on the free enterprise system as a whole.

This proposition is debatable on at least three bases, two purely domestic and the third international.

---

[7] A. W. *Phillips*, "The Relation between Unemployment and the Rate of Change of Money Wages in the United Kingdom, 1861 - 1957," Economica (November, 1958). For the most influential American application, see Paul A. *Samuelson* and Robert M. *Solow*. "Analytical Aspects of Anti-Inflation Policy," American Economic Review (May, 1960).

[8] A particularly apt example in Milton *Friedman*, "What Price Guidepost?" in George P. *Shultz* and Robert F. *Aliber*, eds. Guidelines: Informal Controls and the Market Place (Chicago: University of Chicago Press, 1966), pp. 17 to 39.

[9] Or, if *Mayer* inclines to triakaidekaphobia, this proposition might be substituted for the preference for small models over large ones (his # 6) which seems related only tenuously to the basic monetarist insight.

1. If M is the money stock and B the monetary base, we have:[10]

$$M = \frac{B}{\frac{C}{M} + \frac{R}{D}\left(1 - \frac{C}{M}\right)}$$

where $\left(\frac{R}{D}\right)$ is the commercial banks' reserve ratio and controlled by the commercial banks themselves at least within legal limits and $\left(\frac{C}{M}\right)$ is the public's ratio of currency to total money and controlled by the public. It is the contention of numerous writers (most prominently J. G. *Gurley* and E. S. *Shaw*)[11] that the Federal Reserve's control of B is inadequate to regulate M in either cyclical booms or depressions.

2. The Federal Reserve is a creature of Congress and cannot disregard current political sentiment, however wrong-headed it may be. There have been frequent attempts already, led for three decades by the expansionist Congressmen Wright *Patman* (D., Tex.) as Chairman of the House of Representatives Committee on Banking and Currency, to restrict particularly the system's anti-inflationary clout by limiting methods involving "tight money". (This term refers to rises in nominal interest rates and standards of credit-worthiness, "credit squeezes" on particular companies unusually dependent on borrowed funds, and pressure on savings institutions from "disintermediation", as deposits are withdrawn in search of higher interest incomes.) More recent congressional critics, such as Senator William *Proxmire* and Representative Henry *Reuss* (both D., Wis.) have been more sympathetic to monetarism in their proposals.[12]

---

[10] The derivation below is based on Phillip *Cagan*, "Determinants and Effects of Changes on the Stock of Money, 1975 - 1960" (New York: Columbia University Press, 1965) p. 12

$$M = C + D \quad (C = \text{currency}, D = \text{bank deposits})$$
$$B = C + R \quad (R = \text{bank reserves})$$

$$\frac{M}{B} = \frac{C+D}{C+R} = \frac{\frac{C}{M} + \frac{D}{M}}{\frac{C}{M} + \frac{R}{M}} = \frac{1}{\frac{C}{M} + \frac{R}{D}\cdot\frac{D}{M}} = \frac{1}{\frac{C}{M} + \frac{R}{D}\left(1 - \frac{C}{M}\right)}$$

[11] *Gurley* and *Shaw*, "Money in a Theory of Finance" (Washington: Brookings Institute, 1960).

[12] The belated rise of "monetarist" criticism of the Federal Reserve within Congress itself lends some support to monetarist reproaches against Federal Reserve "fleeing where no man pursueth" in connection with past ineptness.

3. Under a regime of fixed exchange rates and unregulated short-term capital movements, the power of any country's monetary authority is circumscribed by the tendency to international equality of interest rates. Monetary expansionism, lowering short-term rates at home, is thus counteracted by capital outflows, and vice versa. During the 1960's, moreover international aspects of monetary control have been exacerbated for the United States by the rise of the Eurodollar market. This market has become a vehicle for foreign banks, including foreign branches of American banks, to create dollar deposits on a large scale by loans subject neither to reserve nor to reporting requirements, so that the Federal Reserve can only estimate more or less inaccurately the total volume of the dollars outstanding and overhanging the American money market. It is obviously difficult to regulate a quantity when one does not know with adequate precision what that quantity is!

The basis of scepticism regarding monetarism is summarized by a "Wall Street Journal" editorialist:[13] "[A]fter so much government manipulation over so many years, private commerce has become exceedingly adroit in switching to money imports and substitutes, chiefly trade credit and credit cards, both of which are sources of liquidity" i. e., of autonomous changes in velocity.

VII.

Three random comments on *Mayer's* exposition of individual propositions and I close:

During the Great Depression, for example, and under the gold standard, *Friedman* and *Schwartz* deny that the fear of gold drains constituted a rational explanation for Federal Reserve phobia against expansionary open-market operations. Milton *Friedman* and Anna J. *Schwartz*, "The Great Contraction, 1929 - 1933", (Princeton: Princeton University Press, 1965), pp. 103 to 110.

[13] Jude *Wanniski,* "The Mundell-Laffer Hypothesis — A New View of the World Economy", Public Interest (Spring, 1975), p. 28 n., citing Professor Robert *Mundell.* — More generally, the monetarist theory of the international balance of payments seems itself inconsistent with any notion of over-riding power in the hands of domestic monetary authorities. This is because it sees a balance of payments deficit (surplus) as primarily a manifestation of an excess supply of (demand for) money, and an avoidance of the authority's authority. See Donal *Kemp,* "A Monetary View of the Balance of Payments", Federal Reserve Bank of St. Louis Review (April, 1975) and sources cited, (including Professor *Mundell*).

1. On that alleged "black box" — the transmission mechanism between monetary changes and the real economy — *Mayer* should perhaps have spelled out in more detail what he thinks monetarists believe that process to be, or if indeed they seem to him hopelessly divided among themselves. To me, any explanation must involve the proposition, resting on *Pigou* and *Keynes* effects, that money changes effect real variables through price-level changes separately from and in addition their effects through interest changes both nominal and real. If so, it *is* important "whether one formulates the analysis in terms of M or in terms of r", since the effects, despite substantial overlaps, are significantly different. It is easy to criticize monetarist coyness in deciding between the M_1, M_2, ..., M_n concepts of money (I have seen n values as high as 7). But the critics owe Professor *Friedman* in particular the concession of mentioning his belief (unconfirmed, to the best of my knowledge) that all the ratios $\frac{M_i}{M_j}$ would be sensibly constant but for such constraints as the ban on interest payments on demand deposits and the "Regulation Q" interest ceilings on savings deposits.

I likewise have questions about *Mayer's* sentence: "An increase in the real stock of money lowers the *imputed* real interest rate on money balances" (italics his) as a part of the transmission process, unless indeed this statement implies a rise in the price level.[14]

2. It may involve no more than my inflated ego to point out the existence of a compromise proposal (of my own)[15] midway between the *Friedman - Shaw* constant monetary growth rule (*Mayer's* proposition

---

[14] In personal correspondence, *Mayer* has clarified my difficulty here. By "imputed real interest rate" he means what I would call the marginal utility of an increment to real balances. I do not think that our difference is more than verbal.

[15] M. *Bronfenbrenner*, "Monetary Rules: A New Look", J. L. E. (October, 1965). — If we write the standard equation of exchange as:

$$MV = pY = pN\pi \text{ , whence}$$
$$\log M + \log V = \log p + \log N + \log \pi$$
$$d \log M + d \log V = d \log p + d \log N + d \log \pi$$
$$\frac{dM}{M} + \frac{dV}{V} = \frac{dp}{p} + \frac{dN}{N} + \frac{d\pi}{\pi}$$
$$G_m + G_v = G_p + G_n + G_\pi$$

the expression in the text follows, if $G_p = 0$, i e., if price-level stability is maintained.

9) and the complete discretion the Federal Reserve has traditionally sought for itself. This suggested compromise it that the monetary-stock growth rate G_m be set one year at a time as $(G_n + G_\pi - G_v)$, i. e., the estimated growth rate of the labor force *plus* the estimated growth rate of its man-hour productivity *minus* the estimated growth rate of the velocity of circulation (at the real interest rates expected to prevail during the coming year).

3. *Mayer's* proposition 10 reads: "Rejection of an unemployment-inflation trade-off in favor of a real *Phillips* curve." My conception of the monetarists' "real *Phillips* curve" is precisely a natural (but not necessarily invariant) rate of unemployment. *Mayer* clearly means something else, but it is not clear what it is, unless it be a short-run artifact involving money illusion and approaching the natural rate with the passage of time.

To make matters more difficult rather than less, one notes from *Mayer's* summary Figure I that the notion of a natural rate of unemployment enters only to connect "relative unconcern with inflation" (# 11) with the "transmission mechanism" (# 2) by a line labelled "r", and is not connected with the "real *Phillips* curve" in any way. Surely this omission is a slip or oversight — which is not to deny the relation on which *Mayer* concentrates his attention.

VIII.

Four summary questions and answers in conclusion: Is *Mayer's* exercise worth attempting? I think so. Is his proposition set an impressive one? Yes. Is his diagrammatic summary of the multifarious interrelations of the proposition set helpful? Yes, but primarily to one who, like *Mayer*, has worked the components out carefully for himself. Does *Mayer's* study pre-empt the field against further, and possibly quite highly variant, attempts any similar lines by other scholars? No, and *Mayer* as I know him would be the last man to claim otherwise.

Issues of Post-Keynesian Monetary Analysis

A Contribution to the Discussion Opened by
Professor Thomas Mayer*

By Karl Brunner

The "Keynesian cross" and its implicit disregard of monetary processes dominated the analysis of stabilization policies in the early postwar years and reemerged recently in the guise of the Neo-Cambridge theory. Monetary theory, best represented by the work of *Patinkin* in the early 1950's and the classic piece by Lloyd *Metzler*, was safely separated from contamination with the analysis of stabilization policies. *Patinkin* pursued the line introduced by *Hicks* and integrated monetary analysis and "value theory". The seminal work of Lloyd *Metzler* influenced aspects of growth theory, initiated a monetary interpretation of aggregative analysis and shaped the monetary approach to the international balance of payments.

Metzler and *Patinkin* offered important contributions to the gradual evolution of monetary analysis. But this field still suffered under a somewhat schizophrenic state, probably unavoidable in the slow development of a body of knowledge. Monetary theory and the discussion of monetary and credit policy belonged to separate worlds. Monetary analysis offered little basis for the clarification of actual problems confronting policymakers, and the usual discussion of policy and institutions proceeded without benefit of analysis. The "islamic" framework provided no basis for the discussion of "credit" policy and could not cope with the relation between credit and money. Major ideas guiding policymakers' evaluations emerged over many years independently of academic monetary theory and involved views contradicting central and

* See Kredit und Kapital, Vol. 8 (1975) pp. 191 and pp. 293. — This paper forms part of a project supported by a grant from the National Science Foundation. It is based on joint work developed over many years with Allan H. *Meltzer*. The crucial influence of this close collaboration is gratefully acknowledged.

well grounded propositions of economic theory.[1] The professional literature still failed to offer a coherent account for the behavior of monetary
aggregates at the end of the 1950's. We find no analysis about the nature
of the interaction between monetary authorities, the banks and the
public. But without such analysis, supplemented with suitable information, discussions of monetary or credit policy and the views typically
advanced by monetary authorities in public pronouncements of docu-
ments could barely be assigned much relevance. Similarly, the discussion
bearing on interest rates was largely occupied with learned exercises
about stocks and flows and whether such formulations could be con-
ceivably made equivalent. They offered no useful explanation of observable interest rate behavior. We also lacked at the time an adequate
explanation for the simultaneous occurrence of retardation in output,
increasing unemployment and still rising money stock and prices. This
phenomenon could not be explained by Keynesian or monetary theory
without an array of ad hoc assumptions arbitrarily tailored for this
purpose.

Recognition of this state of affairs contributed to the "monetarist
revolution" in monetary and macro-theory. The implicit separation of
our linguistic activities into a policy discussion without analysis in one
volume, and a monetary theory yielding barely any relevant propositions for assessment and interpretation of monetary and credit policy in
another volume, offered a serious intellectual challenge. The struggle for
a monetary analysis applicable to policy problems typically confronting
policymakers evolved into a central concern of the monetarist reexamina-
tion of monetary and aggregative analysis. The monetarist endeavor
thus involved a decisive rejection of the "platonic games" so frequently
cultivated in our professional literature.[2]

The desired connection between policy and analysis explains the other
"sources" of monetarist evolutions. The gradual development of thought
was strongly influenced by a search for broad empirical regularities. This

---

[1] The different versions of the free reserve doctrine should be especially
noted in this respect. These hypotheses are examined in some detail in a forthcoming book on "Theory and Practice of Central Banking" jointly authored
with Allan H. *Meltzer*.

[2] Hans *Albert* presented an excellent critique of the "platonic games" pursued in our professional literature: "Modell-Platonismus. Der neoklassische
Stil des ökonomischen Denkens in kritischer Beleuchtung", in: *Logik der Sozial-
wissenschaften*, ed. by Ernst *Topitsch*, Cologne-Berlin, 1971, pp. 406.

search affected important portions of monetarist thinking and guided the evolving analysis. Lastly, the required aggregative analysis was approached as an extension of price-theory to the aggregative plane and to aggregative issues. This conception contrasted with the prevailing Keynesian views and affected the interpretation of money demand (e. g. irrelevance of a liquidity trap[3]). It also influenced the interpretation of the interest elasticity of aggregate demand for output, views about the multiplier and about the roles of consumption and investment in the process, the rationale of a credit market in a full description of relevant portfolio adjustments and the range of channels transmitting monetary impulses.

Almost a generation has passed since the first questioning doubts in the postwar literature. The accumulated work and the ongoing disputes gradually modified the formulations and substance of monetary analysis. The views of active participants "in the action" hardly stayed fixed at the level of the middle 1960's. It appears thus most appropriate to survey at this time the nature of the issues behind the usual labels. The labels functioned in recent years more often as a psychological obstruction to understanding and searching analysis than as an economic device to summarize alternative conjectures and analytic ideas. *Mayer's* survey of the substantive issues should be welcome therefore as a valuable contribution. It directs attention away from labels burdened after years of dispute with emotive shadows and emphasizes the substantive nature of the questions to be addressed in future work. The following sections of my paper elaborate and clarify some important aspects covered by *Mayer's* argument. They describe in particular some of the crucial problems which will require our future attention[4].

---

[3] A price-theoretical interpretation determines that a liquidity trap means an excess of marginal transaction costs over benefits for any level of transaction. This condition held in the 1930's only for the Federal funds market. Transactions continued on all other financial markets and assured thus the transmission of monetary impulses to economic activity and the price-level.

[4] The nature of the issues has been discussed on several occasions. The reader is referred to "The Monetarist Revolution in Monetary Theory", Weltwirtschaftliches Archiv 1970, "A Survey of Selected Issues in Monetary Theory", Schweizerische Zeitschrift für Volkswirtschaft und Statistik, 1971; note also the papers jointly authored with Allan H. *Meltzer*, "An Aggregative Theory for a Closed Economy" and "Monetarism: The Principal Issues, Areas of Agreement and the Work Remaining", and prepared for the Conference on Monetary Economics at Brown University in November 1974; to be published by North-Holland Publishing Co. in a Conference volume.

The organization of my discussion reflects a definite view of the structure of issues. *Mayer* distinguishes twelve separate aspects:

" 1. The quantity theory of money, in the sense of the predominance of the impact of monetary factors on nominal income.

2. The monetarist model of the transmission process.

3. Belief in the inherent stability of the private sector.

4. Irrelevance of allocative detail for the explanation of short-run changes in money income, and belief in a fluid capital market.

5. Focus on the price level as whole rather than on individual prices.

6. Reliance on small rather than large econometric models.

7. Use of the reserve base or similar measure as the indicator of monetary policy.

8. Use of the money stock as the proper target of monetary policy.

9. Acceptance of a monetary growth rule.

10. Rejection of an unemployment-inflation trade-off in favor of a real *Phillips*-curve.

11. A relatively greater concern about inflation than about unemployment compared to other economists.

12. Dislike of government intervention."

This presentation is somewhat unstructured and fails to convey the dependencies and interrelations between the issues. *Mayer* emphasizes the relative independence of several problems. This is useful and important. But he misses another important aspect, viz. the logical structure between the problems. Issues 1 to 4 form the basic core. Moreover, the basic four are not completely independent. The subsequent discussion reveals some cross connections influencing the actual clustering of analytic positions. Points 5 to 11 are essentially derived issues and depend on the decisions made concerning [issues 1 to 4]. Points 5 and 6 in particular are special aspects of the issues involved under point 4. The indicator (i.e. interpretation) and target (i.e. strategy) problem listed under points 7 and 8 are implications of the answers offered to the questions raised under the basic issues and the specifications introduced for this purpose. Point 9 moreover is only a special form of the strategy problem listed under point 8. Points 10 and 11 form essentially the same problem and the answer is again predetermined by the decisions made with respect to the basic issues. It depends most particularly on the views about the nature of the transmission mechanism. We should also note here that point 11 perpetuates a widespread misconception. The problem is stated as a matter of relative *concerns,* a matter of personal preferences. This characterization is seriously misleading. It would be difficult to deny that preference orderings of social states are not involved. But there is substantially more to the problem. The conflicting positions are sensitively conditioned by the core issues which determine the comparative consequences of activist monetary-fiscal expansionism. The last point covers a range of problems of great importance for the future of western societies. This range is however not closely related to the propositions disputed in monetary analysis. Still, there is probably a statistical association involving more than historical accident between the positions occurring under this point and the core issues. Neither policy nor political problem raised by *Mayer* will be covered in my discussion. This does not impute any lack of significance to policy or political aspects. On the contrary, their importance deserves a more extended analysis in a separate paper.

I. The Nature of the Transmission Mechanism I:
The Range of Asset Substitutions

The "islamic" framework defines a familiar reference scheme for our purposes. It occurs with two distinct interpretations involving substantially different and conflicting hypotheses. The "Hicksian" version imposes a restricted range of substitution relations on money. Money substitutes only with "bonds" representing a class of financial assets. Neither bonds nor money substitute with real assets. Real assets are frozen into portfolios by forbidding transaction costs. The "interest rate" represents a rate of return on financial assets. The textbook presentations of the Hicksian version explain moreover the interest-elasticity of aggregate demand in terms of relative borrowing cost. The comparative magnitude of these costs associated with the different expenditure categories determines the magnitude of this interest-elasticity. The Hicksian version dominated the textbook and particularly also econometric models.

An alternative interpretation is associated with *Metzler's* classic piece.[5] The "Metzlerian" version dominated growth theory and the monetary approach to the international balance of payments. It places money in a wide-ranging net of substitution-relations. Money substi-

---

[5] Lloyd *Metzler,* "Wealth, Saving and the Rate of Interest", The Journal of Political Economy, April 1951.

tutes with all assets in all directions. Substitutability is not constrained to a subset of existing assets. This *general* substitutability is supplemented with a characteristic Metzlerian postulate, viz. that financial and real assets are "perfect substitutes". This assumption reconciles a pattern of general substitutability with the implicit two-asset model of the "islamic" framework. The full portfolio adjustment is again described by a money market equation. The "interest rate" measures in this case however the real rate of return on real assets supplemented with the anticipated rate of inflation. The Metzlerian version generally rejects implicitly the borrowing cost interpretation of the interest elasticity of aggregate demand and the occurrence of a liquidity trap.

The Metzlerian postulate of "perfectly substitutable" financial and real assets admits two interpretations. It may represent a hypothesis that non-money financial assets are comparatively close substitutes with real assets, whereas money exhibits relatively looser substitution relations with both financial and real assets. It could be understood however as an elliptical description of a realm of application confining the analysis. It does not mean in this case that financial and real assets are comparatevely close substitutes. The assumption of "perfect substitutability" only means under the circumstances that the analysis is constrained to experiences exhibiting large monetary variations when compared to the relative variability of financial and real assets.

The alternative interpretations of the familiar paradigm confront us with the first issues in this section. We reject the Hicksian postulate of a restricted substitution range for money and we also reject the first interpretation of the Metzlerian version. We accept on the other hand the second variant of the Metzlerian analysis and find it a useful approximation for periods with dominantly monetary disturbances. We remain however quite reluctant to apply the Metzlerian analysis to problems of the international balance of payments in the manner developed over the past 15 years. The Metzlerian postulate is usually supplemented in this analysis with an assumption of perfectly substitutable financial assets denominated in different currencies. The results is an all-around perfect substitutability removing the analysis from any shorter-run relevance in periods not exhibiting very large inflation.

A more useful approach with a less confined range of application seems properly to emerge from the second interpretation of the Metzlerian version. We postulate thus for money a *general* and *imperfect* range of substitutions in all directions over the whole spectrum of assets.

This postulate is reflected in the analysis by the occurrence of a credit
market equation supplementing the money market equation. Portfolio
adjustments covering simultaneously three classes of assets involve under
a general and imperfect substitutability assumption the explicit interaction between two asset markets. The concentration in our work on
credit and money market does not reflect in this context a matter of
logical necessity. It is determined by the relative convenience of empirical research and the opportunity to analyze directly propositions
bearing on bank credit, credit policy and the role of financial intermediation and disintermediation in the monetary process.[6] An immediate
corollary of the general and imperfect substitutability implies the rejection of a frequent and long repeated characterization of the issue.
The substitutability assumption determines that the slope properties
of the IS-LM curves are neither sufficient nor necessary conditions
for any propositions about the relative efficacy of monetary impulses.
More particularly, propositions about fiscal and monetary policy are not
crucially dependent on the magnitude of the interest-elasticity of money
demand. The dependence of money demand on interest rates forms no
relevant issue, not even the absolute magnitude of this dependence expressed by an elasticity. This analytic fact reflects an important implication of general substitutability. This pattern substantially enlarges
the range of transmission channels conveying monetary impulses to the
pace of economic activity and the price level. The explicit formalization
of this basic idea may vary. The *Brunner-Meltzer* model offers one
particular representation of the basic idea emphasizing the role of relative price adjustments over the whole range of assets, between old
assets and newly produced assets, and between assets and real consumption or yields of assets. Other formalizations of the basic idea
are certainly possible and may be usefully explored in the future.
Mayer's separate reference[7] to the range of substitution relations and
the *"Brunner-Meltzer"* relative price and stock mechanism is somewhat
misleading in this respect. The basic issue centers at this point on the
range of substitution relations and the "B-M mechanism" forms only a
particular attempt at analytic formalization in order to explore the
ramifications of the idea more coherently.

------

[6] A detailed discussion bearing on the aspects covered in the text can be
found in the Comments addressed to the discussion at the Conference on
Monetarism held in November 1974 at Brown University (see the reference
under footnote 4).

[7] Thomas *Mayer*, page 13.

This is not the place to discuss in detail the implications of the alternative substitution hypotheses and their bearing on policy problems, or the choice of research procedures to assess the consequences of policies. These aspects were covered extensively at another occasion to which the reader is referred.[8] Another aspect may be emphasized in passing. One encounters occasionally assertions denying occurrence or relevance of the "substitution issue". But such assertions cannot be reconciled with the analytical facts. A careful examination of the literature cannot fail to demonstrate the *occurrence* of the alternative hypothesis. Moreover, an analysis of the alternative frameworks determines the empirical relevance of this issue and its significance for policy problems. This relevance is reflected by substantive differences in propositions about policy aspects derived from the alternative hypotheses. Our more immediate concern at this state bears on statements advanced by *Mayer* in his overview of the problems. These statements require our explicit attention.

Professor *Mayer* argues on page 25 that a "monetarist ... is concerned with people only as money holders and hence is interested in only one sector, the supply of and demand for money". On page 11 we read moreover: ". . . it is hard to see why a quantity theorist would prefer to use the interest rate in his description of the transmission process, it is not hard to see why a Keynesian may agree with a quantity theorist in looking at the money stock rather than the rate of interest." On page 8 *Mayer* stresses the relative stability of money demand as another issue bearing on the nature of the transmission mechanism. Lastly, detailed attention is directed to the comparative measurability, the comparative measurement errors, of money stock and interest rate. On page 9 we read that "monetarists prefer to use the money stock rather than the rate of interest because they believe that the money stock can be measured much better". The relative measurability of the two magnitudes influences according to *Mayer*'s account the properties of the transmission mechanism.

The first statement exemplifies a subtle shifting of attention to an irrelevant aspect frequently encountered in the literature. The confusion between statements about persons and statements about statements made by these persons occurs unfortunately much too frequently. The first type of statement involves an assertion about persons and not about a

---

[8] The reader is referred to my "Survey of Selected Issues in Monetary Analysis", (see footnote 4.).

piece of analysis. As a statement about persons called "monetarists" the assertion is simply false. "Monetarists" are concerned about many things and their attention roams over many facets of human life. All this may be terribly important for a human story to someone, but remains quite immaterial for the evaluation of monetary analysis. So what should we say about the second half of the statement quoted above after purging the irrelevant personal reference? Indeed, we do find formulations in the professional literature, most particularly in articles exploring the "monetary approach to the balance of payments", centering attention on the money market and the supply of and demand for money. But it is quite false and misleading to use such formulations as a general description of "monetarist analysis". The *Brunner-Meltzer* analysis emphasizes on the contrary the role of the credit market and analyzes extensively the interaction between asset markets and the output market subject to the feedbacks via the government sector's budget relation.[9] It is similarly misleading to characterize "monetarist analysis" as essentially (or only) concerned with an economy's adjustment to an excess supply of money (*Mayer,* page 15). *Brunner-Meltzer* developed over the past years in substantial detail the sort-run and long-run consequences of government debt. They also developed the long-run consequences of rising uncertainty about policy trends or of increasing instability in the "rules of the game" confronting private investors and producers.[10]

The second assertion (quoted above and appearing on page 11) continues an entrenched misconception about the nature of the issue under examination. The terminology used is somewhat unfortunate in this respect. The terms "quantity theory" and "quantity theorist" are quite ambiguous and they are frequently used with a deliberate ideological or political purpose (most certainly not by *Mayer* however). The analytic situation on the other hand is clearly determined by the accumulated publications. Careful examination of the available analysis should indeed reveal that the issues centered on the range of substitution relations cannot be meaningfully described as a choice between "looking at interest rates" or "looking at the money stock". "Looking at" does not characterize in any useful or relevant mode any piece of analysis. It

[9] This theme has been developed jointly with Allan H. *Meltzer* in a series of papers beginning with a paper presented at the First Konstanz Conference on Monetary Theory and Monetary Policy in 1970 and subsequently published in a Conference Volume. "A Monetarist Framework for Aggregative Analysis", Supplements to Kredit und Kapital, Supplement No. 1, Berlin 1972.
[10] The reader is referred to the papers listed under footnote 4.

is not a proposition about statements representing an analysis, but about the behavior of a person at a particular moment, independently of the precise analytic structure under examination. Examination of published analysis clearly establishes that the money stock forms only a minor part of the transmission mechanism. This mechanism is essentially defined by a relative price process covering all assets and yields of assets on the one side as against a narrow range of interest rates on financial assets on the other side of the issue. We note just in passing that the statement on page 8 on the relative stability of money does not bear on the nature of the transmission mechanism and will be considered at its appropriate place under the impulse problem.

Mayer assigns lastly great significance to the measurement problem and discusses in great detail the "relative measurability" of money stock and "interest rate". He argues that monetarist analysis of the transmission mechanism implicitly assumes a comparatively small measurement error for the money stock, whereas Keynesians are inclined to assign this pattern to interest rates. This is simply and clearly false and belongs to the "imaginative interpretation" occasionally cultivated in the literature. Comparative measurement errors have no logical relation whatsoever with the issue circumscribed above. A generalized relative price process is consistent with any distribution of measurement errors and so is also the Hicksian position of a restricted substitution range. The relative errors condition the appropriate strategies of empirical research but do not discriminate in any sense between the alternative views about the transmission mechanism. Measurement errors bear however on the target problem, i. e. the choice of an optimal strategy for monetary policy.

II. The Nature of the Transmission Mechanism II:
Properties of the Phillips Curve

A second range of important problems subsumable under the first issue is centered around the *Phillips* curve and the role of expectations. *Mayer* covers these aspects in points 10 and 11. The emphasis in point 11 is somewhat misdirected and important contributions made in recent years require elaboration. The controversy is characterized by conflicting views bearing on the existence of a long-run and a short-run trade-off between inflation and output (or unemployment). Three positions emerged in the literature. One thesis maintains the persistent occurrence of a trade-off in the shorter-run and over the longer-run exploitable by suitable manipulation of monetary-fiscal policies. Another thesis acknowledges the occurrence of an exploitable trade-off for the shorter-run but denies its persistence over the longer-run. The trade-off is asserted to vanish in the forseeable future before "we are all dead". The second thesis argues in particular that unemployment converges over a longer-range to a natural rate of unemployment determined by prevailing institutions and the patterns of real shocks imposed on the economy. This natural rate of unemployment occurs independently of monetary policy but is responsive to fiscal policies (taxes and transfer policies). The last thesis denies the occurrence of any trade-off over any relevant horizon. It involves a strong assertion of the natural rate hypothesis for output and unemployment.

The three alternative hypothesis yield radically different implications about the transmission of financial impulses to real variables and the price-level. They also determine radically different evaluations about the range of useful policy making. The first thesis is rarely, if ever, accepted by monetarist analysis. It remains a characteristic Keynesian position. Monetarist analysis typically incorporates on the other hand the second or third thesis. The crucial divergencies between the three hypotheses reflect substantially different views about the role of expectations and the patterns governing supply behavior on the output market. The "islamic" framework is somewhat incomplete or implicit in this respect. The description of aggregate supply usually associated with this framework uses essentially two extreme assumptions. The Hicksian version assumes a horizontal supply curve, i. e. prices are constant. The Metzlerian version assumes on the other hand a vertical supply curve, i. e. prices and wages are fully adjustable and output settles at "full output". The *Phillips* relation replaces this simple pattern with a more general analysis. The third thesis yields of course a Metzlerian pattern but offers a rationale for this result.

The "Keynesian thesis" does not necessarily exclude expectations, but they are assigned a comparatively moderate role. They may affect the position of the *Phillips* curve. Substantial shifts in the *Phillips* curve are frequently attributed however to structural changes in the labor market including various "cost-push" processes. This view about the role of expectations also affects explanations of interest rates. The high level of nominal rates recently observed reflects according to a prevalent Keynesian position high levels of real rates. The inflation premium contributes in this view a minor portion of the observed variations in nominal rates. The whole approach to labor and credit market processes seems to emphasize real factors. The *Phillips* curve is therefore comparatively stable or its shifts result mostly from "real events" allowing a long-run trade-off. The second and third thesis emphatically reject these views. The role of expectations and the adjustment of wages and prices move the economy towards a natural rate of unemployment. Moreover, inflationary expectations occur with a major weight in explanations of larger changes of the nominal rate of interest. The third thesis uses furthermore a very special hypothesis about expectation formation. Expectations are formed rationally according to beliefs identical to the model incorporating the expectations and their effects. Psychological expectations are thus identical to mathematical expectations defined relative to a specified stochastic model.[11] The conjunction of rational expectation with a specific class of output supply functions implies that no systematically anticipated monetary impulses can affect the real variables. Output, the real rate of unemployment and the real rate of interest move independently of systematic monetary impulses and follow essentially a random process. Systematic monetary impulses are immediately converted into price effects under rational expectations. The *Lucas-Sargent* output supply conjoined with rational expectation thus removes all opportunities for systematic exploitation of a trade-off by means of financial manipulation. The trade-off vanishes even for the short-run. The actual unemployment rate coincides under the circumstances at any moment with a (fluctuating) natural rate.[12]

---

[11] The idea was introduced by Jack *Muth* in a seminal paper. It has been extensively developed for monetary analysis by Robert *Lucas*, Thomas *Sargent*, Neil *Wallace* and Robert *Barro*.

[12] Consider a *Phillips* relation

(1) $$p_t - p_{t-1} = f\,[s_t, \pi_t]; \quad f_1, f_2 > 0$$

where p_t is the log of the price-level in t, $E_{t-1}p_{t-1}$ the expected (in $t-1$) rate of inflation for the period $(t-1)$ to t, and s designates a state variable depending on output y and real capital K, so that $s = s\,(y, K)$. Assume furthermore that $f_2 = 1$ and $\pi_t = E_{t-1}p_t - p_{t-1}$. It follows that

(2) $$p_t = E_{t-1}p_t + f^*\,(y, K)$$

We obtain under standard constraints on f^* also

(3) $$y = h\,[K, p_t - E_{t-1}\,p_t]; \quad h_1, h_2 > 0$$

Equation (3) represents the type of supply function used by *Lucas* and *Sargent-Wallace*. The same assumptions allow us to derive (1) from (3). Under the assumptions made, (1) and (3) are thus equivalent. They are usually associated

The second thesis recognizes rational expectations in *Muth's* sense as a longer-run phenomenon. It also recognizes that expectations are rationally formed on the basis of available information in the context of some beliefs about the nature of the process generating the expected magnitudes. The conditioning beliefs barely coincide however with the structure of the hypothesis incorporating the expectations. The occurrence of explicit and implicit contracts in labor and output markets reflecting an essentially incomplete information determines a lag pattern preventing a full adjustment of prices and wages to the underlying trend situation. This contractual situation could be interpreted as a deviation from the information state postulated by *Muth's* rational expectations, adjusting in the longer-run to accruing information about the underlying trend. The second thesis emphasizes thus a learning process with systematic revision of information and beliefs. It has been demonstrated that rational expectations in this wider sense can actually be formulated in a Baysian framework to yield an adaptive process of expectations for-

---

however with different economic interpretations. Equation (1) is used whenever one wishes to express that causation runs from output to price-level, whereas equation (3) is used to express causation running from price-level to output.

One could also argue with Stanley *Fisher* that the temporal structure of (formal or implicit) contracts produces a pattern described by output supply equation (3')

(3') $y_t = h\,[K, p_t - E_{t-1}\,p_t, p_t - E_{t-2}\,p_t];\quad h_1, h_2, h_3 > 0$

Fisher assumes for this purpose that wage contracts are made for two periods. In each period one set of contracts is renegotiated. *Fisher* demonstrates that with output supply (3') monetary authorities have an opportunity to influence systematically output and the variance of output. The reader is referred to Stanley *Fisher*: "Long Term Contracts, Rational Expectation and the Optimal Money Supply", The Journal of Political Economy 1976. *Fisher's* analysis directs our attention to an interesting problem bearing on the interpretation of rational expectations. It seems somewhat doubtful that the postulated layering of wage contracts is consistent with rational expectations. I conjecture that rational expectations also induce adjustment in the structure of contracts.

A simple transformation of equation (3') produces a *Phillips* type relation (assuming standard properties of h).

(1') $p_t - p_{t-1} = g\,[y, K: \pi_t, \pi_{t-1}; E_{t-2}\,p_t - E_{t-2}\,p_{t-1}]$

with the properties

$$g_2 < 0, \quad i = 1 \ldots 3$$

and

$$g_3 + g_4 = 1 \quad \text{and} \quad g_4 = g_5$$

mation.[13] The learning and information problems emphasized in this general approach also determine the different interpretations of monetary growth and monetary acceleration. These magnitudes were offered as simple empirical approximations to important analytic categories (anticipated and unanticipated movements). The analysis assigned to monetary growth essentially a price effect and no significant output effect. The output effects were associated with monetary acceleration, and neither with the money stock nor with monetary growth.[14]

Proponents of the second thesis would emphasize that concern about indexation appears irrelevant in a world operating according to *Muth's* rational expectation hypothesis. Moreover, the difficulties we encounter in judging the future course of the monetary authorities or in assessing the credibility of their public announcements about prospective policies suggest some caution with respect to shorter-run applications of rational expectations in the narrower sense. This caution is reenforced by the problems encountered in weighing the correctness of official interpretations bearing on past events and actions. On the other hand, when attending to the "Keynesian position" a proponent of the second thesis may note that actual utilization of resources moves over the longer run with the amount of resources available. Furthermore, the upwards cycling of unemployment and inflation in the typical graph used for descriptions of the *Phillips* curve appears inconsistent with an entrenched "Keynesian position". The Keynesian may refer to the experiences of labor markets in the 1930's to refute both the second and third theses.[15] This experience is indeed a somewhat unresolved problem. But the case remains open and future work may reconcile and subsume under a unified hypothesis both the labor market experiences of the later 1930's and also of the last ten years.[16]

[13] Benjamin *Friedman*, "Rational Expectations are Really Adaptive After All", Harvard Institute of Economic Research Discussion Paper # 430, August 1975.

[14] Robert *Barro* offered recently an interesting suggestion to improve this approximation: "Unanticipated Money Growth and Unemployment in the United States." Research paper, available on request.

[15] Robert *Gordon* emphasized this point in his paper "Recent Developments in the Theory of Inflation and Unemployment", The Journal of Monetary Economics, April 1976.

[16] This issue has been reconsidered by David *Coulter* at Carnegie-Mellon University. He shows that the problems encountered by the *Lucas-Rapping* model and criticized by Albert *Rees* disappear when the government's demand for labor is properly incorporated into the analysis.

It would be a serious mistake to settle comfortably on the middle thesis ("because it is in the middle"). Some important issues moving beyond the old alignments emerge in this range of problems. They involve interpretations of observed fluctuations in real variables and also concerns views about the adjustment in prices and wages. The first and second theses imply in contrast to the third thesis that prices and wages are not fully adjusted over shorter-run horizons to the underlying (and uncertainly comprehended) trend. The second and third theses assert on the other hand the occurrence and operative significance of a natural rate of unemployment independent of monetary manipulation. Moreover, observable fluctuations in real variables are interpreted by the first two theses to contain a systematic component. The third thesis implies in this respect essentially a generalization of *Slutsky's* proposition. Fluctuations in real variables are expressions of a random process without systematic time structure. It should be recognized that the challenging work on rational expectations offered to the profession by Robert *Lucas*, Thomas *Sargent*, Neil *Wallace* and Robert *Barro*, forced us to reexamine the role of accruing information and the consequences of shifting policy patterns. This impact affects in particular recent disputes in the summer and fall 1975 about the course of financial policies.

III. The Nature of the Transmission Mechanism III:
Fiscal Policy and "Crowding Out"

Some attention should be directed at this stage to fiscal policy. Many discussions created the impression that the intellectual conflicts in monetary analysis depend on propositions about fiscal policy. In particular, it has been frequently asserted that "monetarist analysis" assigns no aggregative significance to this policy. There should be little doubt that the analysis of fiscal policy gradually changed over the past ten years in some pieces of "monetarist analysis". The *Brunner-Meltzer* analysis, developed since 1970, assigns distinctive roles fiscal policy for the shorter and the long-run. Their analysis implies a definite impact of fiscal policy affecting output and price-level. But this impact differs substantially between the shorter and the longer-run. Over the short-run increasing government expenditures raise the private sector output. This increase depends inversely on the responsiveness of prices to changes in output. Moreover, this responsiveness depends on the revisions in expectations induced by fiscal expansionism. With price and wage expectations fully adjusted to the fiscal policy, an increase in government demand for labor or private output is completely absorbed by the price-level and produces no change in the private sector's output. An increase in the government sector's demand for output determines under the circumstances even for the shorter run a complete "crowding out". The incremental absorption of output by the government sector implies a matching reduction in output absorbed by the private sector. This analysis contrasts with the usual "islamic" procedure which determines a particular position of the LM curve as a necessary and sufficient condition for short-run crowding out. The *Brunner-Meltzer* analysis assigns on the other hand no particular significance to the properties of the money demand underlying the slope of LM. The critical conditions are placed with the slope of output supply and the responsiveness of money wage and price expectations to fiscal actions. A pronounced short-run impact of fiscal policy on output requires a comparatively flat output supply curve (i. e. small elasticity of price setting with respect to output) and a comparatively small responsiveness of expectations (in the short-run). A genuine multiplier effect (i. e. a negative "crowding out") occurs for approximately flat supply curves, unresponsive expectations and a feedback via the asset markets dominated by positive responses of prices of real assets. Positive crowding out emerges even over a shorter run whenever these conditions are violated.

The feedbacks via the budget relation associates, over an intermediate run, financial consequences with fiscal policy actions. The short-run impact effect is thus supplemented with the effect produced by expanding financial stocks. It follows that the total effect of fiscal policy appears as the sum of a pure fiscal effect (i. e. the impact effect) and a financial effect. The latter effect exceeds according to this analysis the pure fiscal effect. The general patterns shaping the impact effect of fiscal policy on output and price-level also determine the response over an intermediate run containing adjustments of financial stocks to an underlying state of fiscal policy. One would surmise however that an extension of the horizon beyond the short-run increases the change of substantial revisions in expectations. There emerges thus a greater probability for the occurrence of some measure of "crowding out".

These remarks on "crowding out" over a shorter to intermediate run require however some qualifications. They neglected the relative position of the system's state, i. e. they neglected the interaction of an evolving state with the natural rate of unemployment or normal output. For states below normal output fiscal expansion accelerates the approach of the state towards normal output, whereas for states above normal output expansive fiscal action raises output only temporarily. These deviations from normal output involve of course less than fully adjusted expectations and price-level. It follows that fiscal action affects over a shorter or intermediate run the volume of the private sector's output. Shorter-run "crowding out" seems more significant therefore for output levels beyond normal output.

But recent analysis suggests that the problem does not center on "short-run crowding out". The *Brunner-Meltzer* analysis implies that for any given combination of fiscal policies there exists a long-run level of financial stocks and a long-run price-level. There is also associated with each combination of fiscal policies a normal output level depending on long-run capital intensity, normal rate of unemployment and normal labor supply to the private sector. Fiscal policies affect the determinants of normal output. In particular, increasing real expenditures by the government sector lower the private sector's normal output. This reduction in normal output expresses the long-run crowding out induced by government expenditures. These long-run consequences are necessarily built into the system with prevailing budget policies and will be revealed as the years pass. The long-run crowding out eventually appears even with a genuine multiplier effect operating over the shorter-run.

The occurrence of both short and long-run "crowding out" are disputed by *Tobin* and *Buiter* among others. The second author asserts in particular the very opposite, viz. that an increase in real government expenditures raises long-run output and the long run stock of real capital. *Buiter* develops his argument in the context of a Metzlerian model. This issue remains wide open and will certainly require some attention in the future.[17] The description of the budget, the nature of expenditure policies, the responsiveness of tax revenues, and also the assumptions made concerning asset substitutions appear to affect the resulting propositions. The resolution of this issue seriously conditions our evaluation of future developments.

---

[17] The papers listed under footnote 4 develop an extensive analysis. An alternative view can be found in James *Tobin* and William H. *Buiter*, and also in a paper by *Buiter*, "The Long-Run Effects of Fiscal Policy", Econometric Research Program, Research Memorandum No. 187, October 1975.

IV. The Issues of Internal Stability and Impulse Dominance

The Brown University Conference on Monetarism held in November 1974 concentrated explicit attention essentially on matters pertaining to the transmission mechanism. The other basic issues were largely disregarded and occurred only in oral statements made by *Friedman, Meltzer* and *Brunner*. They still exist however. Any survey of the literature, critical examination or analytic interpretation of policy discussions reveals the nature of these issues.[18]

Keynesian analysis traditionally emphasized the fundamental instability of the private sector. This position is partly associated with the Keynesian denial of the natural rate hypothesis. We note in this context one of several connections between the issues listed under the four categories. The assertion of a "fundamental flaw in the price mechanism", or the proposition of an "inherent instability of the private sector" is closely associated with the rejection of the relevant operation of a natural rate of unemployment. Keynesians frequently deny that the private sector is a self-adjusting process. It is argued occasionally that the process is self-adjusting but tends to settle at "unacceptable" levels of unemployment. The criterion of "unacceptability" remains quite vague and unsubstantiated however. The natural rate actually determined by a given institutional situation may indeed be suboptimal The natural rate hypothesis yields no attribution of social optimality. This is a separate and supplementary issue worthy of some closer examination. Proponents of the second and third thesis argue specifically that major and persistent changes in the natural rate of unemployment reflect demographic trends and policies pursued by the government. Their analysis would imply that suitable changes in policies and specific institutional rearrangements could be expected to lower the natural rate of unemployment. But we should also beware of the "Can do fallacy". The fact that it can be done does not establish that the social benefits of such actions necessarily exceed the associated social cost.[19] Proponents of the second (or third) thesis also argue that the

[18] James *Tobin* emphasizes in a paper included in the Proceedings of the American Economic Association, May 1975, the importance of the suspected instability of the private sector. His paper prepared for the Brown University Conference contained no references to this fundamental problem.

[19] Martin *Feldstein* contributed probably most effectively to a clarification of several problems noted in the text. His recent publications on Social Security and unemployment are particularly instructive.

patterns of deviations from the natural rate of unemployment and the level of the natural rate are substantially affected by the increasing instability of the "rules of the game" imposed by legislative bodies, the government sector's bureaucracy. This institutional trend is reinforced by erratic and uncertain policies affecting many branches of an economy.

The view of a fundamental instability of the private sector produces farreaching implications. It determines an activist and highly interventionist concept of policy. The government sector necessarily appears as the "ultimate stabilizer". The instability thesis favors the development of a large bureaucracy attending daily to a wide ranging detail of regulations and programs. The alternative hypothesis essentially reverses the traditional Keynesian view. It argues that the private sector is essentially a shock-absorbing, stabilizing and self-adjusting process. Instability is produced dominantly by the operation of the government sector. It is also argued on occasion that this instability increases with the relative size of the government sector. This view determines obviously radically different implications for rational policy making and institutional arrangements. It is important to recognize in this context that we are confronted here with serious cognitive issues bearing on a fundamental property of the social process. The cognitive aspects of these problems should be recognized inspite of ideological trappings, subterfuges and semi-theological rhetoric frequently cultivated in public discussions.[20] Recognition of a cognitive core beyond all the ideological rhetoric should encourage further examination and research explicating precisely the nature of the issue in order to exploit observations more effectively in discriminating assessments. Simple references to the occurrence of economic fluctuations yield no discriminating evidence. We note here only in passing that all econometric models systematically examined in this respect yield no support for the instability thesis. They describe a highly stabilized and shock-absorbing process.[21] It is also possible to assess systematically whether the "public interest hypothesis" or an "entrepreneurial hypothesis" of established bureaucracies and legis-

---

[20] The public discussion in Germany observed in recent years suffered somewhat from an easy substitution of ideological rhetoric and purpose for a serious cognitive effort.

[21] My review of the two volumes on "Econometric Models of the Cyclical Behavior", edited by Bert *Hickman*, Columbia University Press, in the Journal of Economic Literature, Vol. XI, No. 3, September 1973, contains more detail in this respect.

lative bodies offers more useful explanations of observed behavior and developments.[22] The "public interest" hypothesis yields the view of an essentially stabilizing government sector, whereas the "entrepreneurial" hypothesis implies that the political process dominantly generates de-stabilizing patterns.

Recognition of a basically self-adjusting character of the private sector, either in the limited sense of some Keynesians[23] or in the full sense of proponents of the natural rate hypothesis, directs our attention to the explanation of observable fluctuations in real variables. A central issue reflected in many policy discussions pertains to the systematic occurrence of a dominant impulse pattern. One thesis maintains that as a matter of historical fact (and not as an expression of Ontological Reality) monetary impulses dominate the observable fluctuations of real variables. This impulse hypothesis conflicts of course with the strong thesis of rational expectations and can only be combined with the first and second thesis of labor market processes. The textbook versions of "Keynesian analysis" explicitly assign to fiscal policies the dominant weight. It is argued that an assessment of economic evolution over a shorter-run horizon depends crucially on the course of fiscal variables. A Wicksellian tradition recognizes on the other hand the driving force in autonomous swings of entrepreneurial anticipations. This tradition was occasionally translated into an "animal spirits hypothesis" of economic fluctuations.

The hypothesis of a "dominant impulse pattern" is frequently contested. The alternative is an essentially "eclectic view" propounding the operation of shifting combinations of impulses. We note however once again that the record of econometric models yields little support for the eclectic thesis. Moreover, an eclectic thesis remains essentially empty and offers usually almost no empirical content. This need not be the case however. A modified eclectic view may well systematically combine several of the alternatively listed dominant impulse forces. This combination may produce a systematic pattern subsuming several (possibly)

---

[22] Elements of an "entrepreneurial hypothesis" of the political process and bureaucracies are noted in my Comments on Robert *Gordon's* paper, "The Demand for and Supply of Inflation", to be published as a Conference volume sponsored by the National Bureau of Economic Research in The Journal of Law and Economics. A more extensive development of the hypothesis is presented in a paper by William *Meckling* prepared for the Third Interlaken Seminar on Ideology and Analysis 1976.

[23] The "limited sense" alluded to above means an equilibrium adjustment of real flow variables to the setting of predetermined policy variables.

interdependent factors. The combination of fiscal and monetary policy in recent work developed by *Brunner-Meltzer* offers one example in this respect. It should also be noted that in recent work *Brunner-Meltzer* increasingly emphasized and moved beyond the role of financial policies (or behavior). The whole range of government behavior systematically eroding the predictability, the range and interpretation of the "rules of the game" seems to require more attention in the future. Such attention should also include the systematic attrition of property rights resulting from the political process of all Western countries. This attrition lowers an economy's capital intensity and raises the natural level of unemployment. Both events lower the natural level of output. We need hardly refer to the Third World for exemplification of these trends.

A subject raised by *Mayer* in the section devoted to the transmission mechanism is more properly examined as part of the impulse problem. He correctly emphasizes that the relative stability of money demand was a matter of dispute. The view that money demand is highly unstable has been particularly adopted by some groups in the Federal Reserve bureaucracy. This doctrine replaced the defunct free reserve conception which dominated Federal Reserve thinking over many decades. The possibility of an unstable money demand has been suggestively generalized by James *Tobin*. He argues that autonomously shifting demand and supply over a wide range of financial assets also emit impulses affecting price-level and output. This position fits naturally into an eclectic thesis of the nature of the impulse problem which denies the dominance (over time) of any particular impulse pattern. "Financial market eclecticism" in conjunction with the traditional interest target policy of Central Banks implies however a pattern conflicting with the observed association between monetary acceleration (deceleration) and subsequent expansion (retardation) of economic activity. Furthermore, the accumulated empirical work pertaining to money demand produced no support for the instability thesis. One suspects that the authorities were misled on this point by their usual myopia to overrate the role of random events proceeding over a shorter-run horizon.

The impulse and stability problem also includes the "cost-push" controversy. The term is used somewhat ambiguously in the literature and is occasionally applied to radically different interpretations emanating from conflicting hypotheses. It is necessary therefore to clarify two views encountered in the literature and yielding (under identical value systems) vastly different policy conclusions. The two views involve alternative interpretations of wage-price movements. One view postulates that wages and prices evolve in response to market conditions and are systematically modified by changes in these conditions. Another view asserts that prices and wages move (at least in part) independently of market conditions and reflect the operation of autonomous social forces. The first and essentially price-theoretical thesis subsumes observable wage-price movements under the operation of the transmission mechanism. This yields an interpretation of "cost-push" consistent with the basic price-theoretical view. The term refers to an identifiable phase in the adjustment process. Financial decelerations in the context of inherited inflations determine a simultaneous occurrence of price inflation and retardation of output or rising unemployment. The nature of the transmission mechanism, conditioned by expectional adjustments and past policy experiences, determines in conjunction with the magnitude or persistence of the financial deceleration the length and severity of this intervening adjustment phase. The second view, replacing price-theory with sociological considerations, moves the observable behavior of wages an prices to the range of impulse forces. The "cost-push" in this sense refers to an important impulse explained by institutional arrangements and sociological factors beyond the response patterns summarized by price-theory.

The distinction between a price-theoretical and a "sociological" view of price-wage movements appears analytically more useful than the traditional classification into demand pull and cost-push explanations. In particular, the ambiguity of "cost-push" obstructed the development of adequate empirical tests. The distinction formulated on the other hand in terms of price-theoretical categories encourages analytic formulations yielding discriminating tests bearing on the fundamental issue. It is remarkable to note that many economists fail on occasion to comprehend the issue and deny the occurrence of seriously conflicting (i. e. logically inconsistent) hypotheses in this matter. Robert *Gordon* writes for instance that "monetarists tended to regard any claim that inflation is caused by non-economic factors ... as a contradiction of the monetary approach ...".[24] It seems necessary to emphasize that the "institutionalist" or "sociological view" of observed price-wage movements involving an explicit denial of price-theoretical pattern (i. e. assertion of non-responsiveness to evolving market conditions) is no monetarist illusion. It is actually argued and advanced on many oc-

---

[24] See the paper under footnote 15.

casions. The New York Times has sanctified this view in editorials in an essentially Galbraithian spirit. Science Magazine added in 1975 an editorial arguing this position in most explicit terms. We may disregard that the "sociological view" conforming to an intuitive sense of obviousness (as the Ptolemaic view of the relation between earth and sun) dominates the conception of the intelligentsia. More important for our purposes are the professional economists propounding this view. Abba *Lerner* argued that a deficiency of aggregate demand combined with rising prices reveals the occurrence of special forces operating independently of market conditions. Sir John *Hicks* admonishes us that English "troubles are not of a monetary character and can not be cured by monetary means". Monetary policy is thus dismissed both as a sufficient and necessary condition of inflation. And Roy *Harrod* maintains that "the causes of the wage-price explosion are sociological". A detailed survey of the "sociological explanations" will be presented at another occasion in order to demonstrate their frequent occurrence inspite of assertions to the contrary that "nobody means what is really said". It is noteworthy in this context that Robert *Gordon* usefully contributes to exemplify our case. He formulates in the same paper quoted above a cost-push theory of inflation and unemployment. The significant aspect for our purposes is the circumstance that the cost-push factor introduced into *Gordon's* analysis operates independently of evolving market conditions and is responsive neither to expected policy patterns nor to market conditions. It functions as a completely autonomous factor (relative to price-theoretical processes) shaping wages, unemployment and prices.[25]

The alternative hypotheses outlined above express non-contrived and genuine differences in views about the economic process. They affect substantially the policies deemed appropriate to cope with unemployment and inflation. The occurrence of pronounced differences among policy programs and proposals advanced in public debate should be rather obvious even to an inveterate "consensus seeker". Moreover, these differences cannot be reduced according to the media's usual procedure to "ideological positions" or "differences in values". The conflict in pro-

---

[25] The point is developed in my Comments on *Gordon's* paper to be published also in The Journal of Law and Economics. *Gordon* senses correctly the inadequacy of the traditional classification of inflation theories but fails to recognize the existence of a genuine issue between hypotheses asserting a pervasive and systematic responsiveness of prices and wages (incl. "administered" prices), and "sociological" hypotheses denying such responsiveness.

posals and programs reflects a fundamental conflict in substantive views about the world. It seems more useful to recognize this conflict, direct attention to it and challenge our cognitive energies to asses and resolve it in our future endeavors.

V. The Relation between
Allocative Detail and Aggregative Processes

Mayer's discussion contains some useful characterizations of the issues under this title. These aspects were also essentially neglected at the Brown University Conference on Monetarism. Such neglect would be quite appropriate for an essentially esoteric problem of cosmetic significance. But this is not the case. Alternative views of the relation between allocative detail (across and over time) and aggregative processes reflect fundamentally different conceptions of the cognitive process. They also determine substantial variations in proposals or evaluations of policies.

We find on the one side, particularly among econometric practitioners engaged in large scale model building, an explicit belief linking aggregative behavior with detailed allocative processes. We notice at this stage another interdependence with aspects of other issues. An eclectic position bearing on the impulse problem is frequently used to justify the dependence of aggregative behavior on wide ranging allocative processes. Aggregate fluctuations are understood to emerge from the cumulative effect of changes and disturbances occurring in all corners and parts of the economy. Allocative detail is thus unavoidably required to model effectively the course of aggregate fluctuations. This thesis implies further that large models produce better explanations of aggregate behavior than smaller models. It is particularly believed that the sequence of expanding models converges (stochastically?) to the "true model".

The alternative view rejects this implicitly descriptivist conception of science. It also rejects a pervasive instrumentalist approach to science cultivated by many econometricians. This instrumentalist approach is well expressed by a pronounced emphasis on forecasting (unrelated to test statements) and "sophisticated manipulation" with minor attention to the formulation of assessable cognitive claims about the world. This instrumentalist conception has clearly determined the adjustments made on the "class of Brookings models" over the past years. The concentration on cognitive criteria reveals moreover the dangers associated with a cherished principle, viz. "that everything depends on everything else". The history of our cognitive progress over thousands of years demonstrates that our knowledge expanded as a result of a deliberate disregard of this empty principle. Useful and felicitous formulations of hypotheses involve a differentiation between relevant orders of magnitudes and a systematic exploitation of such differences. The alternative view thus radically rejects the idea that "all allocative detail" should in principle be incorporated in the analysis. It rejects in particular the view that more detail improves the resulting explanation of aggregate fluctuations. It is not asserted that all allocation patterns are of comparatively small order of significance and can be (approximately) disregarded and conveyed to a random residual. It expresses essentially a thesis of analytic parsimony. One selects a small range of allocation patterns considered to be highly relevant and disregards the others. They are not disregarded because an Ontological Law promulgated by a Hegelian "Geist" or "Idee" determines the irrelevance of the discarded detail. One may well recognize that the omitted detail exerts some influence. The omission simply expresses an assessable empirical hypothesis that this influence operates mostly at a minor scale and contributes quite marginally to the power of the explanation. This conjecture remains of course always exposed to new questioning and new rounds of reexaminations. These reassessments may well shift occasionally the range of admittedly relevant or irrelevant detail according to the reformulation of the aggregative hypothesis. But there seems so far little evidence supporting the descriptivist-instrumentalist claim to "all the detail". The performance of larger and larger models offers no ground for support of the basic claim.[26]

The descriptivist-instrumentalist misconception of science guiding the approach to larger models also produces patterns of immunization which protect the evolving constructions from critical exposure to relevant observations. Such immunizations involve of course an implicit denial of cognitive standards and the whole endeavor really abandons under the circumstances any cognitive goal. The concentration on forecasting has distracted practitioners from attention to appropriate test procedures. Moreover, the forecasting procedures with their "sophisticated manipulation" of constants, expected exogenous variables and expected

---

[26] The reader is referred to my review of the *Hickman* volumes (footnote 21). The reader should particularly note that Laurence *Klein's* reformulation of the Brookings model moves in the opposite direction. A smaller structure with more dummy variables emerged.

random terms are simply incompatible with the requirements of an assessable empirical hypothesis. The whole affair becomes, as I indicated
at another occasion, an exercise in numerology.[27] One more aspect
deserves attention in this context. The size of the models frequently
raises a problem of "degrees of freedom" whenever the number of predetermined variables exceeds the number of observation points. In order
to execute estimation and also fill the initially empty formulae with
some content various auxiliary procedures were used. But they all involve the implicit imposition of supplementary hypotheses by com-
putational fiat. The content, structure and meaning of these supplementary hypotheses remains however quite obscure.[28]

The cognitive content of the final construction remains thus essentially
unclear. Immunization is under the circumstances complete. It is logically impossible to determine any relevant test statements and numerology has vanquished science. Recent analytic developments also bear on
the relevance of the ambitious econometric attempts. The discussion
about the role of expectations made us realize that economic agents
interact in a vast and continuous learning process. It follows that
variations in policy patterns and new ranges of experiences modify the
response patterns expressed by the structural detail of an econometric
model. Information about the evolution of interest rates over the past
10 years was absorbed by an expanding sector of the public. We expect
therefore different and more sensitive response patterns to relative interest rate changes than in the early 1960's. Similarly, ten years of inflation with repeated failures of policies modified probably the shorter-
run responses of price-level and output to nominal impulses. This problem was first submitted to the profession's attention in explicit analytic
terms by Robert *Lucas*.[29] His analysis implies in particular that an

---

[27] The point was elaborated in my review article (footnote 21).

[28] The problem has been analyzed in detail by Robert *Basmann* in an important chapter, "The Brookings Quarterly Econometric Model: Science or
Number Mysticism?", in Problems and Issues in Current Econometric Practice,
edited by Karl *Brunner*, Columbus, Ohio 1972.

[29] Robert *Lucas*, "Some International Evidence on Output-Inflation Trade-
offs", American Economic Review Vol. LXIII, No. 3, June 1973; and "Econometric Policy Evaluation: A Critique", Carnegie-Rochester Conference
Series, Vol. I, January 1976, North-Holland Publishing Co. The operation of
the *"Lucas"* effect has been particularly explored for the inflation-output
tradeoff by Michael *Hamburger* in a paper: "Inflation, Unemployment and
Macroeconomic Policy in Open Economies: An Empirical Analysis", Carnegie-
Rochester Conference Series, Volume VI, forthcoming.

economy's response structure is not invariant relative to changing patterns of policies. One surmises that the effect of the learning process affects large models with detailed structural specifications more extensively than smaller and more compacted formulations. Moreover, compacter formulations are less susceptible to immunization from critical tests. They also recognize more easily results of the public's learning process.

The fundamental issue confronting us in this section produces important ramifications. It subtly affects conflicting positions bearing on the relevant explanatory horizon. The emphasis on allocative detail is frequently associated with attempts to explain as much detail as possible across and over time. It is expressed by a concern to explain systematically very short-run movements of wages and prices and other variables. The alternative thesis maintains that these short-run movements contain a major portion of white noise from various origins. It argues in particular that we can reasonably explain with adequate approximation movements and patterns evolving beyond the shorter-run. This seems to apply especially to inflation. It emphasizes moreover that persistent attempts at short-run and shortest-run explanation tend to confuse the unavoidable white noise with systematic effects. One seems to become more prone to interpret observed deviations from a previously fitted short-run regression as evidence that "the world has changed".[30]

---

[30] Many specific disputes should be recognized as exemplifications of the basic issue. This applies to the question of whether or not the details concerning the mode of entry of money and credit into the system really matter. It also applies to the current approaches to an explanation of the price-level. One explanation asserts that the position and form of the frequency distribution of price changes depends crucially on selected segments of price changes under the distribution independent of policy patterns. The other explanation denies this and asserts that the position of the distribution is affected mostly by nominal shocks and wide-ranging real shocks. The difference between the two explanations is probably conditioned to some extent by the difference in the time horizon addressed. The second explanation does recognize a feedback from politically sensitive segments of price-changes to the position of the distribution, provided the Central Bank indulges in accommodative policies.

There remains lastly the perennial controversy about "single equation versus structure" and about "black-boxes". Two aspects should be considered here. The accusation of "black-boxing" made by one side is balanced by the accusation of adducing irrelevant detail by the other side. An ability to write more equations assures no relevant information. Neither does the omission of detail guarantee success. The issue has been stated above. The "single equation versus structure" requires partly the same comment. We should also note that "single

VI. Concluding Remarks

My discussion disregards some issues covered in *Mayer's* wide ranging survey. The policy analysis and the analysis of political-institutional processes which appear in *Mayer's* last point should be reserved for another occasion. The policy analysis is properly centered by *Mayer* on the indicator and target problem. The indicator problem refers to the appropriate interpretation of monetary policy and monetary trends. The target problem describes the choice of optimal policy strategy by monetary authorities. The analysis of both interpretation and strategy problem are essentially predetermined by the basic specifications bearing on transmission mechanism, impulse pattern, internal stability and the relevance of allocative detail. The same range of basic specification determines also wider ranges of differences in policy conception. An activist stance of fine-tuning financial policies is usually based on a combination of specifications stressing internal instability and the relevant operation (with respect to aggregative behavior) of a wide-ranging allocative detail. So are most programs of extensive credit controls or proposals to allocate credit. Both interpretation and strategy problems are still much disputed at this stage. They also affect the evaluation and the proposed course of monetary policy in the summer of 1975 or the winter 1975/76. This state and the wider policy implications of the basic issues guides our attention to the analytic and empirical work still required on major questions and conflicting hypotheses. Such cognitive endeavors will reach in the future beyond the traditional boundaries of policy analysis. Mayer's last point opens this issue. The evaluation of "government" involves more than personal preferences and values. It requires an analysis, in particular empirical hypotheses, about the behavior of bureaucracies, legislative bodies and the consequences of various institutional arrangements. The apparently intractable dispute between advocates of "larger government" and proponents of "very limited government" is ultimately reducible, beyond easy ideological feelings, to different conjectures about man and his behaviour under various institutional structures.[31] It is noteworthy that the conjecture underlying the

---

equations" often provide useful test statements for a "structure" or more particularly a "class of structures". Under such circumstances the controversy becomes pointless.

[31] The issue is confronted in a paper prepared by William *Meckling* for the Second Interlaken Seminar on Ideology and Analysis 1975 and to be published in the "Schweizerische Zeitschrift für Volkswirtschaft und Statistik,"

proponents of limited government emerges as a natural generalization of the price-theoretical basis of the transmission mechanism. Beyond all the "esoteric" analytics loom non-contrived problems and questions bearing on the economic process and the future course of societies. We will need the determined work of many competent researchers in order to meet this challenge.

1976. Two other papers, prepared by Gerard *Gäfgen* — Hans Georg *Monnissen* and Willi *Meyer* for the Third Interlaken Seminar, examine the issue in futher detail.

Monetarism in Historical Perspective

By Phillip Cagan*

The Bullionists versus the Anti-Bullionists, the Currency School versus the Banking School, and now the Monetarists versus the Fiscalists. What jolly good sport to participate in a famous debate. It encourages a flowering of thought and economic research, not to mention conferences and grants. Participants in the former debates were immortalized in numerous Ph. D. dissertations and scholarly histories of thought [9, 16]. Alas, no one cares about the history of economic thought any more. Hence we must provide our own account. Hence this collection of commentaries.

But does any one other than the participants care much about this debate? Perhaps not. Yet the issues have far-reaching implications for the conduct of policy and are a serious matter. In his careful review of the issues, Thomas *Mayer* largely bypasses the historical antecedents to present-day monetarism.** I believe the antecedents merit attention.

I. Professional Opinion in the 1940s and Early 1950s

No one who was not in touch with the economics profession in the 1940s and early 1950s can quite imagine the state of thinking then in the profession at large on monetary theory and policy. The quantity of money was not considered important, indeed was hardly worth mentioning, for questions of aggregate demand, unemployment, and even inflation. Peruse the journals of that period! The analyses may have contained an "LM" curve, following *Hicks'* [4] famous interpretation of *Keynes,* but textual discussions of theory and policy in article after article hardly mentioned the quantity of money at all. Textbooks in basic economics and even in money and banking mentioned the quantity theory of money, if at all, only to hold it up to ridicule. Those textbooks produced an entire cohort of professional economists who became the

---

* Comments from Anna J. *Schwartz* on an earlier draft were most helpful.
** Vol. 8 (1975) pp. 191 and pp. 293.

teachers of hordes of economics students. There were, of course, many exceptions, most notably at the University of Chicago and among some teachers of monetary economics whose intellectual heritage reached back into the 1920s. But if you traveled among the profession at large, mention of the quantity of money elicited puzzled glances of disbelief or sly smiles of condescension.

Monetarism is a reaction to that earlier inhospitable environment. Indeed, if there had not been a time when most of the profession said "money does not matter'," it would never have occurred to anyone to say "money does matter" [7]. Much of the monetarist message at first was intended simply to reacquaint the profession with the principles of money known in the 1920s, which had first been denied and then widely forgotten during the 1930s and 1940s. That purpose has now been accomplished, thanks no doubt more to several decades of inflation than to the preachings of the monetarists. Nevertheless, now that monetarists have come out of the wilderness, few would deny them self-satisfaction for the renewed interest in money and monetary policy and its favorable recognition again in textbooks.

II. The Relative Importance of Money

Indeed, monetarism has gained such attention that its opponents have feared that it might sweep away everything else. They have raised the spectre that monetarists claim that "only money matters". That was never claimed. What the opponents mistook for such a claim, perhaps, was the lesser one implied by some monetarists' writings that, among the list of influences on aggregate demand, money should stand at the top. The supporting argument is that changes in the money stock inevitably affect aggregate demand, albeit often slowly. The other influences have uncertain effects. They depend, unlike money, upon redistributive effects, money illusion, or cooperative changes in the money stock, in which the net results can differ materially from case to case.

This issue was argued at the Brown University Conference on Monetarism in 1974 [15]. No one there disputed the importance of money, and most of the proceedings were devoted to the importance if any to attach to fiscal policy. The fiscalists pointed out that the major econometric models show a large effect from changes in government expenditures or tax rates. But it is not clear how much the effect depends upon the Keynesian structure of the models and the cooperation of an expanding money stock. On a theoretical level fiscal effects (with the money stock constant) depend upon the interest elasticity of the demand for money balances (because the effect of a government deficit on interest rates which induces a more active use of money balances is needed to support an increase in expenditures) and upon the extent to which future tax liabilities of government bond interest are discounted (because government borrowing can be offset by an increase in taxpayers' saving) [5 a]. As I pointed out in my published comments at the conference [15], all this makes the magnitude of the long-run (say over a year or more) effect of fiscal policy uncertain.[1] On the presumption that the initial impact of a change in expenditures from a fiscal action will take place before the subsequent offsets in private spending associated with the financing of the action, the effect is likely to be much greater in the short run. Even so, the short-run effect of a tax cut can also be small if the public views it as temporary, and the size of multiplier effects of fiscal expenditures are uncertain in the short run because of the variable size and speed of associated offsets (not to mention administrative delays).

Monetary policy presents almost the opposite timing pattern. Its effects are delayed and, in the short run, variable from case to case and uncertain. But it builds up to a single long-run effect, aside from usually minor differences in the manner of changing the money stock (open market operations, change in reserve requirements, etc.). A sustained change in the money stock tends to produce a proportional change in aggregate expenditures in the long run. There are no important qualifications or offsets to the effect of monetary changes on aggregate demand in the long run. A change in the demand for money balances due to accompanying changes in interest rates is an offset, but it cannot last forever and is largely a very short run offset. The only qualification to the proposition that changes in money will have inevitable long-run effects on aggregate demand arises when the monetary change is a policy response to actual or anticipated changes in aggregate demand, for in some cases policy may accommodate the money stock to demand changes which have already originated in other short-run influences. In those cases the causal connection between money and aggregate demand becomes muddled, because money is then an endogenous

---

[1] If consideration is given to various wealth effects of fiscal actions, even the direction of the effect becomes uncertain [8]. The main monetarist propositions do not, however, depend upon wealth effects.

variable and not an independent source of disturbances to the economy. But the possible endogeneity of money is not denied by monetarism. All that monetarism holds is that money should be properly controlled and that, if it is, it can control aggregate demand.

Whether or not money belongs at the top of the list of influences on aggregate demand is not a theoretical question to argue about, so long as money is not buried in neglect at the bottom as it once was. The question is an empirical one and will be settled by the weight of evidence. It was the importance of gathering the evidence which motivated Milton *Friedman* and Anna *Schwartz* to undertake their monumental study of U. S. monetary history [3]. They found support for their view that money had been the most important source of disturbances to the U. S. economy over that period. It is hard to imagine taking strong exception to their finding, though many do. If we take another step and conclude that money will continue to be a serious potential source of disturbances unless properly controlled, we enter into monetarist territory.

III. A Fixed Monetary Rule

The preceding empirical proposition about the importance of money supports a strong prima facie case for a policy of constant growth in the money stock, the bête noire of the opponents of monetarism. It is not entirely a new proposal. The immediate antecedent was Henry *Simons'* early arguments in favor of a constant money stock [14][2]. This has the benefit of simplicity of policy management and would avoid the horrendous mistakes of policy that produced devastating fluctuations in the money stock of the past. It has the disadvantage, however, of not stabilizing the price level. Lloyd *Mints* proposed that policy control the money stock with a view instead of stabilizing the price level [10]. His proposal has since lost its appeal, because the price level is not a sensitive indicator for monetary policy, an objection strengthened by experience in recent years. We have learned that money affects prices with a long lag and that movements in prices and activity are not closely correlated in the short run. Consequently, a policy of trying to stabilize the price level would not be successful in the short run and would entail substantial fluctuations in monetary growth.

---

[2] See also *Robertson's* discussion [11] of policy views in the 1920s.

It is natural, therefore, to turn back to the money stock itself as the best indicator of policy, and to propose a constant rate of growth consistent with long-run price stability. Since the long-run trend of monetary velocity changes from time to time, moderate periodic changes could be made in the fixed rate of monetary growth to achieve approximate long-run constancy of the price level.

An argument frequently made against such a proposal is that a discretionary policy must always dominate a fixed rule. If the authorities seek to stabilize the growth of aggregate demand, constant monetary growth will by chance and only occasionally be the optimal policy and therefore should not be specified beforehand. Let the authorities choose the best policy as they go along; if constant monetary growth is the best, it will be chosen. This is a silly argument and misses the point. The monetarist position is based on the fact of our ignorance and the mistakes that are bound to result, whereas the opposing argument assumes optimization of a known model of the economy. Once stochastic terms are added to represent uncertainty, the optimal policy collapses toward virtual constancy of the policy instrument in the short run as the degree of uncertainty increases. As *Friedman* pointed out [1], policy makers must have forecasts and knowledge of the effects of their actions that are very good indeed before they can hope to reduce rather than add to the instability in aggregate demand. Maybe they will someday, but who can be optimistic?

Nor is that all. Besides the effect of stochastic terms in models to represent uncertainty, the structure of models entails an unknown degree of misspecification which can aggravate policy errors well beyond the two standard deviations of normal stochastic terms. In addition, the kind of policy pursued by the authorities will itself affect the response of the economy. *Mints* [10, p. 9 and elsewhere] held the view that public expectations of a constant-price-level policy would help to keep the price level stable. Uncertain, discretionary policies undermine stabilizing behavior by the public. Thus Benjamin *Klein* [5] concludes that the demise of the gold standard in the period between the two World Wars and absence of any clear commitment to stabilizing prices has made the price level more volatile than it used to be. In technical terms, he finds that changes in the price level used to be regressive but now follow a random walk.

The same point is developed further with the new idea of "rational expectations" [6, 12, 13]. If the public bases economic decisions on expectations formed rationally, that is, with all the available information and economic knowledge, they will take into account what is announced or known about government and central bank policy. The consequences are remarkable and intriguing. The standard "Phillips Curve" is vertical (that is, no tradeoff exists between inflation and unemployment), and monetary policy has no effect on output and employment but only affects prices.

Such models based on rational expectations should not be taken as accurate descriptions of economic behavior, but it is an empirical question whether they are worse approximations to reality especially today than are the various econometric models on which discretionary policy proposals are based. These econometric models derive "optimal" discretionary policies to trade off inflation and unemployment; they are able to do so because they are based on lags and ad hoc mechanical formulations of expectations by the public which are distinctly irrational in terms of the models themselves.[3]

But the recent work on rational expectations, though consistent with the monetarist tradition, goes beyond it. Monetarism is not based on rational expectations and does not require them.

Indeed, a monetarist in good standing need not oppose all discretionary monetary policy. It might be beneficial in particular circumstances. The monetarist view is rather that discretionary monetary policy has not been beneficial over-all in the past, that its performance in the future cannot by assumption be taken as beneficial without question, and that in any event discretion should be quite limited and undertaken with caution. (Keeping monetary growth reasonably constant gives the authorities plenty to do, so fixed monetary growth is far from a "passive" policy.)

Monetarists and their opponents disagree on the degree of economic stability to be achieved with a policy of constant or near constant monetary growth. The monetarists say the resulting stability — no longer disturbed by domestic monetary influences — will probably be the best attainable and "good enough", whereas the opponents say "not good enough" and think they know how to do better. This issue goes to the heart of the debate and does not appear capable of being settled to

---

[3] As one who helped to popularize mechanical expectations in a study of hyperinflations done long ago before expectations entered empirical models at all, I welcome work on rational expectations as an appropriate antidote.

everyone's satisfaction by the kind of evidence so far available. We need experience with constant monetary growth. German policy has moved in that direction and, under prodding from Congress, so has the U. S. Federal Reserve. Perhaps the future will bring the needed evidence, but it should be understood that reasonably constant monetary growth, starting in the midst of rapid inflation and world economic disorganization, needs more than a few years to demonstrate its beneficial effects.

Debates tend to accentuate extreme views. It should be emphasized, therefore, that monetarists do not claim that reasonably constant monetary growth (and its necessary corollary, freely floating exchange rates) will produce a millenium free of disturbances to the economy and of fluctuations in economic activity. They claim only that economic instability will be much less than in the past. Monetarists may differ among themselves whether some discretionary monetary policy and short-run variations in monetary growth could, under good management, be beneficial and worth trying. Given the lags in monetary effects, however, discretionary monetary policy will outperform a policy of constant growth at best moderately, and worse results are a real danger.

IV. Is a Discretionary Fiscal Policy Needed?

Monetarists are accused of claiming that fiscal policy has no effect. Not so. The defense of those effects thrown up by fiscalists is in response to a different monetarist argument, namely that the preference generally given to fiscal over monetary policy as a means of moderating economic fluctuations is a mistake, and that the order of priority should be reversed. Fiscal measures, particularly expenditures such as unemployment compensation, obviously do have short-run effects, and nothing in monetarist thought opposes their use for purposes of short-run stabilization, especially in view of the long lags of monetary policy. *Friedman* for one has pointed to the beneficial automatic effects of the government budget for short-run stabilization and proposed that it be nondiscretionary [2]. One might also seriously contemplate an active discretionary fiscal policy. I see no basic conflict of such a view with monetarism on a theoretical level.

The catch is the fiscal performance in practice. Here monetarists are skeptical of a record which fiscalists glorify. As monetarists sum up our experience with fiscal policy, decisions to change the level of government expenditures have administrative lags just as long as the "outside" lag for monetary policy, while cyclical changes in tax rates, on which fiscal stabilization in the U. S. has been forced to concentrate, have uncertain effects on consumption expenditures. Because of forecasting errors, the over-all contribution to the stabilization of mild business cycles is open to question. In severe, prolonged recessions the contribution is more likely to be beneficial and is widely accepted. Tax changes for stabilization purposes, however, are difficult to control in a democracy because of their effects on the distribution of income. The consequence is the well known preference of elected governments for cuts rather than increases and the persistence of deficits when they are not appropriate. Perhaps the management problems of fiscal policy are not insuperable. Yet they are formidable.

As a first step, the monetarist proposals for monetary policy should be inoffensive to a wide range of economists including neo-Keynesians who might nevertheless doubt the degree of success to be achieved with stable monetary growth alone. Whether a discretionary fiscal policy, despite the risks, is also desirable depends upon how unsuccessful a monetarist policy would be. The monetarist position is that, after several years of reasonably stable monetary growth, discretionary fiscal changes would not be needed as a stabilization instrument.

V. Concluding Remark

As is evident from the above discussion, monetarism in my view is more a set of propositions about policy and about the empirical research to support them than a particular theoretical model of the economy. The core of the monetarist view is that money is very important and that reasonably stable monetary growth should be the centerpiece of stabilization policies.[4]

References

1. Milton *Friedman*, The Effect of a Full-Employment Policy on Economic Stability: A Formal Analysis, in his Essays in Positive Economics, Chicago, 1953. — 2. Milton *Friedman*, A Monetary and Fiscal Framework for Economic Stability, American Economic Review, June 1948, 245—64, reprinted in his

---

[4] To avoid misunderstanding I should add that this is a policy for an economy already on its desired path. If we start far off the desired path, as with the inflation of 1975—76, we can only approach the desired path gradually.

Essays, ibid. — 3. Milton *Friedman* and Anna J. *Schwartz*, A Monetary History of the United States 1867—1960, National Bureau of Economic Research, 1963. — 4. John R. *Hicks*, Mr. *Keynes* and the "Classics", A Suggested Interpretation, Econometrica, 1937, reprinted in W. *Fellner* and B. F. *Haley* (eds.), Readings in the Theory of Income Distribution, Philadelphia, 1946. — 5. Benjamin *Klein*, Our New Monetary Standard: The Measurement and Effects of Price Uncertainty, 1880—1973, Economic Inquiry, Dec. 1975, 461—84. — 5 a. Levis A. *Kochin*, Are Future Taxes Anticipated by Consumers? Journal of Money, Credit and Banking, Aug. 1974, 385—94. — 6. Robert E. *Lucas*, Jr., Econometric Policy Evaluation: A Critique, manuscript, 1973, forthcoming in volume edited by Karl Brunner to be published by North Holland. — 7. A. James *Meigs.* Money Matters, Harper and Row, 1972. — 8. Lawrence H. *Meyer* and William R. *Hart,* On the Effects of Fiscal and Monetary Policy: Completing the Taxonomy, American Economic Review, September 1975. 762—67. — 9. Lloyd W. *Mints*, A History of Banking Theory, Chicago, 1945. — 10. *ibid.*, Monetary Policy for a Competitive Society, McGraw Hill, 1950. — 11. D. H. *Robertson*, Lectures on Economic Principles, vol. III, Staples Press, London, 1959. — 12. Thomas J. *Sargent* and Neil *Wallace*, Rational Expectations and the Theory of Economic Policy, Federal Reserve Bank of Minneapolis, Studies in Monetary Economics 2, June 1975. — 13. *ibid.*, Rational Expectations, the Optimal Monetary Instrument, and the Optimal Money Supply Rule, Journal of Political Economy, April 1975, 241—54. — 14. Henry C. *Simons*, Economic Policy for a Free Society, Chicago, 1948. — 15. Jerome L. *Stein* (ed.), Monetarism, North Holland, Amsterdam, 1976. 16. Jacob *Viner*, Studies in the Theory of International Trade, Harper, 1937.

The Theoretical Nondebate about Monetarism

By Benjamin M. Friedman

During the two decades since the publication of "Studies in the Quantity Theory of Money" [20], the debate over the content and relative merits of what has subsequently come to be called "monetarism" first ripened, then matured, and has now even begun to mellow. The thrust of Thomas *Mayer's* [28] excellent taxonomical survey is that perhaps the time for a measured stock-taking has come. What, then, has "the monetarist debate" been all about?

One key to the overall thrust of the discussions involved in the monetarist debate is that most economists today view the macroeconomic process differently than they would have done twenty years ago. In strong contrast to the views which predominated in the wake of the Oxford [3, 29] and Harvard Business School [15] surveys, most economists now believe that what happens in financial markets does play a major role in determining nonfinancial economic activity. The nexus of prices and yields and quantities of assets — not excluding "money" — does "matter".

What too often becomes lost in any economic discussion, however, is the distinction between *empirical* propositions and *theoretical* ones. This distinction is especially important in making an assessment of the monetarist debate because, as key participants in the debate have progressively elaborated exactly what they think on particular questions, it has become increasingly clear that the distinguishing content of monetarism is a set of *empirical* propositions. One corollary to this situation is that, while the debate has encouraged researchers on both sides to sharpen and extend their theoretical analysis, those lessons which economists have thus far learned and accepted from monetarism are

* The author, who is Associate Professor of Economics, Harvard University, is grateful to the National Science Foundation for support under grant SOC 74 - 21027, and to James *Duesenberry,* Michael *Hamburger,* Thomas *Mayer* and Allan *Meltzer* for helpful comments on a previous draft of this paper.

primarily lessons about empirical issues. Another corollary is that the remaining points in dispute today — the monetarist debate is not, and probably never will be, over — are also primarily empirical issues of comparing relative variances and elasticities, distinguishing first-order from n-th order effects, and the like. From a theoretical standpoint the debate has by today achieved the status of a nondebate.

I. Theory and Empiricism in Mayer's Taxonomy

Mayer's survey set forth twelve propositions as the basic building blocks in the belief structure of today's "monetarist" economist. Although much of his paper carefully developed the interrelationships among these twelve propositions, showing why a believer in one may well be a believer in others on the same list, *Mayer* also went to considerable effort to note that belief in or rejection of all twelve propositions together is not a necessary condition for consistent analytical thinking.

Of *Mayer's* twelve propositions, not one is theoretical in its distinguishing content. In other words, while each of these propositions rests on some underlying theoretical structure, in every case that theoretical base is neither more nor less than what most "Keynesian" economists also believe today. What distinguishes most of these "monetarist" propositions from what a "Keynesian" economist would be likely to believe, is their explicit statement about the magnitude of one or more parameters of the common underlying theoretical framework accepted by both monetarists and Keynesians.[1] For the remainder of *Mayer's* propositions, the distinguishing content is of a personal-preference nature; such preferences either are implicit statements about positive issues, like the magnitude of parameter values, or are nondebatable and non-explainable gustes of the non-disputandes kind.

---

[1] One can, of course, trivialize the empirical/theoretical distinction by saying either that all models are special cases of a more general model with certain parameters set equal either to zero or to infinity, or that many theoretical propositions are subject to empirical testing. To do so, however, is to discard a useful concept which seems especially relevant to considering the development of the monetarist debate in general and *Mayer's* current survey in particular. To a certain extent, the process of scientific debate consists of resolving theoretical disagreements about different paradigms into agreement on a common paradigm (which, if appropriate, may be subject to empirical testing).

A brief review of eleven of *Mayer's* propositions, deferring for the moment his treatment of "the monetarist model of the transmission process", indicates the empirical or personal-preference essential nature of each:

The quantity theory of money, in the sense of the predominance of the impact of monetary factors on nominal income (*Mayer's* proposition # 1) is clearly an empirical notion. It rules out no nonmonetary influences but rather simply asserts their subordinance to monetary factors, presumably in the sense of explanation of variance.[2] Furthermore, as *Mayer's* discussion of the quantity theory makes clear, what is relevant here is the net result of monetary influences on nominal income, and not the particular way in which these influences come about. In the conceptual framework of formal models of causation, this is a proposition about the magnitudes of reduced-form coefficients and about the variances of factors taken to be exogenous, but not about the specification of the underlying structural system.

The stability of the private sector (# 3) is also an empirical issue, at least in the context of the monetarist debate.[3] A given system is typically stable or unstable, and in either case oscillatory or monotonic, according to the magnitudes of certain of its parameters.[4] Just as importantly, in light of the relevance of the stability question for the monetarist debate, the time required for a perturbed stable system to return to equilibrium also depends on certain key parameter magnitudes. Hence the question of the stability of the private sector is an empirical issue from the outset.

The rejection of the significance of allocative detail (even in the short run), together with the corollary belief in a "fluid" capital market (# 4), is again a basically empirical matter of separating first-order from secondary effects. Surely *Mayer* would not want to assert that monetarists believe the economic system to be wholly without friction —

---

[2] Subdebates over whether the relevant variable to be explained is the variance of nominal income or the variance about trend, or over the relevant time unit to use in computing these variances, do not alter the fundamentally empirical nature of the quantity theory proposition.

[3] Following *Clower* [13] and *Leijonhufvud* [27], a number of writers have recently explored this question in a theoretical context which has not yet intersected with the monetarist debate. *Tobin's* [45] contribution to this literature comes closest to relating it to questions raised by monetarism.

[4] See *Friedman* [17] for a discussion of this stability issue in the context of *Cagan's* [12] demand-for-money model.

i. e., that for every disappointed would-be homebuilder, unable to find a mortgage loan when short-term market interest rates exceed thrift deposit interest rate ceilings, someone else steps in with an exactly equal amount of nominal expenditure elsewhere in the economy; or that every medical student living in strapped circumstances does so because of personal preference or doubts about future earning power, rather than because of risk aversion reflected in bank lending practices. *Mayer* identified the monetarist approach in this respect as viewing expenditures as determined by the net excess demand for a single stock (real balances), but a quick reference to *Friedman's* [21] "Restatement" shows that net excess demands for other stocks (e. g., productive capital, inventories, houses, consumer durables) can theoretically matter also. Like acceptance of the quantity theory, dismissing the specific compositional detail reflects empirical rather than theoretical judgments.[5]

Since *Mayer's* first four propositions are the most familiar — and the most fundamental — elements of today's "monetarism", it is possible to deal even more briefly with the remaining eight.

Focusing on the overall price level instead of on individual sector prices (# 5) and using small rather than large econometric models (# 6) are elements of research strategy which follow naturally from the empirical dismissal of the importance of allocative detail.[6]

Using the reserve base as the instrument of monetary policy (# 7) and using the money stock as the intermediate target (# 8) constitute optimal monetary policy procedures only given certain parameter magnitudes, as *Poole* [38] and *Pierce* and *Thomson* [37], respectively, have shown in their analyses of these two issues.[7]

A constant money growth rule (# 9) constitutes optimal monetary policy if and only if the variance of some relevant final-form parameter of the economic system is infinite (or if there is infinite risk aversion),

---

[5] A reading of *Mayer's* own discussion of this proposition suggests that "unimportance" may describe what he had in mind better than "irrelevance" which he used.

[6] Parts of *Mayer's* discussion of the price level question seem to suggest a fundamental theoretical issue, but the discussion is highly inconclusive in this regard.

[7] The "indicator" issue has no unambiguous meaning, and no importance for monetary policy, unless the "indicator" is identical to the instrument which the central bank fixes; see *Friedman* [16].

just as a fully activist certainty-equivalent policy constitutes optimal monetary policy if and only if the variances of all relevant final-form parameters of the economic system vanish (or if there is zero risk aversion). As *Brainard* [8] has shown, whether the optimal degree of policy activism in the general case lies closer to the constant no-discretion rule or closer to certainty equivalence depends directly upon the variance-covariance structure of the system's final-form parameters,[8] and so preference for a constant no-discretion policy rule (as a first approximation to the optimal policy) is implicitly a statement about parameter values.

Belief in the absence of an inflation-unemployment trade-off (# 10) is largely an empirical proposition relating to money wage illusion, as a comparison of the *Phelps-Friedman* [23, 35, 36] and *Tobin* [44] views of the *Phillips* curve indicates.

Greater concern over inflation than over unemployment (# 11) and dislike of government intervention (# 12) are clearly personal preferences. They may reflect empirical judgments — for example, that the economy returns to full-employment equilibrium rapidly after a contractionary perturbation, or that a combination of cupidity and stupidity typically leads democratically elected officials to do the wrong thing — or they may reflect more abstract philosophical principles. In either case, they are empty of theoretical content in a macroeconomic sense.

With the exception of "the monetarist model of the transmission process", then, none of *Mayer's* characteristic "monetarist" propositions has a theoretical macroeconomic issue as its fundamentally distinguishing content.

II. Mayer on Monetarists on the Transition Mechanism

What about the "transmission mechanism"? In the context of the debate over monetarism, this term has become a familiar shorthand for the specification of that part of the structural economic system which relates to the effect of money on nominal income (or anything else which money is presumed to affect). Almost by definition, therefore, discussion of the "transmission mechanism" is the heart of whatever theoretical content the monetarist debate has had.

---

[8] *Friedman's* [19] classic treatment of this problem summarizes the relevant part of the variance-covariance structure in a single correlation coefficient.

Mayer's treatment of "the monetarist model of the transmission process" identifies four elements which are variously described as "... substantive difference[s] between the Keynesian and monetarist transmission processes" and "... links between the hypothesis of the primacy of changes in the quantity of money and the monetarist — as opposed to the Keynesian — version of the transmission process": (1) the stability of the demand for money, (2) the relative measurability of money versus interest rates, (3) the range of assets considered, and (4) the relative price effects and stock effects discussed by *Brunner* and *Meltzer*. Because of the centrality of the transmission process proposition to the whole question of the theoretical content — or lack thereof — of the monetarist debate today, it is useful to examine each of these four sub-propositions separately.

First, a quick glance at page 199 of the "General Theory" [26] immediately imposes the burden of proof onto any aspiring exegete purporting to identify a belief in the *theoretical* instability of the demand for money as part of the usual Keynesian baggage. Once it is possible to specify the arguments of a behavioral function, as Keynes did in his famous $M = L_1(Y) + L_2(r)$ expression, then the two most familiar notions of the stability of that relationship — the variance of the implicit additive residual disturbance and the variance-covariance structure of the right-hand-side coefficients — are both empirical questions.

Mayer's distinction between "numerical" and "functional" stability is at its root simply a question of what variables belong on the right-hand side of the behavioral relationship. Most economists would argue that the simple money demand function $M = f(Y)$ used by *Friedman* [22], for example, is unstable in the sense that it omits the systematic influence of the current interest rate as in the inventory-theoretic model of *Baumol* [4] and *Tobin* [40]; the stable relationship would be $M = f(Y, r)$. Similarly, a strict interpretation of *Keynes'* speculative demand model would imply that the function $M = f(Y, r)$ is also unstable in that it omits the difference between the current interest rate and the expected future interest rate; the stable relationship, according to this argument, would be $M = f(Y, r, r - r^e)$. The argument with respect to other theoretically oriented variables, such as the anticipated rate of price inflation, or more strictly institutional influences on money demand, such as deposit interest ceilings (including the zero nominal yield on demand deposits), is exactly analogous. Once there is agreement on the specification of the behavioral relationship, questions of stability become empirical issues in the analysis of variance. Since *Friedman's* "Restatement" presents a theoretical specification of the money demand function which admits of many right-hand-side variables, and since most empirical work on money demand by monetarists[9] has included interest rates as right-hand-side variables just as in the Keynesian approach summarized most recently by *Goldfeld* [25], it is clear that the stability of the money demand function, in any of its various disguises, is an empirical rather than a theoretical issue.[10]

What about either the liquidity trap, which was the object of much attention in the demand-for-money literature of some years ago, or the more recently discussed "crowding out" effects associated with debt-financed fiscal policy? Both involve essentially empirical questions about the stability of the money-demand function as it relates to the presence of a wealth variable, or total portfolio constraint. The Keynesian liquidity trap requires a form of the $M = f(Y, r)$ function which is not single-valued at some point r^* and is not defined for $r < r^*$.[11] By contrast, the continuous and universally defined function $M = f(Y, r, W)$ reflects a liquidity trap if $\frac{\partial M}{\partial W} = 1$ for $r < r^*$. Similarly, as *Blinder* and *Solow* [5, 6] and *Tobin* [46] have shown, the mechanics of the "crowding out" analysis hinge on a shift in the $M = f(Y, r)$ function as the system receives an injection of outside bonds. Simply restated, the point here is that the $M = f(Y, r)$ function is unstable because the correctly specified money demand function should be $M = f(Y, r, W)$. The issue, once again, is not whether the demand for money is a stable behavioral relationship or an unsystematic outcome but, instead, whether a particular specification of this relationship is made to appear "unstable" by attributing to the additive residual and the several included right-hand-side coefficients effects due to systematic variation of an excluded variable. Questions of this kind are empirical and lie far

---

[9] For an early example, see *Meltzer* [30].

[10] A result established in Friedman [16] is that using the money stock as a straightforward intermediate target variable constitutes the optimal monetary policy procedure only if the money demand function is both interest inelastic and perfectly stable in the sense of zero residual variance.

[11] Conceptualizing the problem in this way avoids the difficulties of *Patinkin's* [34, Ch. 14] discussion, which determines that the liquidity trap notion is inherently a logical contradiction.

from the sense of the "stability" issue as *Mayer* related it to the monetarist debate.[12]

The second issue raised in *Mayer's* treatment of the "transmission mechanism" is the relative degree of measurement difficulty associated with "money" versus "the interest rate". As is clear from *Mayer's* discussion, neither of these two concepts necessarily corresponds to a quantity or price which is readily observable. Variation of expected future price inflation and of asset risk differentials complicate the identification of "the interest rate". Variation of asset preferences and of institutional arrangements complicate the identification of "the money stock".

There is no way of knowing, a priori, which sources of variation are more severe in any given economy. The answer must reflect empirical judgments. Furthermore, even if the precise variances of the two respective measurement errors were known, how would one evaluate their relative importance, i. e., their relative contribution to the variance of prediction or control of nominal income or whatever other key variable provides the ultimate criterion for choice? Is a measurement error variance of X_1 per-cent-per-annum-squared for the interest rate more or less troublesome than a measurement error variance of X_2 billions-of-dollars-squared for the money stock? The answer requires empirical information about relevant aspects of the overall economic system.

Yet another potential problem in this context, also not precluded on a priori grounds, is that the respective sources of interest rate and money stock measurement error may bear different comparisons in different time units. How is one to choose if the inflation expectations which lead to measurement error in identifying "the interest rate" change only slowly each quarter but vary greatly over the course of a decade, while the institutional factors which lead to measurement error in identifying any specific observable aggregate as "the money stock" vary greatly from quarter to quarter in ways which largely wash out

---

[12] The *Ando-Shell* appendix to *Ando* and *Modigliani* [2] is somewhat exceptional in this regard, since it attempts to demonstrate theoretically the independence of money demand from a wealth variable (rather than arguing, as did *Goldfeld* [25], that a wealth dependence is reasonable a priori but is empirically insignificant). This position is Keynesian in averting the "crowding out" problem but anti-Keynesian in precluding a liquidity trap. (Both of these propositions require redefinition in a money-shorts-longs world instead of a money-bonds world, however.)

over a decade or so? Even choosing the proper time unit for such a comparison is essentially an empirical problem.

The third "transmission mechanism" issue considered by *Mayer* is the "range of assets" for which the net excess demand may rise (fall) in response to an increase (decrease) in the public's holdings of money balances. An often repeated view, sketched by *Mayer*, is that the monetarist adopts a generalized portfolio approach, according to which the response is nonzero for all "assets" including both securities and "real assets" such as capital goods and consumer goods, whereas the Keynesian adopts, a priori, a segmented approach which assumes zero response for (nondurable) consumption goods. If true, this difference would indeed constitute a genuine point of theoretical difference at the core of the debate over monetarism. Nevertheless, while the "Keynesian" half of this theoretical distinction may be a valid description of the model of the "General Theory" itself,[13] it is in no way a valid description of the modern Keynesian position which is relevant to an assessment of the monetarism debate today.

A key point to note at the outset is that the only category of expenditure in any dispute whatever is that on consumption of services and nondurable goods. Consumer durables and residential dwellings are both analogous to producers' capital goods in their treatment, by Keynesians and monetarists alike, as assets bearing returns (in the form of services) and subject to ready incorporation within a generalized model of portfolio choice. The fact that only this one category of expenditures remains in question is important because, by definition, services and nondurable goods do not comprise an "asset" to be treated analogously with all of the other assets. Like leisure, nondurable consumption is a flow for which the integral over time is not a physical stock which can be bought or sold but is rather simply a cumulant over time of past and/or future activity. Hence it is at best misleading to imply that, in "the monetarist model of the transmission mechanism", increased money balances raise the public's net excess demands for ". . . all types of real

---

[13] Even in the "General Theory", *Keynes* was simplifying on the basis of an empirical judgment that, given the observed variation of interest rates, the interest elasticity of consumption was sufficiently small to render interest-induced consumption effects insignificant in comparison with the income-induced consumption effects which lay at the heart of his multiplier process; see [26, pp. 93-94].

assets", thereby leading the public to equilibrate marginal yields by spending the ". . . excess balances to acquire . . . consumer goods".

Incorporating the determination of a pure flow variable along with asset stock variables within a generalized portfolio model is not necessarily easy, as *Merton* [31] and *Samuelson* [39] have shown in the explicit context of interrelated saving and portfolio decisions. The standard simplification of this problem today is probably the "life cycle" saving model developed by *Modigliani, Brumberg* and *Ando* [1, 33], according to which the value of the stock of consumer wealth (including money balances) is a key determinant of the flow of consumer spending (including nondurables and services). This theoretical model has served as the foundation for a substantial amount of empirical work, often by "Keynesian" economists, investigating the effects of wealth on consumption spending.[14] There is no a priori reason for assuming homogeneity of effects among different kinds of wealth increments and different kinds of expenditures, and so whether money balances have as large an effect as do other assets, and whether nondurable consumption is affected as much as are other expenditures, are both empirical questions.[15] From the standpoint of identifying *theoretical* differences between the monetarist and Keynesian models of the "transmission process", however, the "range of assets" included in the portfolio model demonstrates more agreement than difference.

III. Brunner and Meltzer and Tobin on the Transmission Process

The fourth "substantive difference" between the monetarist and Keynesian transmission processes, in *Mayer's* survey, is the *Brunner-Meltzer* [9, 10] analysis which ". . . focuses on a relative price process and stock effects which tend to bring the system towards a classical rather than a Keynesian equilibrium." Since *Mayer* merely cited this point of dif-

---

[14] See, for example, *de Leeuw* and *Gramlich* [14], *Modigliani* [32], *Tobin* and *Dolde* [47], and *Friend* and *Lieberman* [24]. Much of this empirical literature has emphasized the market value of consumers' equity portfolios, but this focus is natural in view of the relative magnitude and variability of consumers' equity holdings in comparison with money balances or other forms of wealth. The key point is that dependence of nondurable consumption on money balances is not precluded a priori.

[15] *Bosworth's* [7] results, for example, are curious in suggesting that changes in the value of equity portfolios stimulate nondurable consumption but not purchases of consumer durables.

ference without explanation, and since the *Brunner-Meltzer* model is somewhat complicated, this subject bears more extensive investigation. In particular, comparing *Brunner's* and *Meltzer's* "monetarist" model with a "Keynesian" model such as *Tobin's* [43] is a useful way to evaluate the extent of theoretical dispute between alternative models of the "transmission process".

The *Brunner-Meltzer* model consists of explicit representations of economic behavior in three markets — output, bank credit, and money.[16]

The output market equations represent (1) the equilibrium condition for real output of the private sector, y, (2) the determination of private expenditures, d, and (3) the determination of the price level, p:

(1) $$y = d + g$$

(2) $$d = d\,(i - \pi, p, p^*, P, e, W_n, W_h)\,,\ d_3, d_4, d_5, d_6, d_7 > 0 > d_1, d_2$$

(3) $$p = p\,(y, K, w, \Phi)\,,\ p_1, p_3, p_4 > 0 > p_2$$

where g is government expenditures, i is the nominal interest rate, π is the rate of price inflation expected by credit market participants, p^* is the price level expected by producers, P is the price of existing real capital assets, K is the stock of existing real capital assets, w is the efficiency wage rate, Φ is the price level expected by suppliers, and subscripted notations indicate partial derivatives. Subsidiary relationships determine (4) nonhuman wealth, W_n, (5) human wealth, W_h, and (6) the anticipated per-unit return on real capital assets, e:

(4) $$W_n = PK + v\,(i, \tau)\,S + (1 + \omega)\,B\,,\ v_1 < 0$$

(5) $$W_h = W_h\,(y, \tau)\,,\ W_{h_1} > 0$$

(6) $$e = e\,(y, \tau)\,,\ e_1 > 0$$

where v is the price per face-amount dollar of government securities, τ is a vector of tax rates, S is the face-value amount of government securities outstanding, ω is the ratio of the banking system's net worth to the monetary base, and B is the monetary base itself.

The credit market equations represent (7) a market-clearing equilibrium condition, (8) the asset multiplier of the commercial banking

---

[16] The form of the *Brunner-Meltzer* model presented here is from [10]. This model has evolved through various forms and has appeared in several published sources over a number of years.

system, a, and (9) the stock of assets offered to banks by the nonbank public, σ [17, 18]:

(7) $$aB = \sigma$$

(8) $$a = a\,(i, p, P, W_n, W_h, e)\,,\;\; a_1, a_3, a_4 > 0 > a_2$$

(9) $$\sigma = \sigma\,(i - \pi, P, p, p^*, \Phi, e, S, W_n, W_h)\,,\; \sigma_3, \sigma_4, \sigma_5, \sigma_6, \sigma_7 > 0 > \sigma_1, \sigma_2\,.$$

Brunner and *Meltzer* conceptually assigned to the credit market equations the role of (proximately) determining i, along with a and σ.[19]

The money market equations analogously represent (10) a market-clearing equilibrium condition, (11) the money multiplier of the commercial banking system, m, and (12) the nonbank public's desired nominal stock of money, L:[20]

(10) $$mB = L$$

(11) $$m = m\,(i, p, P, W_n, W_h)\,,\;\; m_1, m_2 > 0 > m_3, m_4$$

(12) $$L = L\,(i, p^*, \Phi, e, p, P, W_n, W_h)\,,\; L_5, L_6, L_7, L_8 > 0 > L_1, L_2, L_3, L_4\,.$$

Brunner and *Meltzer* conceptually assigned to the money market equations the role of (proximately) determining P, along with m and L.

The final component of the model is the description of the government's role in the economy. The government budget constraint is

(13) $$pg + \overline{w}lg + IS - t = \dot{B} + \dot{S}$$

---

[17] Although the model as presented in [10] omits any mention of time deposits, time deposits must be present as an additional asset in the model to prevent the banking system's asset and money multiplier functions from being inconsistent; see *Friedman* and *Froewiss* [18]. Some earlier versions of the model included the yield on time deposits, i_t, as an explicit argument of equations (8) and (9) and *Brunner* and *Meltzer* [11] have made clear that the version of the model in [10] assumes i_t to be implicitly present in these two equations.

[18] The earlier version [9] specified $\frac{\partial a}{\partial w_h} > 0$, $\frac{\partial a}{\partial e} < 0$ and $\frac{\partial \sigma}{\partial s} = 1$.

[19] In long-run steady-state equilibrium $i = \frac{p}{P}e + \pi$.

[20] The earlier version [9] specified $\frac{\partial m}{\partial w_h} < 0$ and also included e as an argument of equation (11) with derivative $\frac{\partial m}{\partial e} > 0$.

where pg and $\overline{w}lg$ are government purchases of goods and labor services, respectively, and subsidiary relationships determine (14) interest payments per face-value unit of government debt, I, and (15) tax revenues, t:

(14) $I = I(i),\ I_1 > 0$

(15) $t = t(p, y, \overline{w}lg, \tau),\ t_1, t_2, t_3 > 0 .$

The financing mix of the net deficit follows as

(16) $\dot{B} = \mu\,[pg + \overline{w}lg + IS - t] + v$

(17) $\dot{S} = (1 - \mu)\,[pg + \overline{w}lg + IS - t] - v$

where μ is by definition the portion of a deficit financed by issuing or withdrawing B, and v is the amount of B issued or withdrawn independently of the deficit.

Since one of equations (13), (16) and (17) is redundant, the model in this form is a system of sixteen independent relationships in the sixteen jointly determined variables $(y, d, p, W_n, W_h, e, a, \sigma, i, m, L, P, I, t, \dot{B}, \dot{S})$. This system is capable of generating responses to monetary policy, and *Brunner* and *Meltzer* have elaborated extensively the mechanics of the resulting "transmission mechanism".[21] The key aspect of this mechanism, which *Mayer* cited as constituting a substantive difference from Keynesian models of the transmission process, is the dependence on relative price effects and stock effects. In other words, monetary policy in the form $v \neq 0$ disturbs the asset market equilibrium, thereby causing portfolio adjustments which change P and i.[22] An open market purchase of securities $(v > 0)$, for example, increases commercial banks' supply of deposits and demand for earning assets, and a fall in i and rise in P are necessary to increase the public's demand for deposits and supply of loans, so as to restore equilibrium in the asset markets. These changes in P and i then lead to further adjustments in the goods market because of the direct dependence of d on P and i, a host of indirect effects operating through the direct dependence of W_n on P and i, and finally the dependence of p on y.

---

[21] The *Brunner-Meltzer* model is also capable of generating fiscal policy responses, but a discussion here of the differences between monetary and fiscal effects in the model would not add to the examination of the model's "transmission mechanism" for monetary policy. See the analysis of the "bbe line" in [10].

[22] All other things equal, e varies inversely with P.

How does this "monetarist model of the transmission process" differ from a Keynesian alternative?

Tobin's [43] Model II consists of explicit representations of economic behavior in three markets — capital, (short-term) government securities, and money.[23] Although *Tobin* presented the model more compactly, it is useful here, for purposes of comparison, to describe it in a form analogous to the outline of the *Brunner-Meltzer* model presented above.

The capital market equations represent (I) a market-clearing equilibrium condition in real terms, (II) the public's demand for capital as a fraction of real wealth, f_k, and (III) a definition of the real rate of return on capital, r_k:

$$\text{(I)} \qquad\qquad f_K W = qK$$

$$\text{(II)} \qquad f_K = f_K\left(r_K, r_S, r_M, \frac{Y}{W}\right), \quad f_{K_1} > 0 = f_{K_4} > f_{K_2}, f_{K_3}$$

$$\text{(III)} \qquad\qquad r_K = \frac{R}{q}$$

where K is the stock of real capital; q is the ratio of the market price of capital to its reproduction cost (equivalent to P/p in the *Brunner-Meltzer* model); Y is real income; r_S and r_M are the real yields on government securities and money, respectively; R is the marginal efficiency of capital relative to reproduction cost; and W is the stock of real wealth defined as

$$\text{(IV)} \qquad\qquad W = qK + \frac{S}{p} + \frac{M}{p}$$

where S is the nominal amount of government securities outstanding and M is the nominal money stock.

The government securities market equations analogously represent (V) a market-clearing equilibrium condition in real terms, (VI) the

---

[23] *Tobin's* model also has evolved through various forms over a number of years; see, for example, *Tobin* [42]. The more detailed Model III, also presented in [43], is more comparable to the *Brunner-Meltzer* model in that it distinguishes the public's assets and liabilities from those of the banking system, so that items such as deposits, loans and the monetary base are explicitly identified. For purposes of seeing the analytic principle of the "relative price effects and stock effects", however, the simpler Model II is sufficient.

public's demand for government securities as a fraction of real wealth, f_S, and (VII) a definition of r_S:

(V)
$$f_S W = \frac{S}{p}$$

(VI)
$$f_S = f_S\left(r_K, r_S, r_M, \frac{Y}{W}\right), \quad f_{S_2} > 0 > f_{S_1}, f_{S_3}, f_{S_4}$$

(VII)
$$r_S = i_S - \pi$$

where i_S is the nominal yield on government securities and π is the expected rate of price inflation.

The money market equations analogously represent (VIII) a market-clearing equilibrium condition in real terms, (IX) the public's demand for money as a fraction of real wealth, f_M, and (X) a definition of r_M:

(VIII)
$$f_M W = \frac{M}{p}$$

(IX)
$$f_M = f_M\left(r_K, r_S, r_M, \frac{Y}{M}\right), \quad f_{M_3}, f_{M_4} > 0 > f_{M_1}, f_{M_2}$$

(X)
$$r_M = i_M - \pi$$

where i_M is the (typically zero) nominal yield on money.

Since the adding-up constraints implied by the wealth definition (IV) constrain the derivatives of asset demand functions (II), (VI) and (IX), one of these four relationships is redundant. Hence *Tobin*'s model in this form is a system of nine independent equations in the nine variables $(f_K, r_K, q, W, f_S, r_S, i_S, f_M, r_M)$.[24] This system too is capable of generating responses to monetary policy, and Tobin has also analyzed carefully the resulting "transmission mechanism". In contrast to the implication of *Mayer*'s paper, however, the key aspect of this mechanism is once again its dependence on relative price (yield) effects and stock effects. Monetary policy in the form $dM = -dS \neq 0$ disturbs the asset market equilibrium, thereby causing portfolio adjustments which change r_K, q, r_S, i_S, r_M and W. The "mechanism" is thus essentially identical to that employed by *Brunner* and *Meltzer*.

---

[24] *Tobin* explicitly noted that different interpretations of the model are possible, depending upon the particular set of nine variables assumed to be endogenous.

While *Tobin's* model is explicitly more detailed than the *Brunner-Meltzer* model in its treatment of the asset markets, it is less explicit in incorporating the goods market. Nevertheless, *Tobin* explained clearly that the private-demand-for-goods equation which he graphed as a form of *IS* curve in (R, Y) space depends positively on q.[25] Just as in the *Brunner-Meltzer* model, therefore, the asset market adjustments due to monetary policy lead in turn to further adjustments in the goods market.

Furthermore, both the *Tobin* model and the *Brunner-Meltzer* model adopt the same disaggregation methodology to sidestep completely the "asset aggregation" question which dominated much of the monetarist debate a decade ago. In particular, the issue which attracted so much attention at that time concerned the asset substitution implications of moving from the Keynesian-Hicksian-Metzlerian world, in which the only two assets were money and capital, to a three-asset world including money and capital and securities.[26] Were securities to be treated as (approximately) perfect substitutes for capital, leaving the only (or principal) dividing line that between money and all non-money assets, or were securities (approximately) perfect substitutes for money, leaving the only (or principal) dividing line that between capital and all financial assets?[27] Both *Tobin* and *Brunner* and *Meltzer* have disposed of this question by simply preserving the full three-way asset disaggregation and acknowledging that, in principle, the demand for every asset depends upon (among other things) the yield on all other assets. Relative substitutabilities are therefore an empirical matter of elasticities of functions explicitly included in the model with respect to arguments explicitly included in those functions, rather than a theoretical matter of competing paradigms.

What is one to make of all this? Perhaps *Brunner* and *Meltzer* are not monetarists. Or perhaps *Tobin* is not a Keynesian. Perhaps. A more likely conclusion, however, is that, once monetarists and Keynesians

----

[25] From (III), any variation in r_K requires an inverse variation in q for fixed R; see footnote 22. *Tobin* did not indicate the nature of the supply-of-goods equation which would accompany his model; in the *Brunner-Meltzer* model the price-setting equation (3) describes the behavior of suppliers.

[26] See, for example, the discussion in *Tobin* [41]. The discussion usually assumed that the securities in question were nominally denominated and non-indexed.

[27] See *Leijonhufvud* [27] for an argument which resolves this question according to whether the securities are of short or long maturity.

specify clearly the "transmission mechanism" by which monetary policy has its effect in their respective theoretical models, these alternative mechanisms are by and large identical. On this key issue, which is the essence of the theoretical dimension of the monetarist debate, it is hard to find significant disagreement.

IV. Conclusion

From a *theoretical* standpoint, the "monetarist" label today is an old school tie. Like other such emblems of association, it may convey information about the bearer's institutional affiliations, or about his mode of expressing himself, or about his tastes and preferences, or even about who his friends are. It does *not* bear information about the bearer's theoretical conception of money and its role in the macroeconomic system. Theoretical questions there are plenty, but these are *not* bound up in the monetarist debate. Instead, in part as a result of two decades of discussion, the focus of the monetarist debate today lies with *empirical* issues.

V. References

1. *Ando*, Albert, and *Modigliani*, Franco: "The Life Cycle Hypothesis of Saving: Aggregate Implications and Tests." American Economic Review, LIII (May, 1963), 55 - 84. — 2. *Ando*, Albert, and *Modigliani*, Franco: "Some Reflections on Describing Structures of Financial Sectors." Fromm and Klein (eds.), The Brookings Model: Perspective and Recent Developments. Amsterdam: North-Holland Publishing Company, 1975. — 3. *Andrews*, P. W. S.: "A Further Inquiry into the Effects of Rates of Interest." Oxford Economic Papers III (February, 1940), 32 - 73. — 4. *Baumol*, William J.: "The Transactions Demand for Cash: An Inventory Theoretic Approach." Quarterly Journal of Economics, LXVI (November, 1952), 545 - 556. — 5. *Blinder*, Alan S., and *Solow*, Robert M.: "Does Fiscal Policy Matter?" Journal of Public Economics, II (November, 1973), 318 - 337. — 6. *Blinder*, Alan S., and *Solow*, Robert M.: "Analytical Foundations of Fiscal Policy." *Blinder* et al., The Economics of Public Finance. Washington: The Brookings Institution, 1974. — 7. *Bosworth*, Barry: "The Stock Market and the Economy." Brookings Papers on Economic Activity (No. 2, 1975), 257 - 290. — 8. *Brainard*, William C.: "Uncertainty and the Effectiveness of Policy." American Economic Review, LVII (May, 1967), 411 - 425. — 9. *Brunner*, Karl, and *Meltzer*, Allan H.: "Money, Debt, and Economic Activity." Journal of Political Economy, LXXX (September/October, 1972), 951 - 977. — 10. *Brunner*, Karl, and *Meltzer*, Allan H.: "An Aggregate Theory for a Closed Economy." Stein (ed.), A Conference on Monetarism. Amsterdam: North-

Holland Publishing Company, forthcoming. — 11. *Brunner*, Karl, and *Meltzer*, Allan H.: "Monetarism: The Principal Issues, Areas of Agreement and the Work Remaining." Mimeo, 1975. — 12. *Cagan*, Phillip: "The Monetary Dynamics of Hyperinflation." Ch. 2 in [20]. — 13. *Clower*, Robert W.: "The Keynesian Counter-Revolution: A Theoretical Appraisal." Hahn and Brechling (eds.), The Theory of Interest Rates. London: Macmillan, 1965. — 14. *De Leeuw*, Frank, and *Gramlich*, Edward: "The Channels of Monetary Policy." Federal Reserve Bulletin, LV (June, 1969), 472 - 491. — 15. *Ebersole*, John: "The Influence of Interest Rates upon Entrepreneurial Decisions in Business: A Case Study." Harvard Business Review, XVII (1938), 35 - 39. — 16. *Friedman*, Benjamin M.: "Targets, Instruments, and Indicators of Monetary Policy." Journal of Monetary Economics, I (October, 1975), 443 - 473. — 17. *Friedman*, Benjamin M.: "Stability and Rationality in Models of Hyperinflation." Mimeo, 1975. — 18. *Friedman*, Benjamin M., and Froewiss, Kenneth C.: "Bank Behavior in the Brunner-Meltzer Model." Journal of Monetary Economics, forthcoming. — 19. *Friedman*, Milton: "The Effects of a Full-Employment Policy on Economic Stability." Friedman, Essays in Positive Economics. Chicago: University of Chicago Press, 1953. — 20. *Friedman*, Milton (ed.): Studies in the Quantity Theory of Money. Chicago: University of Chicago Press, 1956. — 21. *Friedman*, Milton: "The Quantity Theory of Money — A Restatement." Ch. 1 in [20]. — 22. *Friedman*, Milton: "The Demand for Money: Some Theoretical and Empirical Results." Journal of Political Economy, LXVII (August, 1959), 327 - 351. — 23. *Friedman*, Milton: "The Role of Monetary Policy." American Economic Review, LVIII (March, 1968), 1 - 17. — 24. *Friend*, Irwin, and *Lieberman*, Charles: "Short-Run Asset Effects on Household Saving and Consumption: The Cross-section Evidence." American Economic Review, LXV (September, 1975), 624 - 633. — 25. *Goldfeld*, Stephen M.: "The Demand for Money Revisited." Brookings Papers on Economic Activity (No. 3, 1973), 577 - 638. — 26. *Keynes*, John Maynard: The General Theory of Employment Interest and Money. New York: Harcourt, Brace & World, Inc., 1936. — 27. *Leijonhufvud*, Axel: On Keynesian Economics and the Economics of Keynes. London: Oxford University Press, 1968. — 28. *Mayer*, Thomas: "The Structure of Monetarism." Kredit und Kapital, VIII (Nos. 2 and 3, 1975), 190 - 218, 293 - 316. — 29. *Meade*, James E., and Andrews, P. W. S.: "Summary of Replies to Questions on Effects of Interest Rates." Oxford Economic Papers, I (October, 1938), 14 - 31. —30. *Meltzer*, Allan H.: "The Demand for Money: The Evidence from the Time Series." Journal of Political Economy, LXXI (June, 1963), 219 - 246. —31. *Merton*, Robert C.: "Lifetime Portfolio Selection Under Uncertainty: The Continuous-time Case." Review of Economics and Statistics, LI (August, 1969), 247 - 257. — 32. *Modigliani*, Franco: "Monetary Policy and Consumption." Consumer Spending and Monetary Policy: The Linkages. Boston: Federal Reserve Bank of Boston, 1971. — 33. *Modigliani*, Franco, and *Brumberg*, R.: "Utility Analysis and the Consumption Function: An Interpretation of Cross Section Data." Kurihara (ed.), Post-Keynesian Economics. New Brunswick: Rutgers University Press, 1954. — 34. *Patinkin*, Don: Money, Interest and Prices. 2nd ed. New York: Harper & Row, 1965. — 35. *Phelps*, Edmund S.: "Phillips Curves, Expectations of Inflation, and Optimal Unemployment Over Time." Economica, XXXIV (August, 1967), 254 - 281. — 36. *Phelps*, Edmund S.: Inflation Policy and Unemployment Theory. New York: W. W. Norton & Company, Inc., 1972. — 37. *Pierce*, James L., and *Thomson*, Thomas D.: "Some Issues in Controlling the Money Stock." Controlling Monetary Aggregates II: The Implementation. Boston: Federal Reserve Bank of Boston, 1972. — 38. *Poole*, William: "Optimal Choice of Monetary Policy Instruments in a Simple Stochastic Macro Model." Quarterly Journal of Economics, LXXXIV (May, 1970), 197 - 216. — 39. *Samuelson*, Paul A.: "Lifetime Portfolio Selection by Dynamic Stochastic Programming." Review of Economics and Statistics LI (August, 1969), 239 - 246. — 40. *Tobin*, James. "The Interest Elasticity of Transactions Demand for Cash." Review of Economics and Statistics, XXXVIII (August, 1956), 241 - 247. — 41. *Tobin*, James: "Money, Capital, and Other Stores of Value." American Economic Review, LI (May, 1961), 26 - 37. — 42. *Tobin*, James: "An Essay on the Principles of Debt Management." Commission on Money and Credit, Fiscal and Debt Management Policies. Englewood Cliffs: Prentice-Hall, 1963. — 43. *Tobin*, James: "A General Equilibrium Approach to Monetary Theory." Journal of Money, Credit and Banking, I (February, 1969), 15 - 29. — 44. *Tobin*, James: "Inflation and Unemployment." American Economic Review, LXII (March, 1972), 1 - 18. — 45. *Tobin*, James: "Keynesian Models of Recession and Depression." American Economic Review, LXV (May, 1975) 195 - 202. — 46. *Tobin*, James: "Long Run Effects of Fiscal and Monetary Actions on Aggregate Demand." Stein (ed.), A Conference on Monetarism. Amsterdam: North-Holland Publishing Company, forthcoming. — 47. *Tobin*, James, and *Dolde*, Walter J.: "Wealth, Liquidity and Consumption." Consumer Spending and Monetary Policy: The Linkages. Boston: Federal Reserve Bank of Boston, 1971.

Monetarism and Monetary Economics

A Delayed Comment

By Helmut Frisch

The strong reaction to Professor *Mayer*'s paper "The Structure of Monetarism"[1] indicates that he has touched upon a central theme of the contemporary theoretical discussion. Th. Mayer by using 12 propositions which are of varying importance has characterized present-day monetarism. In this note I concentrate on his first proposition: the predominance of the impact of monetary factors on nominal income (the Neo-quantity theory of money). My point in chap. I is that the Neo-quantity theory is completely trivial as a theory of nominal income if a monetary impulse cannot be divided in a real effect (output and employment effect) and in a price effect. This is shown by appeal to the so-called accelerations theorem, which is formulated by a merging of two *Friedman* models.[2] The few empirical studies which exist make it, however, questionable, whether one can speak of a "dominance" of a monetary impulse on output and production.

In chap. II a neglected aspect of the monetarist transmission process (proposition 2 in Th. Mayers list): the formation of inflationary expectations is considered. There I claim that the accelerations theorem is compatible with adaptive expectations, but not with the model of rational expectations. According to the latter a monetary impulse would only generate inflationary and no real effects. Newer empirical work conveys the impression that for the USA in the period after the II. World War, the acceleration or deceleration of the rate of monetary expansion has not been anticipated. Therefore the accelerations theorem seems to be more compatible with the empirical evidence than does the model of rational expectations.

---

[1] Th. *Mayer*, The Structure of Monetarism, Kredit und Kapital, Vol. 8 (1975) p. 191 - 215 and p. 293 - 313.

[2] M. *Friedman*, A Theoretical Framework of Monetary Analysis, J. P. E. 78 (1970) p. 193 - 238.
A Monetary Theory of Nominal Income, J. P. E. 79 (1971) p. 323 - 37.

Further it is surprising that Th. *Mayer* neglects the "crowding-out" effect, which some authors (for example J. *Stein*[3]) consider as the main difference between Monetarists and Neo-Keynesians. The crowding-out effect claims that government spending not accompanied by monetary expansion, i. e. financed by taxes or borrowing from the public results in a crowding-out of private expenditure with little if any increase in total spending. The neglect of the "crowding-out" is an expression of optimism concerning the stabilization policy of the government, whereas stressing it emphasize the opposite. Chap. III discusses the "crowding-out" effect as a noticeable difference between Monetarists and Neo-Keynesians.

The fundamental difference, however, between monetarism and monetary economics in general is to be found in the 'stability conjecture' according to which the private sector of the economy is inherently stable (Chap. IV). This postulate or as Th. Mayer often emphasizes "belief" belongs to the "presuppositions" (A. *Leijonhufvud*) of the monetarists and is always formulated as a contrast to the 'instability postulate' of Keynesian economics. After a discussion of a more operational concept of stability it is pointed out that the older monetarists such as K. *Wicksell*, G. *Myrdal* and F. A. *Hayek* used instead of the stability conjecture the concept of the 'cumulative' process which rests on the assumption that the monetary sector of the economy (in contrast to the real sector) is unstable, since a discrepancy between the real rate and the market rate of interest moves the system away from equilibrium by a sequence of expenditures and price changes.

I. The Accelerations Theorem

The recent reformulation of the quantity theory is the accelerations theorem. It implies that only an acceleration or a deceleration of the rate of money growth produces any real effects, i. e. employment and output effects, while a constant rate of growth of the quantity of money determines the rate of inflation. For example Laidler's formulation is: "The effects of a change in the rate of change of money supply are felt initially on the level of real income and the rate of inflation, but in the long run it is only the rate of inflation that is affected."[4]

[3] J. L. *Stein*, Inside the Monetarist Blackbox, in J. L. *Stein* ed. "Monetarism", p. 183 - 232, Amsterdam (1976).
[4] D. *Laidler*, An Elementary Monetarist Model of Simultaneous Fluctuations in Prices and Output, in H. *Frisch* ed., "Inflation in Small Countries",

In M. *Friedman's* (1970, 1971), D. *Laidler's* (1976) and K. *Brunner's* (1970)[5] model the accelerations theorem appears with a further conjecture, namely that the impact of monetary acceleration (deceleration) has only a temporary effect on output and employment. Both propositions can be found in a particularly simple formulation in *Friedman's* model. Merging both his theoretical models (1970, 1971) the following theoretical sketch is obtained:

(1) $$\pi = \pi^* + \alpha\,(y - y^*) + \gamma\,(\log X - \log X^*)$$

(2) $$x = x^* + (1 - \alpha)\,(y - y^*) - \gamma\,(\log X - \log X^*)$$

(3) $$y = y^* + \frac{1}{1 - R\beta}\,(m - y^*)$$

List of Symbols:

π ... rate of inflation

x ... rate of growth of real income

y ... rate of growth of nominal income

X ... level of real income

m ... rate of growth of money

R ... rate of change of the velocity of money

β ... adjustment coefficient for inflationary expectations

This system of three linear differential equations expresses the acceleration theorem very clearly. If in (3) the exogenous rate of growth of the quantity of money increases compared to the expected rate of growth of nominal income $(m > y^*)$, a positive difference $(y - y^*)$ arises. Equations (1) and (2) show how that deviation of the actual rate from the expected affects the rate of inflation π and the rate of growth of real income x. The parameters α and $(1 - \alpha)$ can be interpreted as price elasticities and production elasticities. The system demonstrates a causal direction. An increase in the growth rate of money supply produces real effects via equations (1) and (2), the magnitude of which is set by the ratio $\alpha/1 - \alpha$.

An expectations adjustment process of the type: $\frac{d}{dt}\,(y^*) = \beta\,(y - y^*)$ increases y^* in the state of disequilibrium until $y = y^* = m$. In the new

Lecture Notes in Economics and Mathematical Systems, Springer-Verlag, Berlin-Heidelberg-New York (1976) p. 76.
[5] K. *Brunner*, The Monetarist Revolution in Monetary Theory, Weltwirtschaftliches Archiv, 105 (1970).

steady state the effect of an increase of the growth rate of the quantity of money on the real variables have disappeared and all actual rates of growth are equal to the anticipated. If it is intended to produce real effects again the rate of money growth m has to be raised again. A permanent effect on the real system can only be made possible by a permanent acceleration of the growth of the quantity of money.

The accelerations theorem agrees with the first *Mayer*-proposition concerning the "predominance of the impact of monetary factors on nominal income" and it contains some elements of the monetarist transmission process. Two questions arise immediately:

(1) The accelerations theorem is an empirical hypothesis and thereby examinable. The only study to my knowledge which has attempted to subject the accelerations theorem to a direct statistical test is from P. *Korteweg* (1976) and is based on the Dutch economy from 1955 to 1972. In this study the "monetary impulse hypothesis" competes with the "fiscal impulse hypothesis" and the "foreign impulse hypothesis". P. *Korteweg* concludes: "Not rejected are the weak foreign and monetary impulse hypothesis. That is: changes in output growth without foreign and monetary impulses are highly unlikely".[6]

The empirical results do not oppose the accelerations theorem; however they oppose its interpretation in a causal sense, in that an acceleration of the money supply always generates a change in real production.[7] A change in the real rate of growth is always correlated with changes in the rate of growth of money supply; but not every change in the rate of money expansion induces a change in the real rate of growth.

(2) The duration of the real effects depends on the speed of adjustment of expectations and thereby leads to the question, which concept of expectation formation is compatible with the monetarist theory.

---

[6] P. *Korteweg*, Inflation, Economic Activity and the Operation of Fiscal, Foreign and Monetary Impulses in the Netherlands — A Preliminary Analysis 1953 - 1973, De Economist (1975) p. 616.

[7] According to the weak version of the impulse hypothesis, the phenomenon will not occur without the impulse; according to its strong version, the phenomenon will occur anytime the impulse specified occurs.

II. Endogenous Expectations

The central question concerning the process of expectation formation is not analysed in Th. Mayer's "Structures", although it is precisely the expectations which play a fundamental role in understanding the accelerations theorem, as well as the monetaristic transmission process. The acceleration theorem is compatible with the adaptive-expectations model, which is explicitly or implicitly accepted by the majority of monetaristic authors (M. *Friedman* 1970, 1971), (K. *Brunner* 1970), (D. *Laidler* 1976). If the economic agents behave according to the model of adaptive expectations, the real variables of the system (output and employment) can be changed through a change in the rate of change of money supply, because of the appearance of an unanticipated inflation.

Let us consider the situation in the labor market, which is usually neglected by the monetarists (E. *Claassen*[8]). If we start with a steady state situation in which money wages (w) grow at the rate of increase of marginal productivity of labor g and the expected rate of inflation, π^* we have:

$$w = g + \pi^*$$

The rate of growth of the market real wage, however, is $w - \pi$, where π is the actual rate of inflation:

$$w - \pi = g + (\pi^* - \pi) .$$

If a non-anticipated inflation develops due to the acceleration of money supply, the market real wage drops below the marginal productivity of labor and (assuming profit maximizing firms) the rate of unemployment is lowered below its "natural" level u^* (corresponding to the state of affairs in which inflation is fully anticipated $\pi = \pi^*$). This situation could be demonstrated by the following (linearized) adjustment process:

$$\frac{dN}{dt} = N \cdot \gamma \left(g\,(N) - (w - \pi) \right)$$

The increase in employment is proportional to the rentability difference $g - (w - \pi)$.

---

[8] E. *Claassen*, Short-Period Fluctuations in Nominal and Real Income: A Monetarist Model, in E. *Claassen* and P. *Salin* ed. "Stabilization Policies in Interdependent Economies", North-Holland (1972).

However the adaptive expectations adjustment model implies that money wages rise as long as there is a positive difference $(\pi - \pi^*)$. When $(\pi - \pi^*) = 0$ the previous real wage is reached again, the rate of unemployment is equal to u^* again, but the rate of inflation is permanently higher.

Any further attempt to lower u^* below u requires a higher rate of expansion of the money supply. An acceleration of the rate of growth of the money supply induces real effects only when a non-anticipated inflation results, which temporarily lowers the market real wage below the marginal product of labor.

Therefore we have the following lemma:

The accelerations theorem is explained by the existence of a non-anticipated inflation which is a consequence of the change in the rate of money supply.

While authors as M. *Friedman* (1970, 1971), D. *Laidler* (1976) or J. *Stein* (1976) (in his "synthetic" model) have formulated an adaptive expectations process, another group of authors, monetarists "in a broad sense", — such as Th. *Sargent*[9], Th. J. *Sargent* and N. *Wallace*[10] and R. E .*Lucas*[11] reject adaptive expectations as a waste of information, preferring rather "rational" expectations. The central idea of the rational expectations hypothesis (REH) is that the expectation of an economic variable "depends in a proper way on the same things that economic theory says actually determine that variable" (Th. J. *Sargent* and W. *Wallace*, 1975). More precisely: rational expectations of inflation are unbiased estimators of the actual inflation rate π_t, given all information at the beginning of the period.

From a theoretical point of view "rational expectations" render the accelerations theorem invalid. Since any economic agent knows the model, each change in the rate of growth of money supply leads not only to a change in the actual inflation rate but also in the expected rate of in-

---

[9] Th. J. *Sargent*, Rational Expectations, The Real Rate of Interest, and the Natural Rate of Unemployment, Brookings Paperson Economic Activity, 2 (1973).
[10] Th. J. *Sargent* and N. *Wallace*, Rational Expectations, the Optimal Monetary Instrument, and the Optimal Money Supply Rule, J. P. E. 83 (1975), p. 241 - 54.
[11] R. E. *Lucas*, Jr., Econometric Testing of the Natural Rate Hypothesis, in O. *Eckstein*, ed. "The Econometrics of Price Determination", Washington, D. C. (1972) p. 50 - 59.

flation, so that an impact on the real variables of the system is excluded.

In contrast, the econometric application of the concept of rational expectations seems to support the accelerations theorem. Especially informative is an econometric attempt by R. J. *Barro*[12] for the USA (1976). The work can be considered as an econometric test for the accelerations theorem and the concept of rational expectations. The hypothesis that forms the basis of this study is that only unanticipated changes in money have effects on real economic variables like the unemployment rate and the level of output. That hypothesis was quantified by interpreting the "systematic part" (= anticipated money growth) of the money supply as the amount that could have been predicted based on a reduced form equation, where money growth is explained by the "normal federal budget", the lagged rate of money growth and the lagged rate of unemployment. Unanticipated money growth was measured as actual growth less the amount obtained from this predicted relation $(m_t - m_t^*)$. The current and two annual lag values of unanticipated money growth were shown to have considerable explanatory value for unemployment and output according to the accelerations theorem. The results show that from 1961 - 1967 in a period of relatively constant growth the "unanticipated" rate of money expansion was very small; however the acceleration of the money supply 1968 (+ 2.5 %) was not anticipated and this brought the rate of unemployment down to 3.5 % below the estimated "natural level". An unanticipated monetary contraction 1960 (− 3.9 %) accounted for a sharp rise in the unemployment rate to 6.7 %. The empirical verification speaks for the accelerations theorem and against the REH. R. *Barro*'s result shows that for the USA for the period 1960 - 1975 an acceleration (deceleration) of the rate of money supply was regularly not (!) anticipated and it thereby led to changes in employment and output.

Why does the empirical evidence speak for the accelerations theorem and not for the REH? There are several reasons:

(1) Existing price agreements and wage contracts make short-run changes difficult, so that for parts of the price- and wage system adaptive behaviour again appears realistic.[13]

---

[12] R. J. *Barro*, Unanticipated Money Growth and Unemployment in the United States, A. E. R. 67 (1977).

[13] See W. *Poole*, Rational Expectations in the Macro Model, Brookings Papers on Economic Activity 2, (1976) p. 484 f.

(2) Economic agents might form conditional mathematical expectations using an economic model and information about exogenous
variables in t, but different agents might have different models.
People are rational with respect to their model; but the same information might convey different meanings to different economic
agents.

(3) The regular appearance of a significant unanticipated rate of money supply, whenever the rate of money supply changes, shows that
economic agents know the pre-determined variables of the model
but not all exogenous variables at time t, when they make their
predictions. (For example, the fiscal policy variable in $t-1$, but
not the value of that variable in t).

(4) The accelerations theorem can be viewed as a special variant of
the hypotheses that only the unanticipated part of changes in the
rate of money expansion has effects on the real economic variables.

III. The Crowding-out Effect

It is interesting to note that Th. *Mayer* did not discuss the crowding-
out effect as a point differentiating monetarism from Keynesian economics. The crowding-out effect deals with the different ways of financing a budget deficit. "Whether deficits produce inflation depends
on how they are financed. If, as so often happens, they are financed by
creating money, they unquestionably do produce inflationary pressure.
If they are financed by borrowing from the public, at whatever interest
rates are necessary, they may still exert some minor inflationary pressure. However, their major effect will be to make interest rates higher
than they would otherwise be." (M. *Friedman*, 1972)[14]

The crowding-out effect emphasized by M. *Friedman* and the econometricians of the St. Louis[15] model stresses the fact that government
spending not accompanied by monetary expansion, that is financed by
taxes or borrowing form the public results in a crowding-out of private
expenditure with little if any net increase in total spending.

---

[14] M. *Friedman*, Comments on the Critics, in R. J. *Gordon*, ed., "Milton
Friedman's Monetary Framework", The University of Chicago Press (1974),
p. 140.
[15] L. C. *Andersen* and K. M. *Carlson*, A Monetarist Model for Economic
Stabilization, Federal Reserve Bank, St. Louis Rev. (1970).

According to a hypothesis by J. *Stein*[16] the acceptance or rejection of the crowding-out effect is the point of difference between the two schools, the "Monetarists" and the "Neo-Keynesians". *Stein* considers the following 'Gedankenexperiment". The government reduces taxes and finances the deficit through the sale of bonds, thereby increasing Θ, the bonds/money ratio. Since the budget deficit raises the bonds/money ratio the bond market can only be in equilibrium if the nominal rate of interest rises. On the commodity market the results are two opposite effects: a positive wealth effect on the expenditure function $\frac{\partial E}{\partial \Theta} > 0$, and a negative crowding-out effect $\frac{\partial E}{\partial r} \cdot \frac{\partial r}{\partial \Theta} < 0$, ($\frac{\partial r}{\partial \Theta}$ is the effect of a change of the bonds/money ratio upon the market rate of interest). Three possible developments can come from these effects: the "crowding-out" effect can be stronger, can be weaker or can exactly compensate the positive wealth effect.

These two opposite effects signify the difference between Monetarists and Neo-Keynesians:

$$\frac{\partial \pi}{\partial \Theta} \leq 0 : \quad \text{Monetarists}$$

$$\pi = \text{rate of inflation}$$

$$\frac{\partial \pi}{\partial \Theta} > 0 : \quad \text{Neo-Keynesians}$$

If the effect of a government deficit financed by borrowing from the public on the rate of inflation is non-positive the model is Monetarist, if it is positive the model is Neo-Keynesian.

The "crowding-out" effect is an empirically testable hypothesis. F. *Modigliani* and A. *Ando*[17] have recently attempted to conduct, by means of a simulation study, an assessment of the role of the crowding-out effect. They point out that as a consequence of a "monetary impulse" the crowding-out effect is only one of several effects. Financing an increase in government expenditure (ΔG) by issuing debt will produce the following effects:

---

[16] Jerome L. *Stein*, Inside the Monetarist Black Box, in "Monetarism", J. *Stein* ed., Studies in Monetary Economics, Vol. 1 (1976) North-Holland-Publ.-Comp., Amsterdam-New York-Oxford, p. 193 f.

[17] F. *Modigliani* and A. *Ando*, Impacts of Fiscal Actions on Aggregate Income and the Monetarist Controversy: Theory and Evidence, in *J. Stein* ed. "Monetarism". Studies in Monetary Economics, Vol. 1 (1976) North-Holland, p. 25 f.

(1) an impact effect (direct effect $\Delta G \rightarrow$ real income), (2) an induced consumption effect, (3) an accelerator effect, (4) price effects, (5) wealth effects, (6) crowding-out effect and (7) a real balance effect (*Pigou-Patinkin*). According to *Modigliani* and *Ando* we can assume that the effects (3), (5), (7) are empirically negligible and (6) is contractive. Empirical evidence suggests that the contractive mechanisms tend to work more slowly than the major expansive one.

Hence one would expect that first real income will increase (the peak response in the *Modigliani-Ando* simulation is reached in about 5 quarters) but because of the crowding-out effect in the intermediate run (2 - 3 years) the system moves back to the initial situation. The Neo-Keynesian model's neglect of the crowding-out effect expresses an optimism about a government stabilization policy, whereas the Monetarists expresses exactly the opposite by emphasizing the crowding-out effect. This is undoubtedly an important point of difference between the two schools and of more importance than the following points discussed by Th. *Mayer:* (4) "Irrelevance of allocative detail for the explanation of short run changes in money income, (6) Reliance on small rather than large econometric models, (7) Use of the reserve base or similar measure as the indicator of monetary policy, (8) Use of the money stock as the proper target of monetary policy." Perhaps, however, it belongs to Th. *Mayer*'s point (9): "Dislike of government intervention".

IV. The Stability of the Private Sector

A central theorem of the present-day Monetarism is the stability conjecture of the private sector. *Mayer* states: "Monetarism generally believes that the private sector is inherently stable if left to its own devices and not disturbed by an erratic monetary growth". (Th. *Mayer,* op. cit. p. 204) The hypothesis about the stability of the private sector is a fact accepted by all monetarists. (M. *Friedman*[18]), (K. *Brunner* and A. *Meltzer*[19]), (D. *Laidler* [op. cit. 1976]) Here we have reached the core of the contemporary monetarism discussion. The monetarist model differs from the Keynesian economics by the 'belief' that the economic system exhibits a strong tendency to converge to the equilibrium of its real variables. This difference is usually noticeable at the 'cosmological'

---

[18] M. *Friedman,* The Role of Monetary Policy, A. E. R. vol. 58 (1968) p. 1 - 17.
[19] K. *Brunner and A. Meltzer,* An aggregative theory for a closed economy, in J. L. *Stein* ed. "Monetarism" op. cit. p. 69 - 103.

level — to use A. *Leijonhufvud*'s term — and not explicitly represented by the formal model. The 'vision' — how the economy basically works distinguishes Monetarism and 'Keynesian economics'. Even when one bears in mind Th. *Mayer*'s warning against claiming "that monetarism is basically an 'ideological' doctrine" and his advice to resist firmly the "temptation to play amateur psychoanalyst", (Th. *Mayer*, op. cit. p. 307) the stability conjecture is not included with the propositions which constitute the model but rather with the 'pre-suppositions' (A. *Leijonhufvud*)[20], i. e. propositions underlying the assumptions on which the model is based.

On the level of economic model building the stability problem can be reduced to two questions:

(1) Does the private economy exhibit a tendency to converge to equilibrium?

(2) Does this occur in a monotonic or in an oscillatory way?

The stability concept which has been taken from physics is useable only with important limitations in the social science. Even if a system converges to equilibrium the models differ according to the speed of reduction of a disturbance. G. *Tintner*[21] has recently suggested to introduce the concept of 'half-life' as an operational measure for examinations of stability. If halving a disturbance requires ten years for example the system is economically unstable, if it requires 10 months it might be called stable. This of course concerns only a one-shot impulse. However, every non-anticipated change in the exogenous variables generates a new impulse with resultant fluctuations so that at every point of time a system of overlapping — strengthening or compensating — fluctuations results. So far the system is in the average away from the equilibrium and the usual concept of stability would appear to be devoid of meaning.

The second question is concerned with the stability of the adjustment process. The *Hicks-Samuelson* trade cycle model explains the type of the adjustment process through the lag structure of the variables of the system, which generates as solution a difference (differential) equation

[20] A. *Leijonhufvud*, Schools, "revolutions" and research programmes in economic theory, in S. J. *Latsis* ed., "Methods and Appraisal" in Economics, Cambridge Univ. Press, London (1976) p. 65 - 99.

[21] G. *Tintner*, B. *Böhm*, R. *Rieder*, Is the Austrian Economy Stable?, unpubl. Manuscript, University of Technology (1976) Vienna.

of second order. In accordance with the values of the parameters this equation yields a monotonous adjustment process or cyclical fluctuations, which can be dampened or explosive. If a monotonous adjustment process or dampened fluctuations exist the system is stable. The current monetaristic literature hardly shows experiments with lag-structures. The simplest strict monetarist model which has a lag-structure was formulated by D. *Laidler* (op. cit., 1976). It is formed by 3 equations: a money market equation, an 'expectations augmented' *Phillips* curve and an adaptive inflations-expectation process of the type discussed. The solution of the model yields a differential equation of second order for excess demand. The message of the model is that a change in the rate of monetary expansion or in the anticipated 'full employment' rate of growth of the real GNP will generate cyclical fluctuations. When a simple monetarist model generates cyclical fluctuations by a change in its exogenous variables, it is difficult to understand why stabilisation policy should not be possible and desirable. However, Th. *Mayer's* conclusions, "In any case, if the private sector is inherently stable no countercyclical policy may be needed or be desirable" (*Mayer*, op. cit. p. 306), belong more to the monetarist "cosmology" than to the propositions which are relevant for the model.

The hypothesis of stability is a speciality of present-day monetarism. The older monetaristic school of K. *Wicksell*, G. *Myrdal*, F. *Hayek* and others was in this respect somewhat more cautious. Instead of the stability conjecture this school used the concept of the "cumulative" process. In *Wicksell's* model any discrepancy between the market rate of interest and the natural rate will set in motion a dynamic sequence of spending and inflation which will continue as long as the gap persists.

Wicksell's cumulative process can be "stable" in the sense that it contains a self-correcting mechanism, or it may be not self-limiting but of indefinite duration, in the pure credit system. (Th. M. *Humphrey*[22]) In the monetarist business cycle model of F. A. *Hayek*[23] the cumulative process is clearly unstable and, in contrast to *Wicksell*, inflationary changes and changes in the real sector of the economy develop. In the *Hayek* model, the increase in money supply by the banking system lowers the market rate of interest below the natural rate which would equilibrate real investment and voluntary savings. The creation of money

[22] Th. M. *Humphrey*, Interest Rates, Expectations, and the Wicksellian Policy Rule, Atlantic Economic Journal vol. IV (1976) p. 9 - 20.
[23] F. A. *Hayek*, Prices and Production, London (1932) Lecture III.

leads to a "first round effect": the additional money funds are spent for the purchase of investment goods. This induces an inflationary effect and a restructuring process in the economy. The relative price of investment goods (compared with consumer goods) rises and workers and "non specific" means of production will be removed from their current use to the investment goods sector. During this process, excess demand for labor arises. Rising money wages and the (relative) decrease in the production of consumer goods lead to an increase in the price of consumer-goods. A critical point exists in this expansion process, a point at which the market rate of interest will increase. If voluntary savings do not rise — as *Hayek* assumes — an additional creation of money, i. e. an acceleration of the supply of money would become necessary.[24]

In *Hayek's* model the cumulative process ends in a "crisis", but the upper turning point remains, however, somewhat in darkness.

The private sector in *Hayek's* model is inherently unstable, since a deviation from the equilibrium of the system leads away from equilibrium. The cumulative process is maintained by continuously creating money, the rate of which must accelerate. In contrast to the present-day monetarists, the leading monetarists of the 1920's and 1930's considered the monetary system as immanently unstable, whereby disturbances of the system (= deviation of the market rate from the real rate of interest) induce a cumulative process. If the *Hayek* model would be augmented by a modern expectation-adjustment process, the result could offer a fruitful alternative to present-day monetaristic literature.

---

[24] It is interesting to note that *Hayek* used the accelerations theorem: "All this must mean a return to shorter or less roundabout methods of production if the increase in the demand for consumers' goods is not compensated by a further proportional injection of money by new bank loans granted to producers ... And as long as the banks are going on progressively increasing their loans it will, therefore, be possible to continue the prolonged methods of production or perhaps even to extend them still further" (F. A. *Hayek*, op. cit. p. 80).

Comment on Mayer on Monetarism*

By Harry G. Johnson

Prolonged and serious academic discussion of such concepts as "monetarism" is a potentially dangerous endeavour, for two reasons. The first is that, while *Mayer*[1] gives the credit for popularization of the term to a 1968 article by *Brunner* and a 1970 article by *Fand*, there is some reason to think that the popular use of the term owes more to the desire of newspaper columnists and other fringe personnel to encapsulate scientific controversy into sloganized "schools"; and second, at the very least the encapsulation of the processes of scholarly scientific research and discovery in an "adversary procedure" or "democratic election" paradigm is misleadingly oversimplified. Derived in the context of American economic policy, the rapid popularization of the term "monetarism" reflected the policy problems and the debates over monetary versus fiscal policy that ensued on the political success of the "new economics" of Walter *Heller* and the subsequent "new, new economics" of the first *Nixon* Administration. And consequently, the concept of monetarism is saddled with the dead weight of the historical luggage and political passions of that period. This danger is particularly evident in policy discussions and debates in countries other than the United States — and particularly in the United Kingdom, where such contemporarily illiterate monetary policy amateurs as Nicholas *Kaldor* and J. R. *Hicks* use the term "monetarism" to describe any and all views at variance with their own view of British policy problems. (In Britain, in fact, the majority view bases itself on the axiom "monetarism" = Milton *Friedman* = "The Treasury View" = utter nonsense; in the same circles, incidentally, the corollary is "Keynesianism" = incomes policy.)

Such risks of intellectual stereotyping and historical fossilization unfortunately must be courted if some sense and intelligibility is to be

---

* This "Comment" was written at the London School of Economics, International Monetary Research Programme, sponsored by the Social Science Research Council.

[1] Vol. 8 (1975) pp. 191 and pp. 293.

made of issues that really divide active researchers and writers in the field; and on that understanding Thomas *Mayer* has successfully carried out a careful effort to list the main "monetarist" propositions and determine which are "essential" to the monetarist position and which are "optional" but convenient to or aesthetically harmonious with it.

The key proposition, from the point of view of differentiating monetarism from its contemporary alternative, is the first one. It is also the subtlest. Unfortunately, it is the one that *Mayer* states initially in an ambiguous form, and in the discussion of which he concentrates very narrowly on the post-war II, or "contemporary" literature (excluding the very early post-war literature such as that on liquidity preference versus loanable funds that merely carried on the 1930s debates). The ambiguity referred to lies in the use in the initial list of the undefined term "monetary factors", or "the impact of monetary factors", which could mean either factors leading to change in the demand for money, or factors leading to change in the supply, as the main causes of changes in nominal income. It turns out, however, that *Mayer* means "monetary factors" in the specific sense of (changes in) the supply of money, on the assumption of a stable demand for money; and it is this specification that differentiates monetarism from both the broader stream of the quantity theory of money tradition — in which *Keynes* and the Keynesians also belong — and the older pre-war II generation of quantity theorists, and also requires supplementation of the first proposition by the rest of the first four, six, eight, or whole dozen propositions listed. In a subtle sense, it is the proposition that there is a stable demand for money that differentiates monetarism from the classical quantity theory of money tradition, and "monetarism" from its Keynesian rival. (Both views are differentiable from a third view, or more accurately a mixture of two inconsistent views: that money is in perfectly elastic supply from the private economic system in response to demand for it so that the demand does not matter, and is not worth analysing; and that the monetary authority makes the money supply elastic in response to demand in order to control interest rates, and relies on credit control of some kind to control the economy at these interest rates, with the same implication of the irrelevance of monetary theory.)

In elaboration of this point, it is convenient to digress into a brief and impressionistic account of the development of monetary theory and its purpose in economic analysis. The classical quantity theory, in its equation of exchange formulation, had the useful and necessary purpose of separating the theory of real equilibrium (relative prices and quantities) as determined by factor quantities, technology, and preferences, from the determination of money wages and prices — establishing what came to be known as "the classical dichotomy" or "the neutrality of money" or "the homogeneity postulate". This permitted concentration on "real" analysis, itself difficult when the main problem was to establish the systematic interrelationship of the separate parts of the aggregate of economic activity, while leaving vague the question of the mechanism by which the position of monetary neutrality was established, and the time it would take to establish it (the classical non-calendar-time "long run").

As is well known, two alternative mechanisms were developed in the course of time, the "desired cash balance" mechanism of *Walras* and the Cambridge school and the income-expenditure mechanism of *Wicksell* and *Keynes,* and these alternatives remain a central point of difference between the "monetarist" and the "Keynesian" schools of thought at the present time. Note that both, when properly formulated, involve a full simultaneous equilibrium of stock and flow markets, though this point is masked by the common practice of disregarding or minimizing the processes of accumulation of real and monetary assets in economic growth in order to make the analysis more easily applicable to the calendar-time perspective of business cycle and policy stabilization problems. But the income-expenditure approach concentrates on the effects of stock disequilibrium in setting relative prices (particularly the level of the interest rate) that produce disequilibrium between income and expenditure flows and hence change the magnitude of flows, whereas the desired-cash-balance approach concentrates directly on disequilibrium between desired and actual stocks with changes in flows ensuing incidentally.

Initially, the adumbration of a mechanism to resolve monetary disequilibrium was primarily a question of logical completeness and consistency in a theory designed to show that money was a "veil" over the real economy, and that the presence of money and the existence of a monetary economy made no essential difference to the operations of a barter economy. This formulation corresponded with the classical and neo-classical interest in the long run, and specification of the very longest possible run in terms of "the classical stationary state". With the development of economics as a professional and "practical" (as distinct from philosophical) subject of study, however, and also with the emerging recognition of the trade or business cycle as a characteristic phenomenon of the capitalist system, the focus of monetary-theoretic interest shifted gradually from the long-run demonstration of monetary neutrality to the shorter run problem of "the conditions for monetary equilibrium" — the most important landmarks being the work of *Wicksell, Robertson, Keynes* and *Hayek,* and *Wicksell's* followers in the Stockholm School.

As one heuristic formulation, monetary equilibrium over (successive periods of) time requires equality of the real saving people wish to do out of current income with the real investment they wish to undertake, and equality of changes in the quantity of money demand with changes in the quantity of money supplied by the monetary authority. (This formulation ignores certain obvious difficulties associated with the need for growth of the money supply at a constant price level in a growing economy, and changes in the desire for financial intermediation between saving in the form of monetary assets and investments in terms of real capital equipment). A statement of this problem in this way involves converting the concept of neutrality from a long-run equilibrium tendency of a monetary economy confronted by parametric changes in the nominal money supply (or in real balance demands), to a short-run dynamic policy objective, and in so doing creates the setting in which "monetarism" and "Keynesianism" appear as rival approaches. Note, incidentally, that the necessity for this change of perspective explains why *Mayer,* quite correctly, regards *Patinkin* as not belonging to the monetarist school: *Patinkin's* work has been confined largely to the first phase of interest in the evolution of the quantity theory, which concerned itself with long-run monetary neutrality, and specifically with the construction of an integrated theory of relative and absolute prices in a monetary economy, and has not been concerned with the pursuit of short-run stability as a policy objective.

As the argument has been outlined so far, the dynamic neutrality of money can be described by changes in any one of the four basic constituents of, or factors influencing the dynamic development of, the system: the desire to save (or consume), the desire to invest, the demand for money (the active component of which is "hoarding" or "liquidity preference proper" or "the assets demand" as it has been successively described chronologically), and the supply of money. Conventionally, monetary economists have tended to simplify the problem by treating consumption as passive, and this convention is adopted for simplicity here, though with the necessary warning that to do so consistently would close out some important issues involved in *Mayer's* listed propositions, especially, 3, 4, 12 and possibly 5.

With that simplification — or alternatively, by lumping changes in consumption and investment expenditure together under the general description of "real" disturbances — we can quickly arrive at a classification of approaches to monetary disturbances according to the "normal" or most common type of disturbance: disturbances involving changes in private money-holding behaviour; disturbances involving changes in official (or governmental) money supply behaviour; and disturbances involving changes in private real spending behaviour.

While *Wicksell's* analysis of the "cumulative process" in terms of a divergence of the "money" from the "natural" rate of interest could be interpreted as a case of the second type of disturbance, as could *Keynes's* occasionally expressed view that the monetary authorities were not in fact willing to use monetary policy to the extent required to offset private sector disturbance, and as would certain aspects of *Hayek's* discussion of the business cycle, it is a fair generalisation that none of the leading pre-war II monetary theorists regarded policy-introduced changes in the money supply as a (or "the") major source of monetary disturbance. Instead, either real or monetary private sector disturbances or both, on the demand side, constituted the prime source of instability — *Robertson* indeed went so far as to maintain that a competent central bank should be able to distinguish between changes in hoarding demand for money and changes in the demand for money associated with changes in expenditure.

Partly at least, because monetary theory at that time contained no adequate theory of demand for a stock and of demand influenced heavily by expectations about the future, the possibility of changes in hoarding demand was expressed, not as contemporary theory would tend to express it, in terms of a *stable* function of the values of *expected* independent variables in the function, but in terms of *instability* of the demand for money or instability of velocity, an instability which had to be offset by discretionary monetary management or, for some writers, a monetary rule of conducting monetary policy to achieve price stability. This characterisation, in turn, lent itself easily to ridicule at the hands of *Keynes* and the Keynesians, once *Keynes* had used the multiplier relationship and the propensity to consume to tie changes in aggregate expenditure to changes in investment, themselves partially (but not completely) controllable by the influence of monetary policy on the interest rate.

The modern quantity theory, and the monetarist school based on it, makes several fundamental departures from the neo-classical quantity theory, partly as a broadly political response to Keynesianism and partly as a reflection of improved basic theory largely attributable to the impact of The General Theory itself. (There is, however, one basic difference between the new quantity theory approach and the Keynesian approach, which consists in the explicit incorporation in the demand for money function of the expected rate of change of the price level as a determinant of the relative yield on money, which in turn provides the foundation for the distinctions relevant to monetary policy between real and nominal interest rates and between changes in real and in nominal cash balances.) The most direct departure, whose major constituent is the assumption of a stable demand for money, is the assumption that disturbances originate primarily not in the instability of the private sector's behaviour, either in spending or in cash-demanding behaviour, but in the instability of the behaviour of the monetary authorities. This is associated directly or indirectly with most of the other propositions, specifically 2 - 6, which broadly amount to maintaining that the private sector will look after itself if let alone and does not require detailed specification, analysis or control in the process of monetary analysis and policy stabilization; 7 - 9, which aim at making monetary policy as little amenable to discretionary action and semantic obfuscation as possible, and 12, which is a natural corollary of the assumption that governmental action is the prime cause of monetary disturbance. Note, incidentally, that concentration on the demand for money as the key relationship, and nominal income as the determinate that follows from the determinant of the quantity of money through that relationship, releases the quantity theory from the great incubus imposed on it by Keynesian criticism, that it "assumed" full employment and consequently was irretrievably inconsistent with the observed fact of mass unemployment.

The foregoing paragraph omits reference to items 10 and 11 on *Mayer's* list. As regards the *Phillips* curve trade-off, I would regard this piece of apparatus as a long-post-*Keynes,* and only peripherally Keynesian, piece of apparatus relevant to a particular stage in the breakdown of the Keynesian assumption of rigid or exogenously determined wages, and hence not crucial to the Keynesian-monetarism debate. Further, the expectations-augmented *Phillips* curve (with a trade-off in the short but not the long run following a monetary disturbance) has become an integral tool of frontier theorizing on monetarist lines. As regards inflation, *Mayer's* statement is somewhat imprecise, but I would myself say that monetarists are less concerned about both inflation and unemployment than other economists, partly because they regard both as logical consequence of monetary disequilibrium rather than of inexplicable malfunctionings of the private sector, and partly because they are more apt to subject the alleged social costs to economic analysis.

These two propositions being left aside, as either having a more specific context and reference content than their statement implies or as embodying a general judgment based on *Mayer's* extensive reading of the literature, one must accept *Mayer's* general thesis that the listed propositions do constitute an intercorrelated set, sufficiently so to form a coherent approach to a view of monetary policy, but that it is possible to accept or reject some of them while remaining broadly a monetarist, or a non-monetarist, as the case may be. It remains to add only that (as Mayer himself observes) some combinations of selections from the bill of fare would make a pretty indigestible intellectual meal, whereas there are some eccentric tastes (e. g., the love of large models, or distrust of government) that demand "ketchup with everything".

Mayer on Monetarism: Comments from a British Point of View

By David Laidler

I.

As *Mayer's* paper* has so lucidly shown, the boundaries between "monetarism" and other schools of thought are hazy indeed. Monetarist propositions, though inter-related, are not always logically interdependent. This surely reflects the fact that monetarism is not some rigid orthodoxy but rather an ongoing, expanding, and above all pragmatic body of doctrine. This being so, what is called " monetarism", and what appear to be its characteristics are bound to differ from context to context. *Mayer's* paper — and this is no criticism of it — has dealt with monetarism as it is understood in the United States.

Two aspects of monetarism have been of more importance in British debates about macroeconomic policy than they have in the United States. The question of unemployment versus inflation as competing goals of economic policy has been central to these debates as have questions about the conduct of policy in an open economy. These differences in emphasis stem from two sources. First, it is a fact of British political life that far more emphasis is given to the continuous maintenance of high employment as an aim of economic policy than in the United States. Second, Britain is a small, or at best medium sized, economy deeply involved in foreign trade. Any body of economic doctrine must be adapted to accommodate these facts if it is to be applied succesfully to the British economy. *Mayer* discusses the first of these two matters only briefly and the second not at all. I have little to quarrel with in the substance of his paper, and believe therefore that the most useful contribution that I can make to the discussion and debate that it is bound to provoke is to supplement *Mayer's* commentary on monetarism by dealing with these two questions in some detail. I will take up these two

---

* Kredit und Kapital, Vol. 8 (1975), pp. 191 - 215 and 293 - 313.

problem areas in turn, dealing first with the choice between inflation and unemployment as policy goals.

II.

Mayer argues that monetarists show "a relatively greater concern about inflation than about unemployment compared to other economists" but that differences here hinge largely on ethical judgements and are peripheral to the main thrust of the Monetarist-Keynesian debate. Though he may be right in the context of American debates, British monetarists have always shown as much concern for the maintenance of high employment as have their "Keynesian" opponents; at the same time British Keynesians have on the whole been proponents of the maintenance of a fixed exchange rate, and for that reason if no other have not been vulnerable to the charge of underrating the seriousness of inflation as an economic and social problem.[1] Even so differences of opinion about appropriate policies towards inflation and unemployment are extremely sharp in Britain. They reflect fundamental differences over economic theory and facts, however, not over social values. The British monetarist regards inflation as a macroeconomic problem to be dealt with by macroeconomic means and argues that, given appropriate macroeconomic policies, unemployment becomes a problem for microeconomic analysis and policy. The British Keynesian take a diametrically opposite view.

The basic of the monetarist's case is straightforward enough. It follows mainly from his belief in the quantity theory of money and in a real *Phillips* curve, as well as in the inherent stability of the private sector, again given that the appropriate monetary policy is pursued.[2] The real *Phillips* curve doctrine is equivalent to the proposition that

---

[1] Cf. for example, the *Radcliffe* report, where the whole thrust of the discussion of policy towards inflation is premised on the desirability of maintaining a fixed exchange rate.

[2] This qualification is important: one can believe that the private sector is stable given that a money supply rule is pursued but expect it to be extremely unstable if monetary policy is geared to pegging the level of nominal interest rates. Given the focus on the level of nominal interest rates as the centrepiece of monetary policy in Britain, there has been a good deal of cross purposes in the monetarist debate in that country. Monetarists when they talked of a "given monetary policy" meant holding the money supply on a given time path while Keynesians, meant maintaining a given level of nominal interest rates. On these matters cf. *Laidler* 1973.

there exists at any moment a "natural rate of unemployment" in an economy. This view in turn implies that any attempt to hold the actual unemployment rate below that natural level will involve ever accelerating inflation. At the same time the existence of a stable aggregate demand for money function implies that ever accelerating inflation will be impossible without ever accelerating monetary expansion. Thus these two hypotheses immediately force the monetarist to conclude that the pursuit of a stable inflation rate must involve the abandonment of any attempt to influence the economy's equilibrium unemployment rate by macro policies. Furthermore his belief in the stability of the private sector leads him to conclude that, given the pursuit of a stable inflation rate — which must involve a steadily growing money supply — the economy will in fact converge upon its natural unemployment rate. His view of the stability of the private sector is quite compatible with the Keynesian hypothesis about the relative instability of the marginal efficiency of investment — here perhaps I disagree with *Mayer*[3] — for what is required for stability in the private sector when the money supply is following a steady growth path is that the demand for money function be sufficiently stable and sufficiently interest inelastic for fluctuations in the marginal efficiency of investment to result in interest rate fluctuations rather than in disturbances to output and employment, not that the marginal efficiency of investment schedule remain stable.[4]

Now of course there is nothing here to imply that the natural unemployment rate will always rule. The foregoing argument does not make a complete case for letting the unemployment rate look after itself as far as macroeconomic policy is concerned. Vital to making a complete case is one of those characteristics of monetarism which are pervasive and yet not logically interrelated with others: namely scepticism about how much is known in quantitative terms about the actual economy. The monetarist cannot deny the logical coherence of a policy scheme that would have the natural unemployment rate actively pursued as a target by the use of discretionary monetary and fiscal measures — but in the absence of any reliable evidence as to its value he is pessimistic about the practicality of such a policy.[5] Given his views of the costs in terms

---

[3] Cf. *Mayer*, pp. 204.

[4] Cf. fn. 2 above.

[5] Moreover, there is no reason to suppose that the natural unemployment rate will remain constant over time — it can be influenced by demographic and institutional changes in a manner that, in the present state of knowledge, is ill understood, and hence virtually impossible to predict.

of accelerating inflation that would be involved in underassessing the value of the natural unemployment rate and then pursuing that target he prefers macro, particularly monetary, policy to be geared to achieving a stable inflation rate.[6]

This does not mean that the monetarist must be content to let the unemployment rate look after itself however, for if he believes that the economy will converge on, and fluctuate about, its natural unemployment rate, when steady monetary expansion is maintained there is no reason why he should regard such a natural rate as socially desirable.

In a British context, monetarism is strongly associated with a concern for the design of policies that will lower the natural unemployment rate — that will shift the *Phillips* curve to the left.[7] Such policies of course are aimed at influencing the structure of labour markets and involve measures designed to enhance both the occupational and geographical mobility of labour. In the British context, such policies might well involve the removal of particular government interventions that are thought of as reducing labour mobility — the withdrawal of rent control and public housing subsidies for example — but they might also involve the expansion of government sponsored retraining schemes or indeed of subsidies to employment in depressed regions of the country. Thus British monetarism is far from being unconcerned with unemployment or ideologically committed to a completely free market solution to the problem. Rather, the feature that distinguishes it from Keynesian orthodoxy is that it regards unemployment policy as being fundamentally a matter of microeconomics.

The whole thrust of Keynesian orthodoxy is to make the unemployment rate the central target for aggregate demand policies.[8] It is not

---

[6] In the British context it is important to look at the interconnectedness of monetary and fiscal policy that arises from the government budget constraint. The central government's borrowing requirement is an important source of monetary expansion. The relative independence of monetary and fiscal policy that is so often taken for granted in United States discussions of aggregate demand management is much less a feature of the British economy.

[7] Thus there is nothing inherently monetarist about this aspect of British monetarism. Such concern has been common to all schools of thought. For a discussion of the unemployment problem by one who is usually regarded as a monetarist see *Brittan* (1975).

[8] For an example, see the evidence of the Treasury representatives as reprinted in House of Commons (1974); for an earlier example see the *Radcliffe* report.

always clear whether Keynesians view variations in aggregate demand brought about to influence the unemployment rate as having a systematic influence on the inflation rate or whether they take the view that the time path of wages and prices is determined by sociological factors that operate exogenously on the economic system.[9] Nevertheless they do seem to be united in the view that appropriate policies towards inflation involve direct controls on both wages and prices. In short, the Keynesian's relatively greater concern with the behaviour of individual prices noted by *Mayer* leads him, particularly in a British context, to advocate an essentially microeconomic approach to the control of the price level.

Thus, when discussing macroeconomic policies, the British monetarist emphasises the inflation rate as a policy target and the Keynesian the unemployment rate, not because of any difference in ethical judgement, but because of a straightforward scientific difference about which variable macro policy is best adapted to influencing.

III.

I have already noted that Britain is a relatively small open economy, and any analysis of its policy problems must take note of that. I believe that it is possible to distinguish what we might term *a monetarist view of inflation as an international phenomenon, a monetarist view of the transmission of inflation between countries* as well as *a monetarist view of the central problems of international monetary reform.* None of these views originated in Britain, nor has their recent development been solely the work of British economists. Nevertheless they are particularly relevant to any open economy and hence are important in a British context. *Mayer,* writing in the context of the relatively closed U. S. economy does not deal with these issues, and it will be useful to devote the last few pages of this essay to their discussion.

As *Mayer* has rightly noted, monetarism concentrates on explaining the behaviour of the general price level — which is after all but the inverse of the price of money — and tends to downplay the significance of the behaviour of particular prices; this is part and parcel of the belief

---

[9] *Harrod* (1972) and *Wiles* (1973) are two particularly extreme examples of the view that the causes of inflation are sociological. Reading the evidence of Lord *Kahn* and Mr. *Posner* to the House of Commons expenditure committee, or indeed of the Treasury representatives would suggest that they accord some, albeit marginal, influence on the inflation rate to aggregate demand variations. Cf. House of Commons (1974).

that allocative detail is at best of secondary importance while studying the macro economy. But if one is to study aggregate phenomena, he must form a view of what is the relevant aggregate for study. The existence of inflation and unemployment as national political problems certainly means that data aggregated to the level of the national economy have to be understood and explained, but it does not follow from this that the boundaries of the nation state also constitute the boundaries of "the economy as a whole" to which macro theory is most usefully applied. This problem exists, or ought to exist, for the Keynesian as well as for the monetarist, but the latter, with his emphasis on the quantity of money as a key macroeconomic variable naturally draws the boundaries of his macro economy around the area served by a common currency.

Adherence to the quantity theory of money would necessarily imply that, in a world of rigidly fixed exchange rates between freely convertible currencies, the relevant variable to explain in terms of the quantity theory would be a price index computed for the world economy. Though the Bretton Woods system did not provide either for completely fixed exchange rates or completely free convertibility, British monetarists have nevertheless taken the view that the international monetary system as it existed up to the end of 1971 was a sufficiently close approximation to the theoretical ideal type to make it appropriate to analyse the inflationary process of the level of the world economy. They have then gone on to treat questions about inflation in any one country as having to do with the mechanisms whereby inflationary impulses are transmitted into particular "regions" of the world economy rather than as being matters to be dealt with by theories of the generation of inflation.[10]

This approach to the problem of inflation in the world economy is markedly different from that taken by Keynesians. They do not ignore the international aspects of inflation, but do not seem to regard the concept of a "world price level" as a useful one. In their discussions of inflation as a world-wide phenomenon they concern themselves instead

---

[10] The seminal work on the monetary theory of the balance of payments is, of course, by *Johnson* (1973) — but written and widely circulated much earlier — and *Mundell* (1971). The most coherent account of these matters as they influence the Monetarist debate is given by Harry G. *Johnson* (1972). See also *Laidler* and *Nobay* (1975). A good deal of empirical work testing the stability of a "world" demand for money function and a "world" real *Phillips* curve has been carried out by my former colleagues at Manchester. Cf. *Gray* et al. (1975), *Duck* et al. (1975).

with the behaviour of the prices of particular commodities for which world-wide markets exist: oil and other raw materials, agricultural products and so on. They focus on these individual markets as sources of inflationary pressures that are common to all open economies.[11] The contrast between the monetarist and Keynesian approach to inflation at the level of the world economy thus reflects a distinction already referred to above, and noted by *Mayer*. The monetarist is mainly concerned with the behaviour of an aggregate price index and the Keynesian puts more emphasis on analysing the behaviour of the prices of individual goods.

But the monetarist cannot stop his analysis at the level of the world economy; national inflation rates are of vital importance, and he must therefore have a view about the way in which price behaviour in the world economy impinges on the individual country. A key element here is a theory of the international distribution of the world money supply.[12] The monetarist emphasises the influence of inflows and outflows of foreign exchange reserves on domestic money supply behaviour. He attaches less importance than does the Keynesian to the individual central bank's capacity to sterilise such influence by way of offsetting open market operations. While not denying the logical possibility of successful sterilisation in the short run, the monetarist takes the view that the effects of such operations on international interest rate differentials will be sufficiently important to ensure that capital movements accentuate the initial balance of payments disequilibrium and quickly undermine any sterilisation operations.

It would be wrong to attribute to the monetarist the view that inflationary impulses are transmitted to particular countries solely or even mainly through the operation of flows of reserves on domestic money supplies. If it makes sense to talk of a world price level, it must also

---

[11] This certainly seems to be the view of Sir John *Hicks*. Cf. *Hicks* (1974), (1975) it is worth noting in passing here that in the latter paper *Hicks* agrees that the core of the difference between Keynesians and Monetarists (implicitly in a British context) lies in their views on the manner in which the labour market works and in particular in their views on the *Phillips* curve. Unfortunately he then attributes to monetarists a belief in a nominal rather than in a real *Phillips* curve so that his subsequent criticism of his opponents becomes completely misplaced.

[12] Not to mention a theory of the generation of the world money supply'. Monetarists have been slow indeed to provide a properly worked out analysis of this aspect of their position. However such work is now forthcoming cf. *Swoboda* (1975) and *Parkin* et al. (1975).

make sense to talk of a world market for goods and services — or at least in so-called tradable goods and services. The domestic prices of such tradables must then be viewed as being determined in world markets; fluctuations in the world inflation rate thus impinge directly upon the domestic inflation rate by what may be termed a direct "price transfer mechanism". Flows of foreign exchange reserves ensure that domestic money supplies accommodate to variations in domestic prices thus induced, rather than in any sense causing them.[13]

There are several variations on the broad outlines of the mechanisms just sketched. Some monetarists view the price transfer mechanism as simply reflecting the proposition that the law of one price holds true across national boundaries for any good which can be arbitraged; others focus on the way in which inflationary expectations enter the expectations augmented (or real) *Phillips* curve, and argue that the time path of prices in the world economy exerts an important influence on price setting behaviour in domestic markets.[14] Though there is no uniformity here, monetarist analysis is nevertheless rather sharply distinguished from the Keynesian approach to the international transmission of inflation. This either focusses upon rising import prices particularly of food and raw materials as a "cost push" factor influencing domestic inflation as already noted above, or upon somewhat ill specified demonstration effects transmitting labour force "militancy" across national boundaries.

The foregoing discussion was premised upon the existence of a system of fixed exchange rates, and such a system broke down in 1971. There

---

[13] If this view of the international transmission of price level fluctuations is correct, then the possibility of sterilising reserve flows, though it might give an individual country power over its money supply, will not give it complete power over its price level. The sterilisation of reserve inflows in the face of a world-wide inflation can influence the domestic level of income and employment and the domestic prices of non-tradables, but nothing else. Perhaps this factor accounts for the failure of Germany to keep out world-wide inflation without resort to revaluation in the early 1970's.

[14] The first of these views is also the earlier, underlying such papers as *Dornbusch* (1973) and *Mussa* (1974). *Cross* and *Laidler* (1975) found that such a view did not perform well empirically and were able to show that the expectations based approach to the international transmission of inflation, though not without problems, was strongly to be preferred on empirical grounds. Note that subsequent work reported in *Laidler* (forthcoming) showed that the expectations approach performed better than a "cost push through import price inflation" hypothesis of the international transmission of inflation.

is now a rapidly growing monetarist literature on flexible exchange rates, based, as would be expected from the above analysis, upon the quantity theory of money determining national price levels, and some variant or other of the purchasing power parity doctrine determining exchange rates. This literature is still in a tentative state. Moreover there is no unified monetarist position on the relative merits of fixed and flexible rates.[15] However, there does seem to be a distinctively monetarist view of the nature of current international monetary problems and the steps that must be taken in solving them, as I shall now argue.

A combination of the quantity theory of money and the monetarist view of the international transmission of inflation discussed above imply that, in the long run, a country can only control its own inflation rate if it can control its own money supply and hence only if it operates a flexible exchange rate. Pessimism about the possibilities of sterilising reserve flows suggest that, at least for relatively small countries, this "long run" represents a fairly short time horizon. Taken alone, this argument would push monetarists in the direction of favouring flexible rates, but other aspects of monetarism are important here. The view that money is a social device for economising on the use of resources in generating information underlies much monetarist analysis, particularly that which stems from the work of *Brunner* and *Meltzer*.[16] Thus the monetarist is acutely aware that exchange rate volatility is a source of inefficiency in the international economy.

If a flexible exchange rate scheme was associated with such volatility, and the opponents of such a regime frequently argue that it is, then the monetarist would find it hard to defend flexible rates. However his analysis tells him that flexible exchange rates will be volatile only if domestic monetary policies are volatile and divergent as between countries. He sees no reason for exchange rates to be volatile if all countries follow monetary rules. According to his view of the matter there would be an array of national rules which would ensure that flexible rates would in fact be essentially constant over time. In short, the very factor — the adoption of rules for domestic monetary expansion rates — that would ensure the stability of flexible rates would also make a regime of fixed rates feasible.

---

[15] The papers given at the 1975 Saltsjöbaden conference, to be published in the 1976 Scandinavian Economic Journal are an excellent source of recent Monetarist — and Keynesian — analysis of flexible exchange rates.

[16] See in particular *Brunner* and *Meltzer* (1971).

Given this argument, some monetarists go on to urge that fixed rates be adopted, and a world-wide rate of monetary expansion fixed by some supranational body, because of the greater efficiency that this would introduce into the international economy; they look to fluctuations in official holdings of reserves to absorb the consequences of short term variations in individual countries' output and inflation rates about their long term trends. Others prefer that it be left to market forces to allocate such effects between fluctuations in private speculators' reserve holdings and variations in exchange rates around their long run equilibrium values. Yet others note that a degree of exchange rate flexibility confers an extra policy tool on the authorities and hence regard a so-called "dirty float" as a desirable regime.[17]

Thus there is disagreement among monetarists about the most appropriate exchange rate regime, but this is secondary to the proposition upon which monetarists agree: namely that the key to achieving exchange rate stability lies not in the manner in which the foreign exchange market is organised but in finding a way of co-ordinating monetary policy between countries. The contrast between this view and the prevailing Keynesian orthodoxy which still accords central importance to the foreign exchange rate regime itself, and pays little if any attention to the problems, both economic and political, inherent in harmonising domestic monetary policies, is a strong one.[18]

IV.

These comments need no long concluding summary. I have tried to elaborate on and extend *Mayer's* discussion in a constructive fashion. It will be apparent that the key features of "monetarism" seen from a

---

[17] The monetarist case for fixed exchange rates is forcibly argued by *Parkin* (1973). *Friedman's* classic paper (1953) is still an excellent source on the case for flexible rates. *Boyer* (1975) who perhaps would not wish to be characterised as a monetarist, prefers to view fixed and flexible rates as extreme cases of a spectrum of regimes and argues, on the basis of an essentially monetarist model, that the optimal exchange rate regime will frequently lie between these two extremes.

[18] For example the 1974 Economic Report of the President devoted a great deal of attention to the international monetary system and the matter of alternative exchange rate schemes without ever mentioning the role of incompatible monetary policies in various countries as a source of exchange rate instability. For a lucid account of the issues involved in the debate about the problems of the international monetary system, see *Zis* (1975 a, 1975 b).

British point of view differ somewhat — albeit more in matters of emphasis than substance — from the American version of the doctrine. However, as with the propositions analysed by *Mayer*, the matters highlighted in this comment overwhelmingly concern questions of fact and logic. Hence they can be settled, in principle at least, by reference to economic analysis and empirical evidence. To the extent that the classification of particular propositions as "monetarist" and "anti-monetarist" hinders their scientific assessment, such classification process is to be deplored. There is, as *Mayer* says a good case to be made for abolishing the use of the term "monetarism", but I share his pessimism on the likelihood of this being possible.

References

Boyer, R.: Optimal Dirty Floating, University of Western Ontario, mimeo 1975. — *Brittan,* S.: Second Thoughts on Full Employment Policy, Centre for Policy Studies, London, 1975. — *Brunner,* K. and *Meltzer,* A. H.: The Uses of Money, Money in the Theory of an Exchange Economy AER 61, 5 (1971), pp. 784 - 805. — Committee on the Working of the Monetary System; Report (The Radcliffe Report) London, HMSO, 1959. — *Cross,* R. B. and *Laidler,* D. E. W.: Inflation, Excess Demand, and Expectations in Fixed Exchange Rate Open Economies: Some Preliminary Evidence in *Parkin,* J. M. and *Zis,* G. (eds.) Inflation in the World Economy, Manchester, Manchester University Press, 1975. — *Dornbusch,* R.: Currency Depreciation, Hoarding, and Relative Prices JPE 81 (1973), pp. 843 - 915. — *Duck,* N. W., *Parkin,* J. M., *Rose,* D. E. and *Zis,* G.: The Determination of Rate of Change of Wages and Prices in the Fixed Exchange Rate World Economy: 1956 - 1970 in *Parkin* and *Zis* (eds.) op cit. — *Friedman,* M.: The Case for Flexible Exchange Rates in Essays in Positive Economics, Chicago, University of Chicago Press, 1953. — *Gray,* M. R., *Ward,* R. and *Zis,* G.: World Demand for Money in *Parkin* and *Zis* (eds.) op cit. — *Harrod,* R. F.: The Issues: Five Views in *Hinshaw,* R. (ed.) Inflation as a Global Problem, London, John Hopkins Press, 1972. — *Hicks,* J. R.: The Crisis in Keynesian Economics, Oxford, Blackwell, 1974. — *Hicks,* J. R.: What is Wrong with Monetarism, Lloyds Bank Review, October 1975, pp. 1 - 13. — House of Commons, 9th Report From the Expenditure Committee, Public Expenditure, Inflation and the Balance of Payments, London, HMSO, 1974. — *Johnson,* H. G.: Inflation and the Monetarist Controversy, Amsterdam, North Holland, 1972. — *Johnson,* H. G.: The Monetary Approach to Balance on Payments Theory, in *Johnson,* H. G.: Further Essays in Monetary Economics, London, 1973. — *Laidler,* D. E. W.: Monetarist Policy Prescriptions and their Background, Manchester School 41, March 1973, pp. 59 - 71. — *Laidler,* D. E. W.: Alternative Explanations and Policies Towards Inflation: Tests on Data Drawn from Six Countries in *Brunner*, K. and *Meltzer*, A. H. (eds.) Proceedings of the Third Carnegie Mellon Rochester Conference on Economic Policy (forthcoming). — *Laidler*, D. E. W. and *Nobay*, A. R.: Some Current Issues Concerning the International Aspects of Inflation in *Laidler*, D., Essays on Money and Inflation, Manchester, Manchester University Press, 1975. — *Mundell*, R.: Monetary Theory: Inflation Interest and Growth in the World Economy, Pacific Palisades, California, 1971. — *Mussa*, M.: A Monetary Approach to Balance of Payments Analysis, Journal of Money, Credit and Banking 6, August 1974, pp. 333 - 352. — *Parkin*, J. M.: The World Monetary System in Transition, ANZAS Lecture, St. Lucia, University of Queensland Press, 1973. — *Parkin*, J. M., *Richards*, I. and *Zis*, G.: The Determination and Control of the World Money Supply nder Fixed Exchange Rates 1961 - 1971, Manchester School 43, September 1975. — *Swoboda*, A. K.: Gold, Dollars, Euro Dollars and the World Money Stock mimeo from the Institute of International Studies of the University of Geneva, 1975. — *Wiles*, P.: Cost Inflation and the State of Economic Theory, Economic Journal 83, June 1973, pp. 377 - 98. — *Zis*, G.: Inflation: An International Monetary Problem or National Social Phenomenon?, British Journal of International Studies 1 (2), 1975. — *Zis*, G.: Political Origins of the International Monetary Crisis, National Westminster Bank Quarterly Review, August 1975.

Monetarist, Keynesian and Quantity Theories

By Allan H. Meltzer*

In economics as in other developing sciences, change erodes the value of popular terminology. Monetarism is a name that has been given to a particular set of propositions at a particular point of time. Like Keynesianism, fiscalism, or the "Treasury view," the particular set of propositions called monetarism does not fully describe the body of thought accepted by a loosely knit group of practicing economists anymore than terms like Chicago, Cambridge or Austrian School describe the thought of all to whom the terms are applied. In the humanities, such connections are the subject of treatises; most economists are usefully employed at other, no less valuable, occupations.

Thomas *Mayer's* statement** of the set of propositions constituting "monetarism" and their interrelations takes the form of an inventory of a now successful counter — revolution in economic thought. *Mayer's* critics and commentators — Martin *Bronfenbrenner*, Karl *Brunner*, Phillip *Cagan*, Benjamin M. *Friedman*, Harry G. *Johnson* and David *Laidler* — appear to accept his inventory, although each would delete, de-emphasize, or combine some of the items; and some critics, correctly, add to the list propositions about exchange rates, balance of payments position, and determinants of the stock of money and the rate of inflation in open economies.

That the counter-revolution has been successful, there can be little doubt. Jerome *Stein* now writes that "a Keynesian can be a monetarist" (*Stein*, 1976), and James *Tobin* analyzes the conditions for the "crowding out" of private expenditure by debt finance (*Tobin* and *Buiter*, 1976, p. 296). Several central banks choose specific target rates of growth for

* This paper reflects many discussions with Karl *Brunner* and more recently with Edward *Prescott*. I am indebted to *Brunner* and *Prescott* and to André *Fourçans*, Benjamin *Friedman*, Robert *Hodrick*, David *Laidler* and particularly to Thomas *Mayer* for comments on an earlier draft. Wolf *Becker* Jr. drew the charts.

** Kredit und Kapital, Vol. 8 (1975) pp. 191 and pp. 293.

some monetary aggregate and, more importantly, they have shown greater ability to reach the targets than they once admitted or believed feasible.

It was not always so, and the history of science suggests that the particular set of propositions that *Mayer* has listed will not draw the same agreements and disagreements a year, or more surely, a decade from now. The meaning of "monetarism" will change if the term remains useful.

There is, also, general agreement between *Mayer* and the commentators on his paper that the remaining areas of disagreement are not analytical issues but are empirical issues related to policy. The point is, at times, implicit in *Mayer's* paper, at times explicit. *Brunner, Johnson* and *Laidler* support the point with examples of empirical differences about the effects of policies. Although Benjamin *Friedman* concentrates on analytic issues, he too notes that the "distinguishing content of monetarism is a set of empirical propositions" (*Friedman*, 1977, p. 347). *Cagan* and *Bronfenbrenner* discuss a particular policy arrangement — a fixed monetary rule — that has been closely associated with monetarism in the wirtings of mony non-monetarists and some monetarists. But *Bronfenbrenner* is emphatic also about the broader policy implications that constitute the monetarists' "vision."

To the extent that resolvable differences about policy remain, they result from two distinguishable types of empirical judgment. One is the value of parameters in particular equations; the second, and much more basic, empirical issue concerns the societal effects of government policies, including the relative costs and benefits of collective and private decision-making. The costs include any loss of freedom and increases in the nature and extent of uncertainty, loss of incentives and the like. *Mayer's* proposition 12, "dislike of government intervention" suggests that the differences about the appropriate roles for private and government decisions are solely a matter of taste. James *Tobin* (1976, p. 336) writes that "monetarist policy recommendations stem less from theoretical or even empirical findings than from distinctive value judgments."

I disagree with both statements. Both ignore the empirical and analytical bases of monetarist policy recommendations, and both take a very restricted view of the range of empirical issues in the Keynesian-monetarist debate. In some ideal world, differences between the

effects of government and private action may vanish, but many monetarists believe that, in practice, expansive fiscal policies "crowd out"
real capital, lower the long-run value of output per man, encourage
the growth of government and reduce freedom.

Discussions of counter-cyclical policy reflect more than differences
in values and differences in emperical judgments about the long-term
effects of Keynesian policies. Different conclusions are drawn about
short-term effects. Many of these issues are not fully resolved at this
time. Monetarists and Keynesians assign different meaning or interpretation to unemployment. Consequently, they differ about the costs
and benefits of reducing or removing the risk of unemployment by
government policy or collective action. The policies recommended by
monetarists and Keynesians reflect empirical judgments about the effects of policies and, also, differences about the operation of labor markets and the meaning and interpretation of the fluctuations in employment. Differences about the interpretation of unemployment are
basic to the Keynesian-monetarist discussion, but the differences are
unresolved. Below I state the issues and their relation to the discussion.

Monetarist and Keynesian policy differences also reflect different
assessments of evidence and differences in beliefs. Beliefs affect the
judgments and decisions of scientists and policymakers, but evidence
changes beliefs. Some experiments are judged a success; others are
regarded as failures. The history of the first twenty-five postwar years,
when the economic policy of many countries was inspired largely by
Keynesian interpretations of events, constitutes a body of evidence. So,
too, is the history of the past several years when countries, faced with
the same real shock, adopted alternative strategies and achieved different outcomes.[1] Historical evidence of this kind may seem more tenuous
or insubstantial than the output of some large, quarterly econometric
model of the economy. It is, nevertheless, a main reason that beliefs
and policies change.[2]

---

[1] An assessment of some of these experiences can be found in Michael
Hamburger and Rutberg *Reisch* (1976) and David *Laidler* (1976).

[2] This interpretation is by no means unique. See, for example, *Coddington*
(1976, p. 1264) who describes the period of the fifties and early sixties as a
period of "Keynesian enthusiasm", then adds picturesquely that Keynesian
ideas "faltered sometime in the middle sixties and stumbled into the seventies". Historical evidence is most useful when there are claims and counter-
claims as in the monetarist-Keynesian discussions of the sixties.

Change does not mean that the positions or beliefs of some past era are restored intact. Monetarism does not now deny all short-run real effects of fiscal policy on relative prices and real demands, whatever incorrect or incautious statements may have been made earlier. But, monetarists questioned the reliability and durability of fiscal effects and the long-run costs of achieving short-run increases in output by fiscal expansion. These conclusions — once scorned as error — are now widely held.[3]

Monetarism is neither the quantity equation rediscovered nor the quantity theory reborn. Thomas *Mayer's* comparison of quantity and Keynesian theories suggests that the quantity theory and monetarism are related but distinct.[4] I share this view. Resolution of policy issues in the monetarist-Keynesian debate does not depend on the truth of the traditional interpretation of the quantity theory or the belief that all relative prices are forever constant. Nor does it depend solely on the slopes of *IS* and *LM* as in Keynesian or neo-Keynesian theories. To advance the discussion and resolve issues, new elements have been introduced.[5] The new elements move the discussion beyond the discussion of quantity versus Keynesian theory.

In the following section, I consider the relation — and emphasize some differences — between quantity, Keynesian, and monetarist theories of the adjustment of economic activity and prices to nominal and real shocks. Then, I discuss the interpretation of unemployment, a subject on which many monetarists and quantity theorists have views that are distinguishable from the Keynesian view. My interpretation of unemployment has not, as far as I know, been presented in its present form but it will not seem startling to those who have followed recent developments in the theory of employment. I conclude by discussing

---

[3] On the general point about the type of change in "beliefs" I find myself close to agreement with *Blinder* and *Solow* (1976 a, p. 502) although we may differ about the size and durability of short-run responses. The MPS (or FRB-MIT) model also shows that real effects of fiscal policy vanish after a short period.

[4] Among the commentators *Brunner* and *Johnson* share this view; *Cagan*, however, appears to regard monetarism as a return to the principles of the twenties — i. e. to some type of quantity theory.

[5] The government budget equation is a principal example. Among recent models formally incorporating the government budget equation are: Alan S. *Blinder* and Robert M. *Solow* (1973), Karl *Brunner* and Allan H. *Meltzer* (1972, 1976), Carl *Christ* (1968), Jerome *Stein* (1974) and James *Tobin* and William *Buiter* (1976).

some remaining differences about the meaning of unemployment and the role of government.

I. Adjustment in Monetarist and Quantity Theories

The term "monetarism" was coined in Karl *Brunner's* (1968) article, but many of the issues in the monetarist-Keynesian controversy had been brought to professional attention much earlier by *Friedman* (1956). Unfortunately, *Friedman* did not follow the promising path he developed but, instead, blurred the distinction between his new approach and the quantity theory. In this section, I distinguish monetarism from quantity and Keynesian theories.

Friedman's quantity theory of 1956 is neither Keynesian — as that term was understood at the time — nor a classical, quantity theory. Recognition of the role of interest rates in the demand function for money accepted one of *Keynes's* arguments that classical economists did not stress and may not have accepted. In other important respects, *Friedman's* demand function for money departs from Keynesian theory, *as that term was understood at the time,* in at least three ways.

First, *Friedman* (1956, pp. 4, 5, 10, 19) directs attention away from current income and toward wealth as a determinant of the demand for money. The concept of income relevant for his analysis is the capitalized value of all sources of "consumable services" — surely a long-run concept to be distinguished from the concept of "income as it is ordinarily measured" (1956, p. 4).[6] The quantity of real balances that households desire to hold depends on wealth and income, not on current receipts.

Second, the way in which money affects economic activity differs from Keynesian analysis. *Friedman* discusses, at length, the effect on the demand for money of changes in yields on bonds, equities, physical goods and human wealth. Most of these yields were not, and often are not yet, arguments of the Keynesian demand function for money.[7]

---

[6] This issue is not settled. Albert *Ando* and Franco *Modigliani* (1975) attempt to prove analytically that wealth does not affect the demand for money. They claim that only current income and short-term interest rates are relevant. *Selden* (1956) showed years ago that income velocity is more closely related to equity returns than to bond yields or bill rates, although he did not pursue the analysis. See *Hamburger* (1977) for more recent evidence on this point.

[7] One need only compare the recent empirical work by *Goldfeld* (1973, 1977) and *Hamburger* (1977) on the demand for money to see that the

Friedman's view of what is now called the transmission mechanism of monetary policy is distinct from the views expressed by Keynesians at the time. Most Keynesian theorists then claimed that changes in the stock of money are adequately summarized by the response of short-term interest rates to money, and of investment to interest rates. Many still do.[8] The Keynesian view is now found in the statement that the relative responses to monetary and fiscal policy are summarized by the interest elasticities of investment (or *IS*) and the demand for money (or *LM*). Monetarists, at least from the time of *Friedman's* essay, stressed the role of other relative prices and wealth in addition to interest rates and insisted that policies affect economic activity through many different channels.[9]

Third, the liquidity trap has much more importance in Keynesian theory than in the *General Theory*. Monetarists deny the relevance of the liquidity trap. One reason is that the demand for money depends on many relative prices or rates of interest in addition to the rate on short-

---

differences are substantial and affect interpretation of past events and policies. *Goldfeld* chose the period of the early seventies to test the "stability" of demand functions for money. The test results are clear and *Goldfeld's* interpretation of his results is incorrect. He does not show that the demand for money is unstable. Comparison of the papers by *Hamburger* and *Goldfeld* shows that the traditional Keynesian demand function in which money substitutes only for "bonds" is less reliable than a function that allows a broader range of substitutes.

[8] *Tobin* is a partial exception. His general equilibrium framework (*Tobin* 1969 and *Tobin* and *Buiter* 1976) is often used as evidence that there are few remaining differences about the transmission or adjustment process. One of *Mayer's* commentators, Benjamin *Friedman* (1977) develops this argument, and it is correct as a statement about general equilibrium models. Although there are differences in detail and in method of presentation, there is little *formal* difference between the general equilibrium framework in *Tobin* (1969) or *Tobin* and *Buiter* (1976) and the models of wealth or relative price adjustment proposed in *Brunner* and *Meltzer* (1963) and developed in *Brunner* and *Meltzer* (1968, 1972, 1976). Here the similar ends. As *Tobin* (1976) points out, there are substantial differences in policy conclusions. *Tobin* appears to draw his policy implications from an IS-LM framework in which there is only a single rate of interest. The general equilibrium, relative price adjustment, of his formal model, appears to be neglected. The rate of price change seems to be determined by a *Phillips* curve that shifts slowly or not at all in response to all, anticipated and unanticipated, fiscal and monetary policies. *Brunner* and *Meltzer* do not neglect relative price changes and make the expected rate of inflation depend, *inter alia*, on past rates of monetary growth.

[9] The effect of wealth on the demand for money is mentioned by *Marshall* (1923); the neglect of wealth by *Keynes* was recognized early by *Haberler* (1952).

term securities. Keynesians selected the short-term rate as the only interest rate relevant for the demand for money (*Ando and Modigliani, 1975*). Hence, the allegation that the market interest rate on short-term securities approached a lower asymptote was sufficient evidence for many Keynesians to declare that a liquidity trap existed in the thirties. *Friedman's* insistence on the many rates relevant for portfolio choice denied the relevance of evidence of this kind.

The transmission process of *Friedman's* quantity theory (1956) not only differed from the Keynesian theory of the time he wrote, but the formal structure differs from the classical quantity theory. The quantity theory in *Thornton, Ricardo* or *Hume* relies mainly on the effect of changes in the quantity of money on expenditure and much less, if at all, on changes in relative prices and interest rates.[10] One reason is that, in the absence of changes in the conditions for producing gold, classical theorists expected the gold standard to keep the price level fluctuating around a value that remained constant for decades.[11] Fluctuations in interest rates, therefore, meant either long-run changes in real rates or short-run, temporary changes resulting from cyclical fluctuations of the price level around a long-run constant value. Fluctuations in the equilibrium real rates were treated as small, so the discussion of economic fluctuations centered on the consequences of departures of the price level from the long-run level determined by tastes, productivity, and real resources on one side and the quantity of money on the other.

This section presents a simple model to illustrate the adjustment mechanism in the classical quantity theory and the differences between

---

[10] A recent, excellent reconsideration of classical theory of the balance of payments is *Frenkel* (1976). *Frenkel* discusses the role of relative prices (interest rates) in the classical theory of the balance of payments and contrasts two approaches to adjustment. One requires shifts in expenditure relative to income. The other requires changes in relative prices. See also *Viner* (1965). I believe classical theorists mainly discuss the first of these adjustments whereas *Friedman* (1956) emphasizes the second in his essay. *Friedman* (1956, p. 19), however, mentions the classical explanation and it is this approach that he followed subsequently.

[11] Persuasive evidence on the views of classical economists about the proper relation of price levels to money is the Report of the Committee on the High Price of Bullion written in 1810. The report urged the resumption of specie payments at the 1797 price of gold. The policy, adopted several years later, required a 50 % reduction in the price level. A century later, in 1919 - 25, the Bank of England deflated again to restore the 1797 price of gold in pounds sterling.

monetarist, Keynesian and quantity theories. In the classical quantity theory, portfolio theory is deemphasized; the principal alternative to holding money is spending to buy goods. In monetarist theory, as in Keynesian theory, money is held in portfolios, but the determinants of the demand for money and the response to changes in money differ.

The quantity equation sets aggregate spending, MV, equal to nominal output, py. Classical economists treated cyclical fluctuations in velocity as small, relative to changes in M, and minimized the effect on velocity of interest rates or relative prices and output. Equation (1) makes velocity constant, so fluctuations in spending are entirely the result of changes in money. A trend rate of change of velocity could be added to recognize improvements in payment arrangements.

(1) $$MV = py$$

(2) $$y = F(K, L) + \varepsilon$$

Equation (2) has two components. The first, called permanent output or permanent income, is equal to full employment output. The second recognizes that real shocks cause current real output (y) to depart from steady state equilibrium output. Deviations, ε, are assumed, here, to be normally distributed with zero mean and constant variance, σ, a modern interpretation of the classical view that output fluctuates around a stationary value (or trend rate of growth if technical change is admitted).

(3) $$M = D + R$$

The money stock is base money and is the sum of domestic assets (D) and foreign reserves (R). The meaning of "money" changed from the 17th to the 19th century. Bullionists certainly did not include domestic earning assets as part of the money stock or monetary base. By the early 19th century, however, the effect on prices of issuing "paper credit" was recognized widely. Many writers included domestic earning assets as a source of base money (*Viner*, 1965).

The next equation tries to capture the spirit but not the letter of a classical theory of fluctuations. Changes in reserves depend on the difference between the domestic price level (p) and foreign price level (p^*). The exchange rate (X) gives the number of units of domestic currency that exchange for a unit of foreign currency. The response to prices separates Keynesian from classical and monetarist economists. Keynesians assume that short-run price changes are small. Prices are inflexible. Most classical economists disagree. Changes in the relative prices of domestic and foreign goods have a large role in the classical theory of adjustment, (*Frenkel*, 1976; *Viner*, 1965).

(4)
$$\frac{dR}{dt} = h\,(p - p^* X)\quad h' < 0$$
$$h\,(0) = 0$$

The steady state equilibrium price level with fixed exchange rates is the world price level (p^*) denominated in domestic currency units.[12] The price level and exchange rate fluctuate around the world price level in the short run. In this version of classical theory, the exchange rate fluctuates within limits set by the adjustment of prices. Equation (5) determines the exchange rate.

(5)
$$p = p^* X$$

The complete system has eleven variables. Five — $p, y, M, \frac{dR}{dt}$, and X — are determined by equations (1) to (5). V is a constant. If R is formally described as an accumulated stock, we are left with three predetermined variables — K, L, and p^* — and one policy variable, D. The system determines steady state values and adjusts to real (ε) and nominal (D) shocks for given technology and resources, $F\,(K, L)$, and for given anticipations of long-run output.

As the system stands, output fluctuates in response to real shocks but is unaffected by changes in monetary policy, D. In the absence of relative price changes, a response of output to nominal disturbances occurs only if output depends on the price level or the quantity of money. This is the point made in *Patinkin's* (1965) criticism that classical economists failed to provide a mechanism or relation by means of which changes in money affect output and the price level. His criticism is applicable in a closed economy in which the relative prices of all currently exchangeable goods — new production or existing assets, durables and non-durables — are unaffected by changes in money. The composite good theorem applies to all exchangeables.

---

[12] *Frenkel* (1976, pp. 32 - 36) quotes from classical writers and neoclassical interpretations to show that the "law of one price" was an accepted proposition.

Many classical economists discussed the relation of money prices and output, but none are clearer than *Thornton*. The price level and output respond to changes in money, according to *Thornton,* because money wages adjust more slowly than the price level (1965, pp. 118 - 9. Italics in the original):

> "It is true, that if we could suppose the diminution of bank paper to produce permanently a diminution in the value of all articles whatsoever, and a diminution ... in the rate of wages also, the encouragement to future manufactures would be the same, though there would be a loss on the stock in hand. The tendency, however, of a very great and sudden reduction of the accustomed number of bank notes, is to create an *unusual* and *temporary* distress, and a fall of price arising from that distress. But a fall arising from temporary distress, will be attended probably with no correspondent fall in the rate of wages; for the fall of price, and the distress, will be understood to be temporary, and the rate of wages, we know is not so variable as the price of goods. There is reason, therefore, to fear that the unnatural and extraordinary low price arising from the distress of which we now speak, would occasion much discouragement of the fabrication of manufactures."

A lengthy footnote to the passage (1965, p. 119) indicates why, under the assumed conditions, the fall in prices and output must be temporary. "The general and permanent value of bank notes must be the same as the general and permanent value of that gold for which they are exchangeable, and the value of gold in England is regulated by the general and permanent value of it all over the world; ... the gold price must, in a short time, find its level with the gold price over the rest of the world."[13] The content of this quotation is summarized by eq. (5).

A modern economist would be inclined to characterize as "unanticipated" the changes that *Thornton* describes as "temporary". The change in terminology is acceptable if unanticipated refers to the size and timing of the change. *Thornton* and many other economists after *Hume* regarded fluctuations in receipts as part of the adjustment required under the gold standard.[14]

Under *Thornton's* hypothesis, temporary or unanticipated price changes affect the level of output by temporarily changing real wages. Let the money wage be W and let

---

[13] *Thornton* (1965, pp. 96 - 7) also discusses changes in velocity and mentions the opportunity cost of holding money as a factor affecting velocity. *Thornton* emphasizes the role of confidence (or uncertainty), however.

[14] *Phelps* and *Taylor* (1977) develop a modern form of this argument for a world of rational expectations.

$$L = L\left(\frac{W}{p}\right) L' < 0$$

describe the demand side of the labor market. The demand for labor is a derived demand. Real and monetary shocks shift the demand for labor along the supply curve, thereby changing the level of employment and output. Substituting for L in eq. (2) makes the short-run output supply curve depend on the domestic price level. Output and the price level are positively related along the aggregate supply curve.

(2')
$$y = F\left[K,\, L\left(\frac{W}{p}\right)\right] + \varepsilon$$

The quantity equation is the classical spending equation. If we substitute $R + D$ for M and solve for y as a function of p, the spending relation is a rectangular hyperbola in the p, y plane that shifts position as R and D change. Equation (2') and the quantity equation jointly determine p and y. Adjustment of the balance of payments in response to relative prices provides the driving force in fluctuations.

A problem with this approach is that M is the home country stock of base money and py is domestic output at market value. By assuming constant velocity, we have eliminated any effects of relative prices on the distribution of purchases between foreign and home markets.

Brunner (1976) has shown that the rigidity of the quantity theory can be relaxed, and the theory can be brought into closer correspondence with observations showing cyclical changes in the current account balance. Rewrite eq. (1) as

(1')
$$\Phi MV + (1 - \Phi^*) M^* V^* X = py$$

where Φ is the proportion of domestic spending to domestic output and $(1 - \Phi^*)$ is the proportion of exports (foreign spending) to domestic output,

$$\Phi = \Phi\,(p, p^* X) \quad \Phi_1 < 0 \ ; \ \Phi_2 > 0$$

$$\Phi^* = \Phi^*\,(p/X, p^*) \ \Phi_1^* > 0 \ ; \ \Phi_2^* < 0$$

Differentiating (1') with respect to y and converting the results to an elasticity, we obtain the slope of the spending relation in an economy with fixed exchange rates.

(6)
$$\varepsilon\,(p, y) = \frac{1}{\Phi^2\, \varepsilon\,(\Phi, p) - \Phi^*\,(1 - \Phi^*)\, \varepsilon\,(\Phi^*, p) - 1} < 0$$

The elasticity of p with respect to y, $\varepsilon\,(p, y)$, depends on the relative response of domestic and foreign purchases, and the shares of total spending.

Equation (6) shows that the expenditure equation, EE, obtained from (1') has the negative slope shown in Figure 1. The position of EE depends on M and M^*. Equation (2') is the aggregate supply curve, yy. Intersection of EE and yy determines the price level and level of domestic output.

Figure 1

Classical Adjustment to a Real Shock

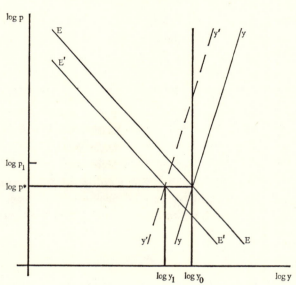

Figure 1 shows some features of the classical system. At output y_0 and price level p^* the system is in flow equilibrium. Real output is at a long-run equilibrium value, y_0, and $p = p^*$, so y_0, p^* is a long-run equilibrium position with $X = 1$. Suppose a real shock reduces output and raises the price level to the position shown by the intersection of $y'y'$ and EE. The amount of domestic spending on home goods falls as p rises. Exports fall and imports rise. The shift of the yy curve along the EE curve brings the economy to a short-run flow equilibrium in the output market at p.

At price level p_1, home prices exceed world prices, and there is a current account deficit. Equation (4) implies that the home country < 0. The loss of reserves lowers R, thereby loses foreign reserves; $\dfrac{dR}{dt}$ reducing expenditure and the domestic price level. When p reaches $p^* X$, the flow of reserves ceases, $\dfrac{dR}{dt} = 0$, and the decline in expenditure ends. A new short-run equilibrium is shown at the intersection of $E'E'$ and $y'y'$. In Figure 1, the level of output is shown as y_1; X is assumed to be unity.

If the real shock is permanent, money wages must fall for output to move from y_1 toward y_0. *Thornton's* analysis suggests that an unanticipated, one-time shock induces a smaller adjustment of money wages than of prices, so I hold money wages fixed in this example. Once the shock passes, the short-run supply of output returns to yy.[15] If spending remains at $E'E'$, the domestic price level is less than $p^* X$, a position inconsistent with equilibrium of the balance of payments. Exports rise and imports fall; spending is reallocated from foreign to domestic markets increasing R and shifting the spending curve along yy. Reserves accumulate; the money stock rises; the price level rises; and long-run equilibrium is restored.[16]

The classical quantity theory treats the output of each country as a composite good in both the short-run and the long-run. Emphasis is on short-run changes in the relative prices of domestic and foreign goods and in cost of production (wage) relative to market price. A partial revival of this line of reasoning is found in the monetary approach to the balance of payments where the "law of one price" is invoked to minimize the effect of short-run changes in relative prices and, often improperly, extended to world prices.[17] Emphasis in the monetary ap-

---

[15] After the recent temporary disappearance of the Peruvian anchovies and maintained increase in the money price of imported oil, the difference between temporary and permanent real shocks is familiar.

[16] The wealth loss during the adjustment from one long-run equilibrium to the next is ignored here. The quotation reproduced above from *Thornton* (1965, p. 118) shows that, contrary to *Patinkin's* (1965) claim, real wealth effects of price changes were recognized by (some) classical writers. *Thornton* recognized that wealth changed, but he appears to have regarded the changes as a secondary effect and the change in real wages and the quantity of output as the primary effects. We can presume that *Thornton's* reference to "all articles whatsoever" includes money balances, although he does not dismiss or mention real balance effects separately.

[17] A difference between recent and older work is the role assigned to interest rates in the demand function for money and in the adjustment

proach is often restricted to the determinants of the long-run stock of
reserves and the supply of money. Such emphasis may, at one time, have
served the useful role of freeing the theory of balance of payments
adjustment from its Keynesian heritage, but neglect of short-run adjustment seems a step back from the level of sophistication achieved by
classical economists like *Thornton*.

Keynesian theory introduced asset adjustment as the principal adjustment to monetary policy. The slow adjustment of money wages,
recognized by *Thornton*, received more emphasis, but prices were also
assumed to adjust slowly. Classical emphasis on adjustment of domestic
prices relative to foreign prices was replaced by changes in the market
rate of interest. The effect of relative price changes on the goods
market was minimized (elasticity pessimism). Relative prices became
identified with the market rate of interest and market rates with costs
of holding money in lieu of short-term assets or costs of borrowing.
The response of spending to interest rates, or the slope of *IS*, determined
the effectiveness of monetary policy, and the response of the demand
for money to interest rates, or the slope of *LM*, determined the effectiveness of fiscal policy. This argument has become familiar with
frequent repetition and has been made recently by *Tobin* and *Buiter*
(1976). Many textbooks elaborate the details of the Keynesian transmission mechanism, and I shall not repeat them. Neither do I play on the
now familiar distinction between Keynes and the Keynesians. That
distinction was not part of the discussion during the first twenty-five
years or longer (*Johnson*, 1961). The main points of the monetarist
critique were fully developed by the time the distinction became
prominent.

Monetarist analysis places much greater emphasis on the role of relative prices in the transmission of monetary policy than either the
quantity theory or the Keynesian theory. Interest rate changes are not
confined to changes in the cost of borrowing but include the relative
prices of many different assets and output. Fluctuations in relative
prices and the components of real wealth are the principal means by

---

of the balance of payments in modern work. Since p^* is the anticipated
price level, we can rewrite eq. (4) as $\dfrac{dR}{dt} = r\left(\dfrac{p^*}{p}\right)$, describe p^*/p as an
interest rate and introduce p^*/p as an argument of the demand function for
money and therefore of velocity. Since spending in eq. (6) depends on p
relative to p^*, no important change in the formal model results from the
introduction of "interest rates".

which the response to government policies spreads from asset markets to output and the price level. The classical mechanism of adjustment — changes in the price level — reappears in monetarist analysis, but now changes in the price level induce substitution between new production and existing assets as well as between domestic and foreign assets and output. Substitution over a broad range of existing assets changes relative prices of assets and the prices of assets relative to new production as in *Brunner* and *Meltzer* (1963, 1976).

The importance given to relative prices in Keynesian analysis differs with the level of abstraction. Much emphasis is given to a broad range of substitutes in general equilibrium macro models, but there is much less emphasis in discussion of policy or policy implications. (See Footnote 8.) Keynesian economists frequently assume away the classical mechanism of adjustment by holding price levels constant during periods of less than full employment, (*Tobin* and *Buiter*, 1976). A fixed price level leaves portfolio adjustment, often narrowly conceived as substitution between money and short-term securities, to do the work elegantly described in the general equilibrium macro model. The additional assumption that bonds and real capital, or bonds and money, are perfect substitutes brings the formal model into closer correspondence with policy recommendations.

The interest rates in *Friedman's* (1956) demand function for money cannot be reduced to a single rate of return, "the interest rate" of Keynesian theory, by assuming than all rates of price change are fully anticipated. The difference between the rate of interest on bonds and equities is approximately (1956, p. 9)

$$r_b - r_e = \frac{1}{r_b}\frac{dr_b}{dt} - \frac{1}{r_e}\frac{dr_e}{dt} + \frac{1}{p}\frac{dp}{dt}$$

where r_b and r_e are interest rates on bonds and equities, $\frac{1}{r}\frac{dr}{dt}$ is the capital gain or loss anticipated (or received) on bonds or equities and $\frac{1}{p}\frac{dp}{dt}$ is the anticipated (or actual) rate of inflation.

The "rational expectation" that actual and anticipated rates of inflation are equal is not sufficient to equate real returns to bonds and equity. Fluctuations in earnings streams, particularly the anticipated earnings accruing to owners of real capital, induce short-run changes in the relative prices of assets and output. Government policies affect anticipations of future earnings by changing the applicable tax rates, by altering perceived risks, by raising or lowering the net benefits accruing to those who bear risk, and in other ways. Cyclical fluctuations, whether induced by real shocks or by changes in the stocks of financial assets, affect the current and future prices of assets and output.

Moreover, a change in the anticipated rate of inflation affects *Friedman's* demand for money by changing the prices of the goods held as inventories relative to the value of the services of the goods. *Friedman*, like *Thornton*, dismisses the wealth effect of a change in asset values, but I know of no evidence that this channel is less important than others for short-run adjustments. If we denote the prices of assets as P and the price of the output (or services) by p, as before, the per period relative rates of change of the two price levels enter the demand for money and become part of the adjustment process.

Some economists who do not regard themselves as monetarists for policy purposes accept what I have called the monetarist theory of adjustment, just as many economists once accepted the Keynesian theory of adjustment without fully accepting policy statements about the impotence of monetary policy. Theories of adjustment, or transmission, provide a framework for assessing evidence and drawing conclusions about relative effects and about the size and timing of adjustment. Keynesian conclusions may continue to be drawn, and Keynesian policies recommended, by those who accept a monetarist transmission theory in general if they deny specific aspects or make assumptions about empirical magnitudes. *Tobin* and *Buiter* (1976) assume that the price level or rate of inflation remains fixed when there is unemployment. Thus, they deny an important piece of the monetarist adjustment process without denying the validity of the theoretical framework. *Ando* and *Modigliani* (1975) deny that the demand for money depends on wealth and on many of the relative prices just discussed.

Brunner and *Meltzer* draw monetarist policy conclusions from their framework and their judgments about relevant responses. In their version of monetarist theory (1972, 1976) the response of output to changes in money and in debt financed fiscal policy depend on the elasticities of the price level with respect to the monetary base and the stock of government debt. The larger the response of the price level to the base, the larger is the response to monetary policy. The smaller the response of the price level to government expenditure and to debt issued to finance deficits, the smaller is the response to fiscal policy. Judgments about the relative response of the price level to monetary and fiscal variables lead *Brunner* and *Meltzer* to monetarist policy conclusions. *Stein* (1974) reaches very similar conclusions in a different way.[18] Acceptance of a common theory of adjustment neither eliminates differences in policy nor makes all remaining differences depend on value judgments.

II. Interpreting Unemployment

The monetarist-Keynesian debate is not restricted to differences about the ways in which aggregate spending, output and the price level are brought to a new equilibrium. The meaning and interpretation of measured unemployment differs. This section relates the alternative interpretations to theories of employment.

Keynesians follow Keynes and regard all cyclical unemployment as involuntary, the result of insufficient spending by the private sector. Even if the unemployed receive compensation equal to the prevailing money wage, society loses all of the output that would have been produced at full employment. Hence, government policies to eliminate unemployment have low costs and large social benefit. If the rate of inflation remains at the fully anticipated rate following the recession, there are few costs to offset the benefits of expansionist policies.

In Keynesian theory, not only is cyclical unemployment involuntary, it is uncertain as to timing, duration and frequency. Workers cannot reduce unemployment by reducing money wages, or at least they do not. Downward rigidity of money wages explains the excess supply of labor, and slower adjustment of wages than of the price level explains why real wages rise in periods of recession.

Social policy is based on the Keynesian interpretation. The current legal definition of unemployment treats all cyclical unemployment as "involuntary". A worker is unemployed if he is described as having looked for work at least once in a four week period.[19]

---

[18] *Stein* (1976), *Meltzer* (1977) and Korteweg and Meltzer (1978, forthcoming) present evidence showing that in all countries and time periods examined the response of domestic prices to domestic fiscal policy is small.

[19] *Feldstein* (1975) discusses some of the ways in which the definition is expanded.

The problem starts from the ambiguity in *Keynes's* definition of involuntary unemployment. *Keynes* (1936, p. 15) called unemployment "involuntary" if a rise in the price level that reduces real wages increases employment. The definition and its subsequent use by Keynesians and policymakers ignores two distinctions. One is the distinction between anticipated and unanticipated price and wage changes, the other the distinction between anticipated income and current receipts. The first distinction has been clarified in the extended discussion of the *Phillips*-curve, but the degree to which fluctuations in employment are anticipated remains.

The classical interpretation of unemployment differs from the Keynesian interpretation. The quotation from *Thornton* (1965, pp. 118—19), reproduced above, does not deny the possibility of cyclical unemployment. On the contrary, *Thornton* describes unemployment as "unusual and temporary distress" arising for reasons that are widely known as Keynesian: Money wages are more rigid downward than are prices. For *Thornton,* however, money wages are rigid upward as well if anticipated inflation remains constant.

Thornton's characterization of unemployment as "unusual and temporary distress" is no lessambiguous than *Keynes's* term, "involuntary." The mechanism producing employment is clearer, however. For classical theorists, cyclical fluctuations in employment and output are a consequence of real shocks acting on the quantity of commodities currently demanded by shifting supply and of monetary disturbances acting on spending. Shifts in aggregate spending and in aggregate supply induce larger fluctuations in prices than in money wages, so real wages change inversely to the price level when spending increases and change directly with the price level when supply increases. Unemployment and real wages are positively related following a reduction in spending but are negatively related following a reduction in supply. *Thornton* (1965, pp. 237 - 9) is explicit about the relation of prices and output.[20]

---

[20] *Thornton's* argument (pp. 237 - 9) has a modern ring. A producer confounds the extra gain resulting from the rise in the price of his inventories "with the other profits of his commerce and is induced, by the apparent success of his undertakings to pursue them with more than usual spirit." *Thornton* subsequently quotes approvingly from *Hume's* Essay on Money (italics in *Thornton*): "'In my opinion, it is only in this interval or intermediate situation between the acquisition of money and the rise of prices' (Mr. Hume must mean, no doubt, the completion of the rise, and not the commencement

Classical and monetarist interpretations of unemployment differ from the Keynesian interpretation in a similar way. Both treat the type of unemployment observed during mild cycles as a temporary or transitory phenomenon. The monetarist interpretation antedates recent formal work on the theory of employment and fluctuations by *Azariadis* (1975), *Baily* (1974), *Lucas* (1977), *Phelps* (1970) and *Phelps* and *Taylor* (1977). However, recent work by these and other economists, many of whom are not monetarists, provides a better foundation for the monetarist interpretation.

The monetarist interpretation starts from *Friedman*'s (1957) distinction between permanent and transitory income — or between income defined as an expected stream and current receipts.[21] Suppose a worker, who behaves according to the permanent income hypothesis, experiences a cyclical "lay off". The permanent income theory implies that, at first, he has no reason to search for alternative employment or to reduce his real wages. As long as his experience remains consistent with the anticipations he held when he chose his job or career, as modified by subsequent experience, he regards the lay off as a drawing from the anticipated distribution of time between labor and leisure that he used to determine permanent income and lifetime consumption. Each day of lay off contains information leading to a revision of his anticipated income, but each day of lay off has little effect on workers in industries subject to cyclical swings in employment and output.

---

of it) 'that the encreasing quantity of gold and silver is favourable to industry.'" A footnote to this passage criticizes *Hume* for suggesting that the increased money changes relative prices at home. *Thornton* argues for the mechanism discussed in a previous section. The increase in money sends money abroad by rising "the gold price of articles above their level in other countries, allowing for the charges of transportation." But this takes time, as *Thornton* reminds his readers in the same footnote. "[I]t is affirmed by French writers that the notes of Mr. Law's bank appeared for a time to have a very powerful influence in extending the demand for labour, and in augmenting the visible ... property of the kingdom."

[21] *Friedman*'s important contribution to the theory of employment (1968) does not rely on this distinction between permanent and transitory income but, instead, emphasizes the difference between anticipated and unanticipated changes in wages or nominal income. Unanticipated and transitory changes are related, of course, and both affect real wages. As used in economics, the two are not the same. The distinction between anticipated and unanticipated separates current or future from past effects of inflation on real values; the distinction between permanent and transitory applies to the effects of fluctuations in economic activity on current receipts and employment.

Every day of lay off is counted as part of measured unemployment, but, as long as income anticipations are not revised, permanent income remains unchanged and the worker is not unemployed *in an economic sense.* There is no loss of aggregate output.

A worker becomes unemployed when he revises, downward, his permanent income. He no longer anticipates that current leisure and future earnings are consistent with his consumption plan. He faces the choice of reducing *income* and consumption either by remaining idle or by reducing his current real wage. If his anticipation is correct, his loss of *income* is a measure of the loss of output to society.

The distinction between measured and economic unemployment is the familiar distinction between current receipts and income, basic to classical and modern theory. For classical economists, as for *Friedman* (1957), anticipated income is known; the timing of receipts is uncertain. Receipts flucttuate around anticipated income, but, as long as anticipations are firmly held, the present value of every negative deviation is offset by anticipated positive deviations. When negative deviations are not offset, anticipations change; workers are unemployed.

There are two sources of uncertainty about the timing of receipts relevant for the aggregate — the real and nominal shocks introduced into the classical model summarized by equations (6) and (2'). Both shocks change current output, y, relative to anticipated output, $F(K, L)$, in equation (2'). Nominal shocks change the price level relative to money wages, and real shocks change current output by ε. If the observed fluctuations in current output are drawings from the anticipated distribution, the deviation of current output from

$$y_0 = F(K, L)$$

does not cause a revision of plans in the aggregate. Any changes in individual plans cancel. The community's anticipated income remains consistent with productive capability, y_0.[22]

---

[22] This statement requires adjustment to take account of (1) differences between monetary and barter economies and (2) any differences in the non-pecuniary services of debt and real capital. The reason is that the services of money and any non-pecuniary services of debt and capital are part of income available for consumption but are not included in the market value of the income produced. (The term income used here is, as in the text, distinct from current receipts.) The qualification does not affect the main point in the text if the non-pecuniary services are like y_0, a long-term independent of current receipts.

Classical writers did not, as far as I know, provide an economic explanation of the slower adjustment of wages than of prices. *Keynes,* like *Thornton,* first assumes that wages are slow to adjust, then offers an explanation based on a particular set of assumptions about anticipations (1936, Chap. 19).

The permanent income theory of employment starts by recognizing the difficult inference problem faced by individual workers and employers in an economy subject to real and nominal shocks. Relative prices and the general price level change. A worker who is laid off cannot be certain whether the change is permanent or temporary, whether he will soon return to work at his previous employment, as many do (*Feldstein,* 1975), or must seek new employment. An offer to reduce real wages in recession to maintain employment introduces variability into *income* for the purpose of smoothing current receipts. Unless the worker is certain that the reduction in income resulting from lower real wages today can be fully offset by increases in future real wages and income, lifetime consumption and utility are reduced. The permanent income theory gives no reason for workers to reduce real wages as long as anticipations are unchanged.

Figure 2 shows the effect of changes in expenditure on output and prices. Anticipated income remains at full employment, y_0, but current output and receipts fluctuate. A nominal shock reduces spending to E_1 E_1; current production falls to y_1, and the price level falls to p_1. At p_1 y_1, the economy reaches temporary, short-run equilibrium. The demand for labor falls. The amount of the labor supplied depends in p, so the quantity supplied increases as p falls. Money wages, w, fall if the assumption that wages change less than prices is correct. Employment is less than L_0, the level of employment when output is y_0, so there is temporary measured unemployment. As long as aggregate anticipated income remains y_0, anticipated lifetime earnings for the labor force remain fixed. The difference between current earnings and anticipated earnings is transitory income.[23]

Measured unemployment varies cyclically in the permanent income theory. At y_1 p_1, employment is less than full employment, L_0, but

---

[23] For periods of inflation and growth, the classical and permanent income theories of employment should be recast in terms of rates of wage change relative to rates of price change and rates of change of output. This modification is ignored in the text and has no importance for the analysis presented here.

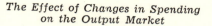

Figure 2

The Effect of Changes in Spending
on the Output Market

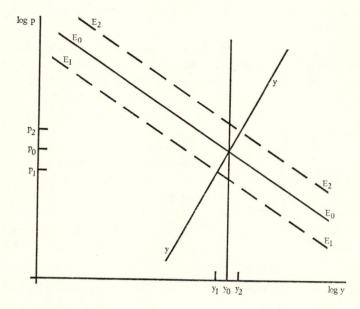

greater than "Keynesian employment" because w falls. In the Keynesian theory, money wages are completely rigid, and the labor supply curve is drawn as a reverse "L" at the full employment wage. In the permanent income theory, workers do not reduce real wages by lowering money wages in recession, unless anticipated lifetime income changes. Neither do they maintain money wages at the full employment money wage, w_0. To maintain w_0 requires workers to accept more reduction in employment than is consistent with their lifetime plans and current anticipations.

Money wages are "rigid" downward in the permanent income theory but are also "rigid" upward as long as anticipations of future prices and permanent income remain unchanged. In periods of high expenditure, shown as $E_2 E_2$ in Figure 2, output is y_2, and the price level is p_2 at the intersection of $E_2 E_2$ and yy; employment and money wages rise. If *Thornton's* assumption is correct, money wages rise less than prices, so real wages fall. Workers could raise the real wage rate to a level equal to $\frac{w_0}{p_0}$ by reducing the supply of labor. Instead, they regard the reduced real wage and increased employment during this period as part of their experience that includes increased real wages and lower employment following nominal shocks that bring recessions, lower real wages and reduced employment following negative real shocks, and higher real wages and higher employment following positive real shocks. As long as the present value of the gains and losses of real income remains consistent with anticipated lifetime income, there is no reason for the supply curve of labor as a function of the real wage to shift.[24]

The permanent income theory of employment does not deny that workers can speculate on real wages, offering more employment when real wages rise, and reducing employment when real wages fall. The theory suggests, however, that workers as a group must forecast wages and the demand for employment, separating temporary from permanent shocks and real from nominal shocks. This task is easier in a classical world, where relative price changes are restricted to the relative price of domestic and foreign output. In a monetarist economy, relative prices of existing assets and new production of home country goods and services also respond to real and nominal shocks and induce changes in the allocation of spending and in output that must be separated from the aggregate effects. The inference problem is more difficult.

The permanent income theory implies that real wages rise if recession is induced by a nominal shock and fall if recession is induced by real shocks. The simple correlation between real wages and unemployment discussed by *Modigliani* (1977, p. 7) contains no information about the permanent income theory (or any other theory) until it is combined with a statement about the dominant cause of recessions and booms. A positive association between real wages and unemployment during recessions supports the permanent income hypothesis if recessions are mainly the result of shifts in aggregate demand.

Monetarists' policy statements distinguish one large, negative real shock in recent years — the oil embargo and subsequent rise in the relative price of oil in 1973/74. All other post — World War II recessions are attributed to government policies and mainly to monetary policies

---

[24] *Feldstein* (1975) shows that during relatively mild cycles a rise in measured unemployment does not lead many workers to search. Workers anticipate, correctly, his study suggest, that most will return to work at their previous employment after a short time. For them, as for Thornton, actual and anticipated unemployment is a temporary phenomenon.

as a principal driving force in the economy. A comparison of turning
points in real wages and in economic acttivity is not a decisive test of
the permanent income theory, but it provides some evidence on a principal implication of the theory.[25] Table 1 compares the peaks and
troughs in the economy to the troughs in real wages from 1948 to 1974.

In the first five postwar cycles in the U.S.-real wages rose during all or
most of the contraction as the hypothesis implies. In four of the five,
the trough in real wages comes at the peak of the preceding expansion
or earlier. In the 1957/58 contraction real wages fell for the first
months of contraction, but started to rise before the trough in the
economy.

Table 1

Dates for Turning Points in Real Wages
and Economic Activity 1948 - 1974 (USA)

Trough in Real Wages	Peak in Economy	Trough in Economy
2nd qtr. 1948	Nov. 1948	Oct. 1949
2nd qtr. 1952	July 1953	May 1954
1st qtr. 1958	Aug. 1957	April 1958
2nd qtr. 1960	April 1960	Feb. 1961
4th qtr. 1969	Dec. 1969	Nov. 1970
4th qtr. 1974	Nov. 1973	March 1975

Source: BCD, June 1976, pp. 112 and 93; BCD, Feb. 1977, p. 105.

The sixth contraction combines a real shock and a monetary contraction. The monetary contraction came almost a year after the real
shock and followed a sharp reduction in the growth of money. Real
wages fell following the real shock, reached a trough during the monetary contraction, fourth quarter 1974, then rose. The movement of real
wages during this contraction is consistent with the permanent income
hypothesis also.

Quarterly data on real wages are not available for earlier periods in
the century. The three highest rates of change of real wages during

---

[25] Judgment enters in the choice of troughs in real wages. Real wages do
not fall in 1953 and 1960. The rate of change becomes near zero or zero in
these two cases. I have omitted a peak and trough in real wages following
the start of the Korean War. There was no recession.

the years 1900 - 17 are in years of recession. In two the economy reached a trough during the year (1904 and 1908), and in one (1913) the contraction lasted for the entire year. The highest rates of increase in real wages come during the only recessions that occurred. Again, the evidence seems consistent with the permanent income theory of employment, although more detailed tests are required to separate the effects of nominal and real shocks.

Workers as a group cannot expect to find a set of consistent contract provisions that maintain both employment and real wages when there are unanticipated real and nominal shocks that change relative prices and the composition of spending and output. The best they can do is reduce the cost of fluctuations in receipts to the minimum cost consistent with the risks inherent in nature, trade and monetary arrangements. Contractual arrangements distribute the cost of bearing risk among the labor force. Seniority provisions of formal and informal contracts permit experienced workers to reduce variability in employment by accepting variability in real wages. The discussion of Figure 2 above shows that slow adjustment of money wages and fluctuations in aggregate spending imply counter cyclical fluctuations in the real wages of the employed. For the employed the excess of receipts over income during recessions offsets the excess of income over receipts in expansions. For the unemployed, the situation is reversed. They take unemployment in periods of relatively high real wages and work during periods of low real wages. Seniority rules impose this choice on new workers but also permit new workers to anticipate a different future. Where training costs are high, one can expect employers to offer seniority provisions so as to receive the delayed benefits of early training.[26]

Seniority clauses are not the only means by which workers adjust to the risks inherent in nature, trade and monetary or social arrangements. Those with a strong preference for stability of receipts enter occupations or industries where anticipated variability is low, as in the civil service, or predictable, as in teaching, utilities, or most consumer non-durables.

---

[26] *Gordon* (1977) shows that women and teenagers have been prominent in the groups of workers willing to offer labor services at times of high employment. Rising prices and less flexible money wages induce employers to hire workers with less training and experience, and seniority provisions assure that such workers will not be retained when spending declines and real wages increase. Seniority provisions give the firm a means of reducing real wages paid to such workers without reducing money wages.

Workers in industries subject to fluctuations in activity could, in principle, sign contracts for payment of real wages, and to some degree they do. Indexation of wage contracts reduces the cost of nominal price changes, but ignores the costs imposed on workers and owners of firms by changes in relative prices. Monetarist theory assigns considerably more importance to fluctuations in relative prices of assets and output than Keynesian or classical theory and suggests reasons for the absence of contracts for payment of real wages. A more difficult problem is to explain why firms and workers do not agree in advance to adjust real wages *ex post* by compensating the lossers for losses arising from unanticipated real and nominal shocks.

In the labor market theories of *Azariadis* (1975) and *Baily* (1974), workers who receive variable streams of earnings demand additional return for bearing the risk of fluctuations in receipts. Whether such compensation is demanded or paid depends on the type of income streams available, the preferences of workers at the margin and on social arrangements for sharing risks.[27]

The amount of compensation demanded and paid for accepting the cost of fluctuations in receipts affects the structure of wages but does not affect the interpretation of unemployment. If the variability of receipts (earnings) is correctly anticipated, the timing of receipts is uncertain, but anticipated income is known. Measured unemployment affects lifetime consumption only if it changes the value of the permanent or anticipated income stream. Teachers are not typically regarded as "involuntarily unemployed" in the summer; construction workers are not involuntarily unemployed when it rains; industrial workers are not involuntarily unemployed in mild cycles of short duration.

Social policies that reduce measured unemployment during recessions increase measured real income only if workers substitute current labor for current and future leisure. If permanent income is unaffected by employment policies, the long-run supply of labor is unaffected also. Employment today is exchanged for future leisure. Workers gain from the exchange to the extent that they prefer to choose periods of employment and leisure or if they have positive time preference and are permitted to reduce the variability of receipts without sacrificing income.

[27] Professors and civil servants influence the rules governing unemployment compensation and defining unemployment. Both groups probably include a disproportionate number of workers with strong preferences for low variability of earnings. Who bears the cost of unemployment insurance?

Permanent income theory makes the supply of labor depend on real wages and anticipated lifetime income, not on real wages alone. The theory explains why money wages appear rigid downward and upward (when anticipated inflation remains constant) but does not require errors in anticipation, or disequilibrium to explain wage rigidity. The theory does not require auction markets for labor, a main point of *Modigliani*'s (1977) criticism of rational expectations. Much more important for our results is consistency in workers, plans. Workers must expect to supply lator at real wages that permit them to earn the income required by their anticipated consumption.

Labor market data appear to show that voluntary terminations of employment, "quits," rise in periods of sustained high demand for labor. Quitting is not required to search for employment, as *Gordon* (1977) and others have insisted. Workers "quit" for many reasons but one such reason is to adjust the distribution of hours between labor and leisure — to return to the supply curve of labor implied by their permanent income. The data on "quits" appears to support the theory.

Permanent income is not immutable for individuals or for society. During this century, experience in Britain during the twenties and thirties and in many countries during the thirties or the sixties may have changed anticipations of lifetime earnings. A long depression probably reduces anticipated income and the rate of increase of real wages; a long expansion probably increases anticipated income, thereby encouraging workers to anticipate fewer layoffs. Quitting and increasing "absenteeism" are some of the means workers use to distribute increases in permanent income between goods and leisure.

Fluctuations in economic activity and in employment change receipts. Keynesian theory treats all cyclical changes in receipts as involuntary unemployment. Unemployment compensation is paid to redistribute the private costs of unemployment more evenly. The loss of unemployment becomes mainly a social loss — the output we would have had in a fully employed economy.

Classical theorists described cyclical unemployment as unusual and temporary. The permanent income theory provides a firmer foundation for their interpretation and an explication of the terms "unusual" and "temporary." If anticipated or permanent income remains constant during mild cycles, there is no loss of output. Cyclical fluctuations change receipts relative to income, but do not change income. Unemployment compensation smooths receipts but can change incomes only to the extent that real wages do not fully adjust to the reduced variability of receipts.

Monetarist policy recommendations are closer to classical than to Keynesian theory. This is shown by the emphasis placed on real wages and the "natural" rate of unemployment and by many denials that employment and output move independently of prices during business cycles.

Classical and monetarist theories of fluctuations recognize risks inherent in nature and trade. To these risks, they add the uncertainty introduced by social arrangements. The gold standard, once regarded as a means of minimizing fluctuations imposed by monetary arrangements, ended in the depression of the thirties. The Bretton Woods system and the widespread use of Keynesian policies encouraged a belief in the fifties and sixties that the new policy arrangements reduced risk. This belief ended for many with the world inflation of the early seventies and the subsequent experience of economies that abandoned "fine tuning" and fixed exchange rates.[28]

III. Conclusion

Thomas *Mayer's* summary of monetarist propositions captures much of the spirit as well as the substance of the monetarist position and the basis of monetarist policy recommendations. The commentators on his paper criticize specific aspects but accept the general argument. All agree that the remaining issues in the monetarist debate are empirical, not analytical.

Monetarists and some modern Keynesians accept rather similar theories of adjustment to real and nominal shocks. I compare this common framework to the early Keynesian and classical theories and indicate some of the principal changes that distinguish the common framework from the earlier theories.

---

[28] In a recent paper, *Mayer* (1977) shows that average unemployment and loss of output in 1900 - 29 are not significantly larger under the gold standard than under the dollar standard from 1948 or 1953 to 1975. *Mayer* recognizes that the average unemployment rate or its variance is not an entirely adequate measure of fluctuations induced by policy arrangements when differences in the extent of real shocks and changes in social arrangements are neglected. Moreover, the risks or costs introduced by social arrangements depend not only on the variability of output but on the variability of prices.

Differences in monetarist and Keynesian policy recommendations are not entirely explained by differences about the size of relative responses, although these differences receive considerable attention in discussions of monetary and fiscal policy. Two related issues have, until recently, remained in the background during the monetarist controversy. Yet, they are the basis of many of the differences in policy and, I believe, help to explain why economists who accept the same formal analysis can be identified as monetarists or Keynesians.

One of the issues is the nature and meaning of unemployment. Keynesians, like *Keynes,* treat all cyclical unemployment as "involuntary," a loss of output to society and, if not compensated, a loss of income to the individuals who are unemployed. This reasoning ignores the distinction between income and current receipts basic to the model of time preference that economists use. Monetarists, like mainstream classical economists, distinguish between current receipts and income and regard much of the unemployment observed during mild cycles as a consequence of fluctuations in receipts. Cyclical unemployment alters permanent or anticipated income streams and consumption only if fluctuations in receipts cause a reevaluation of the mean level or variability of earnings from particular occupations and in the aggregate.

Social arrangements can inncrease or reduce the risks inhepent in nature and trade. Government policies that change the relation between risk and return, that socialize or collectivize risk, or that reduce fluctuations, change anticipated income and the variability of income streams. Optimal social arrangements minimize fluctuations in a society dominated by individuals who prefer smooth to variable streams. The extent to which macro policies reduce fluctuations and lower risk without reducing returns is the analytical and empirical issue familiarly known as "rules versus authority." That issue, long in the background of the monetarist debate, now emerges as a central issue in discussions of the policy implications of a theory incorporating rational expectations *Lucas* (1977), *Prescott* (1977), *Phelps* and *Taylor* (1977).

Bibliography

Ando, Albert and *Modigliani,* Franco (1975). "Some Reflections on Describing Structures of Financial Sectors," in *Fromm* and *Klein* (eds.) The Brookings Model: Perspectives and Recent Developments. Amsterdam: North-Holland. — *Azariadis,* Costas (1975). "Implicit Contracts and Underemployment Equilibria," Journal of Political Economy, 83, pp. 1183 - 1202. — *Baily,* Martin N.

(1974). "Wages and Employment under Uncertain Demand," Review of Economic Studies, 41, pp. 37 - 50. *Blinder*, Alan S. and *Solow*, Robert M. (1973). "Does Fiscal Policy Matter?" Journal of Public Economics, 2, pp. 319 - 37. — *Blinder*, Alan S. and *Solow*, Robert M. (1976). "Does Fiscal Policy Matter? A Reply," Journal of Monetary Economics, 2, pp. 501 - 10. — *Brunner*, Karl (1968). "The Role of Money and Monetary Policy," Review Federal Reserve Bank of St. Louis, 50, pp. 9 - 24. — *Brunner*, Karl (1976). "A Fisherian Framework for the Analysis of International Monetary Problems," in M. *Parkin* and G. *Zis*, (eds.) Inflation in the World Economy. Manchester, pp. 1 - 46. — *Brunner*, Karl and *Meltzer*, Allan H. (1963). "The Place of Financial Intermediaries in the Transmission of Monetary Policy," American Economic Review, Papers and Proceedings, 53, pp. 372 - 82. — *Brunner*, Karl and *Meltzer*, Allan H. (1968). "Liquidity Traps for Money, Bank Credit and Interest Rates," Journal of Political Economy, 76, pp. 1 - 37. — *Brunner*, Karl and *Meltzer*, Allan H. (1972). "Money, Dept and Economic Activity," Journal of Political Economy, 80, pp. 951 - 77. — *Brunner*, Karl and *Meltzer*, Allan H. (1976). "An Aggregative Theory for a Closed Economy," in Monetarism, J. L. *Stein* (ed.) Amsterdam: North-Holland. — *Christ*, Carl (1968). "A Simple Macroeconomic Model with a Government Budget Restraint," Journal of Political Economy, 76, pp. 52 - 67. — *Coddington*, Alan (1976). "Keynesian Economics: The Search for Fist Principles," Journal of Economic Literature, 14, pp. 1258 - 73. — *Feldstein*, Martin S. (1975). "The Importance of Temporary Layoffs: An Empirical Analysis," Brookings Papers on Economic Activity, pp. 725 - 45. — *Frenkel*, Jacob A. (1976). "Adjustment Mechanisms and the Monetary Approach to the Balance of Payments: A Doctrinal Perspective," in E. *Classen* and P. *Salin* (eds.) Recent Issues in International Monetary Economics. Amsterdam: North-Holland. — *Friedman*, Benjamin M. (1977). "The Theoretical Non-Debate About Monetarism," Kredit und Kapital, 9, pp. 347 - 67. — *Friedman*, Milton (1956). "The Quantity Theory of Money — A Restatement," in Studies in the Quantity Theory of Money, M. *Friedman* (ed.) Chicago: Univ. of Chicago Press. — *Friedman*, Milton (1957). "A Theory of the Consumption Function." Princeton: Princeton University Press for the National Bureau of Economic Research. — *Friedman*, Milton (1968). "The Role of Monetary Policy," American Economic Review, 58, pp. 1 - 17. — *Goldfeld*, Stephen M. (1973). "The Demand for Money Revisited," Brooking Papers on Economic Activity, pp. 577 - 638. — *Goldfeld*, Stephen M. (1977). "The Case of the Missing Money," Brookings Papers on Economic Activity, 3, pp. 261 - 280. — *Gordon*, Robert J. (1977). "Structural Unemployment and the Productivity of Women," Carnegie-Rochester Conference Series, 5, suppl. to Journal of Monetary Economics, pp. 181 - 229. — *Haberler*, Gottfried (1952). Prosperity and Depression. New York: United Nations. — *Hamburger*, Michael J. (1977). "Monetary Aggregate Targets: Are They Still Useful?" (multilithed). — *Hamburger*, Michael J. and *Reisch*, Rutbert (1976). "Inflation, Unemployment and Macroeconomic Policy in Open Economies: An Empirical Analysis." Carnegie-Rochester Conference Series, 4, suppl. to Journal of Monetary Economics, pp. 311 - 38. — *Johnson*, Harry G. (1961). "The General Theory after Twenty-Five Years," American Economic Review, Papers and Proceedings, 51, pp. 1 - 17. — *Keynes*, J. M. (1936). The General Theory of Employment, Interest and Money. London. — *Korteweg,* Pieter and *Meltzer,* Allan H. (1978). "Inflation and Price Changes: Some Estimates and Tests," Carnegie-Rochester Conference Series, 8, (forthcoming). — *Laidler,* David (1976). "Inflation — Alternative Explanations and Policies: Tests on Data Drawn from Six Countries," Carnegie-Rochester Conference Series, 4, suppl. to Journal of Monetary Economics, pp. 251 - 307. — *Lucas,* Robert E. Jr. (1977). "Understanding Business Cycles," Carnegie-Rochester Conference Series, 5, suppl. to Journal of Monetary Economics, pp. 7 - 29. — *Marshall,* Alfred (1923). "Money, Credit and Commerce.. London: Macmillan. — *Mayer,* Thomas (1977). "A Comparison of Unemployment Rates Prior to the Great Depression and in the Postwar Period" (multitithed). — *Meltzer,* Allan H. (1977). "Anticipated Inflation and Unanticipated Price Change: A Test of the Price-Specie Flow Theory and the Phillips Curve," Journal of Money, Credit and Banking, 9, pp. 182 - 205. — *Modigliani,* Franco (1977). "The Monetarist Controversy or, Should We Foresake Stabilization Policies," American Economic Review, 67, pp. 1 - 19. — *Patinkin,* Don (1965). Money Interest and Prices, 2nd cd. New York: Harper and Row. — *Phelps,* Edmund S. (1970). Microeconomic Foundation of Employment and Inflation Theory. New York: W. W. Norton. — *Phelps,* Edmund S. and *Taylor,* John B. (1977). "Stabilizing Powers of Monetary Policy under Rational Expectations." Journal of Political Economy, 85, pp. 163 - 90. — *Prescott,* Edward (1977). "Should Control Theory Be Used for Economic Stabilization?" Carnegie-Rochester Conference Series, 7, suppl. to Journal of Monetary Economics, pp. 13 - 38. — *Selden,* Richard T. (1956). "Monetary Velocity in the United States," in M. Friedman (ed.) Studies in the Quantity Theory of Money. Chicago: University of Chicago Press. — *Stein,* Jerome L. (1974). "Unemployment, Inflation and Monetarism," American Economic Review, 64, pp. 861 - 889. — *Stein,* Jerome L. (1976). "A Keynesian Can Be a Monetarist," in Monetarism, J. L. *Stein* (ed.) Amsterdam, North-Holland. — *Thornton,* Henry (1965). "An Enquiry into the Nature and Effects of the Paper Credit of Great Britain" (1802). New York: Kelley. — *Tobin,* James (1969). "A General Equilibrium Approach to Monetary Theory," Journal of Money, Credit and Banking, 1, pp. 15 - 29. — *Tobin,* James (1976). "Is Friedman A Monetarist?" in Monetarism, J. L. *Stein* (ed.) Amsterdam: North-Holland. — *Tobin,* James and *Buiter,* William (1976). "Long-run Effects of Fiscal and Monetary Policy on Aggregate Demand," in Monetarism, J. L. *Stein* (ed.) Amsterdam: North-Holland. — *Viner,* Jacob (1965). "Studies in the Theory of International Trade (1937)." New York: Kelley.

Index

177